Not having Children

HELEN MARSHALL

Melbourne

OXFORD UNIVERSITY PRESS

Oxford Auckland New York

OXFORD UNIVERSITY PRESS AUSTRALIA

Oxford New York Toronto
Delhi Bombay Calcutta Madras Karachi
Kuala Lumpur Singapore Hong Kong Tokyo
Nairobi Dar es Salaam Cape Town
Melbourne Auckland Madrid

and associated companies in
Berlin Ibadan

OXFORD is a trade mark of Oxford University Press

National Library of Australia
Cataloguing-in-Publication data:

Marshall, Helen Margaret
Not Having Children.

Bibliography.
Includes index.
ISBN 0 19 554969 4.

1. Childlessness—Australia. 2. Family—
Australia. 3. Choice (Psychology). I. Title.

306.8

Cover painting (detail): *La Jardinière* by Raphael.
Reproduced with the kind permission of the Louvre, Paris.

Typeset by Syarikat Seng Teik Sdn. Bhd.
Printed by Elite in Hong Kong
Published by Oxford University Press,
253 Normanby Road, South Melbourne, Australia

contents

· · · · · · · · · · · · · · · · · · · ·

acknowledgements   vii

1. INTRODUCTION   1
why this topic?   2
what have other studies found?   6
how to study the voluntarily childless?   11

2. IDEOLOGY: THE THEORETICAL CONTEXT   14
Marx on ideology   15
ideology after Marx   19
ideology in this study   26
defining the ideology of parenthood   28

3. VOLUNTARILY CHILDLESS COUPLES   39
two couples' stories   40
the social location   45
commitments and allegiances   47
little mothers and frightened onlies?   54
early decisions and postponing parenthood   63
summary   67

4. THE CHILDLESS AND IDEAS ABOUT PARENTHOOD   68
is parenthood natural?   69
does parenthood require commitment and responsibility?   72
does parenthood require sacrifice?   76

5. NEGOTIATING WITH IDEOLOGY 85
pictures of the social world 86
explaining childlessness 88
who moves off the proper path? 92
the explanations as a whole 103
focusing on ideology 105
Diane and the ideology of parenthood 106
awareness of the ideology of parenthood 108

6. NEGOTIATING WITH PEOPLE 113
how much pressure is there? 116
dealing with pressure through dealing with people 121
the networks of the childless 122
conversational techniques 123
network management 128
reference groups and ideology 130
reference groups of one? 132
positive referents or awful warnings? 134

7. WHERE TO FROM HERE? 137
what has been shown? 138
theoretical issues 141
policy issues 143
personal issues: implications for activists 148

APPENDIX 1   METHODOLOGY 151

APPENDIX 2   FIGURES AND TABLES 155

ENDNOTES 183

BIBLIOGRAPHY 188

INDEX 196

acknowledgements

. . . .

This book has taken a decade of my life and many people have given me help with it. I am grateful to them all, especially those mentioned below.

The twenty-two childless people in the case-study group and all the anonymous respondents to my questionnaire bore patiently with my intrusion into their lives and in some cases showed generous hospitality to me. I hope that nothing in the book betrays their trust in my discretion and that I manage in it to convey some sense of how much I learned from their stories.

My family, including my former husband, were also patient and supportive during my time as a post-graduate student. Their faith in my capacity to see the thing through (even when I was working in most mysterious ways) was heartening. Special thanks to my sister Alison who knows what it's like to write a thesis.

The Royal Melbourne Institute of Technology has provided me with two periods of leave connected with this project. I gratefully acknowledge a grant from the Department of Social Sciences, which helped me to pursue a childless couple who had fled to Queensland, and the assistance of my former head of department, Dr Norman Blaikie, who took a request for money to go to Surfers Paradise in his stride.

I have received warm support and helpful comment from many colleagues at RMIT especially Judy Smart and Helen Molnar, whose proofreading I appreciate.

Members of the School of Social Sciences at La Trobe University helped in a variety of ways with the thesis on which this book is based. I am especially grateful to Bob Powell and Kerry Exton of the Computer Centre, who gently introduced me to computers, and the mysteries of SPSS. I gratefully acknowledge the research grants for transcripts from both the School and the Department of Sociology.

Pat Morrigan and Yoland Wadsworth of Thesis Writers Anonymous kept me moving theoretically with insightful comment and kept me writing with sisterly support. Marg McKenzie and Freya Headlam, my other TWA group, enabled me to keep a sense of proportion about the enterprise. All these women read drafts or proofread chapters, discussed theoretical, methodological and practical issues and poured generous glasses of wine on many occasions.

John Biddington drew a wonderful cartoon for use in the third interviews, Veronica Trayford did a splendid job as the typist of a long manuscript for the thesis, and Scott Howard of RMIT was very helpful with the business of transferring material from system to system. Cathryn Game was a helpful and efficient editor for Oxford University Press.

Lyn Richards and David Hickman who supervised the thesis are among the most talented researchers and finest teachers I have ever met. Lyn's flights of metaphor set me off on fruitful quests for ideas, David's trains of logic made me give order to the ideas, and their joint insistence on the rigorous analysis of ideas and data helped to give the project substance. Both of them contributed ideas and insights throughout the project. They spent several hours a week reading my drafts in addition to time spent in meetings with me and in the administrative chores associated with a thesis student. The thesis (and hence the book) would not have been written without them, and my debt to them is enduring.

Three other people were crucial to this book. During the writing of the thesis Marg Taylor fed me, rejoiced with me, listened to rehearsals of arguments in which she had no interest, let me cry on her shoulder and occasionally bullied me into keeping on, just as she has for the thirty years of our friendship. She also proofread. Paul Brick, also a friend of longstanding, did all that and more. The love and help of these two people meant that eventually I finished the thesis. The book would have been finished without Ern Reeders' support, but it would, I think, have been a different kind of text; certainly my conclusions about the possibility of active negotiation with ideology rather than passive submission to its dictates would not be so optimistic. *Not having Families* is written for him, and for our daughter Ruth, with love and hope for the future.

1

. . . .

introduction

WHY THIS TOPIC?

This book is about people and ideology. It describes a set of ideas that have a constraining impact on most of us and a group of people who negotiate an unconventional behaviour pattern vis-à-vis those ideas without necessarily abandoning them.

It did not begin as a book or as a book about ideology but as an academic thesis about voluntarily childless couples. Gradually, the thesis moved towards studying how such couples negotiate with the ideology of parenthood, and eventually the thesis became a book with a similar focus.

How did I become interested in voluntary childlessness? And how did the interest in ideology emerge? Like most researchers, my motives were a mixture of personal interests, concern for a particular public issue and theoretical interest in a particular set of ideas.

My initial interest in studying voluntarily childless couples was completely personal. When I married, aged 20 and still a student, I took it for granted that I wanted children and would some day have them. (Two, one of each sex for preference. We had even discussed possible names before our wedding.) But 'some day' was in the fairly remote future, after we had finished our degrees, found secure jobs, travelled, bought a house and generally 'got set up' before we 'got tied down'.

By the time the setting-up was nearly completed, we were both in our late twenties, and the issue of parenthood began to loom on the near horizon. We shared the then-prevalent notion that for woman, childbearing over the age of 30 was nearly out of the question, and that I was 'up against the clock' and had better get on with it. But after seven years of childless marriage, I had become aware of all the difficulties facing women when they become mothers. The certainty that one day we would have children had given way to a question: will we ever have them? And for me especially the question was becoming more and more salient as couples I knew became parents and made jokes about who was next on the list.

Having Families, a study of the changing norms about marriage and child-bearing in Australia (Richards 1978, 1985), pointed out that there was virtually no data on the voluntarily childless in Australia and suggested to me that my private dilemma could be studied as a social issue. The personal interest in voluntary childlessness formed the questions with which I began the research. I had no great interest in the question of *how many* people there were who had chosen childlessness, but I was anxious to know *what sort* of people they were, and what kind of lives they led—rather as if they were a club and I was considering membership.

And, to some extent, it was my personal interests that led me to think about negotiating with ideology. By half way through the research, I knew that, although I liked most of the people I was interviewing and found their lifestyles agreeable, I did not want to join their club. That realization steered me towards thinking about ideas and how they influence behaviour and, in tandem with my interest in feminist theory, led to a dawning conviction that ideology was a useful concept for explaining the phenomenon of voluntary childlessness.

While my interest was the result of private and autobiographical factors, voluntary childlessness has also been a recurrent public issue in Australia and similar countries. In Australia the basic assumption in population policy since the earliest days of European settlement has been that the country was one of great promise, 'requiring only the human resources and the capital to realize its potential' (Refshauge 1979). The demographic transition of the late nineteenth century, which saw a marked decline in family size, caused considerable alarm to governments. The issue of deliberate childlessness was raised by the New South Wales Royal Commission on the Decline of the Birthrate and on Mortality of Infants (1904). That commission came to the conclusion that:

> ... the people, led astray by false and pernicious doctrine into the belief that personal interests and ambitions, a high standard of ease, comfort and luxury, are the essential aims of life, and that these aims are best attained by refusing to accept the consequences which nature has ordained shall follow from marriage—have neglected, and are neglecting, their true duty to themselves, to their fellow countrymen and to posterity.

While this commission is evidence that there was an official attitude of pronatalism, it is also clear that the social climate was not universally favourable to uncontrolled population increase. Governments took no action to make large families more popular, but turned to immigration as a policy area where the deficiencies in natural increase could be remedied. Attitudes to contraception among the medical profession and the population in general were not uniform. Alongside those who saw it as reflecting only the selfish desire for pleasure, there were those who thought that limiting and spacing of births was acceptable and even desirable. There was pronatalism, but it was ambiguous, favouring many children for the sake of the nation, but suggesting fewer children for the sake of individual couples and more especially individual women.

The issue of childlessness seemed to disappear from public consciousness as the century wore on, although concern about keeping up population growth remained. But it re-emerged in the 1970s with some vigour. This time the publicists were proponents rather than opponents. Articles appeared with titles like 'A vote against motherhood' and 'Why we don't want children'.[1] Several popular books put the case against couples becoming parents,[2] and the term *childfree marriage* came into use to describe the voluntarily childless couple. Those words give a clue to the changed attitude. The term child*less* implies lack but a child*free* union sounds as desirable as a fleafree bed.[3]

Organizations for the voluntarily childless were set up in the USA and Britain. In Australia, a meeting was held in Melbourne in 1978 that discussed the possibility of an organization for the voluntarily childless but matters went no further. Clearly, there was an emerging phenomenon of childlessness, but it also became clear that Australian pronatalism was not quite dead. In November 1979 the Liberal Minister for Immigration and Ethnic Affairs, Mr MacKellar, said that declining birthrates among some groups and high rates of increase among others meant that 'the very future of the sort of Western civilization that has been built up over the past millennium is open to question' (*Age*, 13/11/79). He argued that social attitudes, including the growth of equal opportunities for women at work, had accelerated the decline in fertility by making women feel guilty about raising families rather than getting jobs. Though this was a lone and very small voice, compared to the thunderings of the 1904 Royal Commission, throughout the next decade voluntary childlessness continued to be of public interest, and comments about it appeared at intervals in the media. For example, in 1987 the Australian Institute of Family Studies released a prediction that 20% of women born between 1951 and 1956 would remain childless, sparking off comment from newspaper columnists, liberal and conservative alike, which regretted this apparently 'selfish' trend.

Such comments often stressed two themes, which relate ambiguously to each other. On the one hand, writers noted the statistics which showed a falling birthrate, thus evoking memories of earlier pronatalist 'populate or perish' concerns. On the other hand, they gave basically sympathetic accounts of the lives of some childless couples, stressing the right of individuals to choose their own paths in life and suggesting that childless couples faced rather unfair pressure from society at large.

So there is no doubt that voluntary childlessness has recently been an issue of public concern and that attitudes today are as ambivalent as they seem to have been in 1904. The issue thus warrants research, which could produce material of use to policy-makers. There is also no doubt that the issue of childlessness is related to another issue of public concern: the role of women. This seems to have been the case in the early years of the century and is certainly true now.

The resurgence of debate about childlessness in the 1970s took place in a context of extensive and heated debate about women's liberation and is closely connected to that wider debate. The second wave of twentieth-century feminism produced a variety of trenchant analyses of society, and in all of them the position of women in the family was identified as a central factor in female subordination. For those who relied mostly on theories of roles and socialization, the problem lay with the overemphasis on women's roles as wives and mothers. For Marxism-inspired feminists, it lay with the capitalist organization of production—in terms of public work, which was male-oriented and private, reproductive work, which was seen as exclusively feminine. Radical feminists, on the other hand, saw motherhood as being so central to the oppression of women that only a total overthrow of the nuclear family would suffice for liberation. Despite the enormous differences between them, all these feminists agreed that 'the family' in abstract was central to the problems of women. And, in concrete terms, this meant that having children was likely to be a problem for any individual woman who wanted greater freedom than her mother had had. It appeared possible that refraining from having children, even if you thought there were things which you might enjoy about the job of motherhood, might be the only way to what was described as 'ultimate liberation' (Movius 1976).

By the 1980s new tendencies were evident within feminism, including a re-evaluation of motherhood as a fulfilling and even powerful status for women, despite its manifest effect on earning capacity and career mobility. A number of women began to talk about choosing motherhood—sometimes single motherhood—as desirable, and to berate feminists for being sucked into the masculine value system which equated career success with personal fulfilment. But the new debate about motherhood did not make it any easier to decide whether to have children!

Studying the voluntarily childless, then, could throw light on two public issues. The first question, what causes people to choose childlessness, is likely to be of interest to policy-makers (whether they wish to see the birthrate increase or to remain low). The second, the question of whether childlessness is liberatory, is of more interest to those concerned with other policy questions affecting women's lives.

As well as being relevant to issues of public concern, this study of the voluntarily childless can throw some light on a central debate in social theory. That debate has a variety of names. Recent shorthand describes it as the question of *social structure* and *human agency*. An older formulation is that of Marx, who said that people 'make their own history but they do not make it just as they please; they do not make it under circumstances of their own choosing' (Marx 1852). A feminine version of the same dichotomy is offered in a short story, 'The Quilt Maker', by Angela Carter, who uses the metaphor of patchwork to stand for the ways in which we take the material available to us and manipulate it. She says that this image 'synthesizes perfectly both the miscellany of experience and the use we make of it'.

How far can we go in creating our own lives and how much are we constrained by the social structure in which we live? And just how is this process of making our own history within social constraints carried out? One way of understanding the process is through the study of those who seem to have gone a long way towards breaking out of the constraints of social structure by not doing what most people in a similar situation have done. The voluntarily childless are just such a group, and my description of them as negotiating with ideology is a description of people working within a structure of ideas and at the same time resisting it. Of course I cannot finally resolve the debate about freedom and constraint, but my study may help to elucidate some of the factors that enable some people to be more in control than others of (some of) their own history.

WHAT HAVE OTHER STUDIES FOUND?

The project called 'Not Having Families' arose out of and was shaped by this background of personal, public and theoretical interests. It was also shaped by some of the existing material on voluntarily childless couples.

There is quite a large international body of recent research on people who choose to be childless, reflecting public interest in the issue. While every author has an individual perspective on the topic, composed of personal inclinations, discipline and orientation or perspective within disciplines, there are three main approaches to childlessness in the literature: the demographic, the social–psychological and the feminist approach.

The demographic approach

The demographic approach, found in most of the early literature mainly in the US, documents two aspects of childlessness, usually from examination of census data. Firstly, demographers were able to show that rates of childlessness had apparently increased in the 1970s; secondly, they were able to demonstrate some correlation between 'new-style' families, including voluntarily childless ones, and certain social location factors affecting individuals. Roughly speaking, the factors that seemed to be most important as associations of voluntary childlessness were: lack of formal religious commitment,[4] high educational level,[5] high-status occupation and/or high income level[6] and urban location.[7] This was not startling news; it had been a lament for decades that those who could most easily afford large families were those least likely to have them, but the confirmation of popular suspicion is a valuable contribution from the demographic school.

A problem that besets all the demographic work on childlessness is that, because the large-scale surveys on which they rely for data do not include the right questions, they cannot differentiate the voluntarily childless from those who want children but have none. This has two effects. Firstly, it means that the real size of the voluntarily childless population in any country remains unknown, although estimates have been attempted and a variety of figures offered. Veevers (1981) suggests that between 5 and 7% of marriages in the US and Canada are voluntarily childless; Bernard (1974) quoted another estimate of 9%; and Den Bandt cited a Dutch estimate of 2–3% (1977). In Australia, the National Population Inquiry estimate was about 5% (Borrie 1978) in the 1970s and the Institute of Family Studies suggested a figure closer to 20% in

1987. But in the absence of data that links completed fertility of couples with intentions, such calculations remain provisional.

A second effect of the inability of the large-scale demographic studies to distinguish the voluntarily from the involuntarily childless is that their findings about their social locations must also be regarded as provisional, because they are frequently based on inference about which people in a set of data are voluntarily childless; although studies that do sample the voluntarily childless tend to support the conclusions of the demographers. More critically, because their interest is in whole populations rather than in individual lives, the demographers have not been able to explain why *some* educated, affluent, urban-dwelling couples with high incomes and low religious adherence should choose to be childless while others opt for parenthood. The population-based approach cannot illuminate the process by which individuals move into voluntary childlessness and in the end can only offer a preliminary account of the voluntarily childless.

The social–psychological approach

The social–psychological approach, unlike the demographic approach, relied on small samples of those known to be voluntarily childless. These ranged from a clinical case study of six women to a questionnaire study of 374 individuals.[8] The groups studied were, on the whole, volunteers responding to media appeals,[9] although there was research on the American organization for non-parents and some studies relied on college students.[10]

While the demographers had looked for correlates of childlessness in terms of social location, the researchers who focused specifically on groups of the voluntarily childless were able to ask more complex questions. They also studied the family backgrounds of their respondents and they were concerned with the attitudes of the childless and the relationship between attitudes and behaviour, thus approaching the topic from a psychological as well as a social angle.[11] There were studies of the attitudes of the voluntarily childless towards children, which showed a variety of reasons for not wanting them.[12] While the exact formulation of reasons tended to vary with the technique used to elicit them, packages of ideas that seem to be important had to do with the problems of commitment to children and what it entails rather than concern for overpopulation or dislike of children.[13]

Several studies focused on the attitudes of the voluntarily childless to marriage. Expectations of marriage, adjustment to marriage and perceived satisfaction with marriage were all studied.[14] The general tendency of these studies was to suggest that the marriages of the childless are characterized by what could be called 'dyadic intensity' (Veevers 1980) and certainly to discredit any notion that voluntarily childless marriages are unhappier than marriages which involve children. The social–psychological research on the voluntarily childless painted a picture of marriages that conformed quite well to the stereotype of a romantic relationship.

This kind of research, with other work on topics like the contraceptive behaviour and attitudes of the voluntarily childless, their attitudes to sterilization, and 'mental health' of the childless,[15] was a valuable addition to the demographic approach. It began to suggest a more precise description of the voluntarily childless than had been possible using the research on demographic trends. Even more useful was the work that examined the decision to be childless as a process and attempted to specify the routes by which people come to non-parenthood.[16] Other researchers focused on the difference between the 'early articulators' and the 'postponers' (Veevers 1980).[17] This research, together with studies which looked at the pressures facing the childless,[18] and those which examined social attitudes towards the voluntarily childless,[19] enabled a more complex and satisfying explanation for voluntary childlessness than the demographic approach.

The dictum of Lord Peter Wimsey, 'When you know how, you know who', applies to explaining social phenomena as well as bodies in the library. 'How' in this case had a variety of dimensions: coming into marriage or a partnership with the intention of delaying child-bearing, meeting the pushes and pulls of life as a worker and a family member, being dragged this way and that by attitudes to childrearing, marriage, etc., and meeting various reactions from others to which reaction is demanded. By raising the question 'how', social–psychological researchers began to suggest an answer to the question 'who'. The people who are at the intersection of all the pressures suggested in the 'how' research—pressures from their own ideas and those around them, from their own decisions about marriage and jobs, from the actions and reactions of others—are the ones who might become childless if the pushes and pulls are in the right combination. That answer, of course, does not enable prediction about individuals, but it is a considerable advance on the demographic picture.

Although it advances understanding of the voluntarily childless, the social–psychological approach suffers from two problems. At a methodological level, reliance on volunteer samples as a way of 'stalking an invisible minority' (Veevers 1980) creates a problem for generalizing the results of any one study—even though some studies have attracted samples of several hundred each. Censuses have not, to date, sought to know about the voluntarily childless, so there is no way of knowing whether the characteristics reported in the social–psychological research are indeed represented in the population of the voluntarily childless. It is encouraging that the studies tend to be fairly consistent and that the social–psychological findings do not contradict the demographic ones, but the problem of generalizing from samples of a population whose characteristics are unknown remains.

While the technical weakness of sampling in the social–psychological approach is a problem, it is not, to my mind, the major weakness of the approach. A graver problem is the way in which the social–psychological research ignores or treats too simplistically the elements of constraint and conflict in explaining childlessness.

The social–psychological research notes potential conflicts between the childless and socially accepted ideas, or between women and men about not having children, but tends to depict individuals as acting autonomously against a background of consensus. This creates two sets of problems. First, it assumes a more-or-less stable society, characterized by universal norms, with which all agree, rather than a society which is marked by tensions between the interests, values and ideas of different groups. Second, it assumes that those who disobey a widely held norm are manifesting individual will, rather than responding in ways patterned by social structure to sets of social tensions. Parenthood is seen as a matter of taking up a role or perhaps of following a norm. The concepts of role and norm are characteristic of a 'consensus' view of society and have been criticized for concealing or ignoring the existence of conflict and power struggles between groups. As Connell points out, the concept works by ignoring social conflict and runs into problems when it tries to deal with it:

> Role theory plainly appeals to those who like to think that the social order works by mutual agreement; that people ought to do what they are told, and there is something wrong with people who don't; that force, oppression, and exploitation aren't very important in the everyday working of society; and that the constraints that do operate on people reflect some kind of wisdom ... (Connell 1979)

It is this underlying paradigm that leads the social–psychologists to oversimplify the social background of childlessness and to overemphasize the importance of individual volition in fertility decisions. For, although role theory has been criticized for social determinism, or presenting a picture of 'oversocialized' humanity (Wrong 1961), of people who would disappear if all the masks of their roles were removed, it rests actually on *individual* determinism:

> What is it that sticks the components of a role, the position and the actions, together? Unless the role exists wholly and solely in the head of the theorist, it is the expectations of people in counter-positions to the said role. What gives their role-definition its force? It is, and can only be (within role theory), the application of sanctions by those people to enforce their expectations. What determines the application of the sanctions? This cannot logically be regarded generally as a role-prescription for the holder of the counter-position for that way we get into an infinite regress ... Somewhere ... the application of sanctions must be rested on the will of the incumbent of a counter-position, on her personal willingness to apply the sanctions. The ultimate determinism in role theory, that is to say, is psychological, not social. (Connell 1979)

The same problem occurs with the concept of 'norm'. How is obedience to a norm made obligatory if not at some point by the willingness of individuals to take action against norm-breakers? If the answer is that norms and roles are internalized and become part of an individual's nature, then this simply pushes the will to apply sanctions back in time to early socialization into the role.

This hidden inheritance of the social–psychological literature tends to prevent it from being able to get a grip on questions of power, and thus hinders its understanding of the voluntarily childless.

The feminist approach

Studies of voluntary childlessness influenced by feminist concepts are rare. The few articles that do exist are of great interest because they begin to place childlessness in the context of social conflict which both the demographic and the social psychological literature neglect. While *feminist* is a term covering a multitude of positions, a key element in all of them is the perception that women have been, and are still, in a subordinate social position and that this should be changed.

One study, for example (Marciano 1978, 1979), looks at the decision to remain childless against the background of differences between the sexes with regard to power in marital disputes and argues that differences in socialization tend to give husbands more bargaining power in a marriage than wives get. This might explain the pattern shown in a questionnaire study of forty couples belonging to the American National Organization of Nonparents (NON), twenty of whom had experienced conflict over the decision to remain childless. Broadly speaking, when there was conflict over childlessness, it seemed to be the husband's will that prevailed. While the study is exploratory, deals with relatively small numbers and raises more questions than it answers, it suggests that in order to understand childless couples, we must see them in a context of deep-seated (though socially created) differences between men and women and of (on the whole) unequal power between them.

Probably the best-known comment about voluntary childlessness from a feminist perspective is the description of it as 'ultimate liberation' (Movius 1976), which has been cited by other researchers on childlessness and by researchers on motherhood to strengthen suggestions that voluntary childlessness should be seen as a more-or-less revolutionary alternative to parenthood. Wearing (1984) describes it as the possible 'utopian' counter to the 'ideology' of motherhood. I disagree with this view of childlessness but agree with Movius' contention that the conflict between paid work in the 'public' sphere and the demands placed on women by motherhood is at the heart of women's decisions to be childless. Movius is describing the situation correctly when she says that:

> A woman who wishes to succeed to the same degree as a man must give herself the same advantages enjoyed by a man. In our society, one of the most

predictable ways of assuring these advantages is by remaining childless. (Movius 1976)

While I also disagree with the implication that this is a perfectly satisfactory prescription as a description of the current situation, Movius' work points to the necessity of seeing childless couples against a background in which the woman's chances of gaining high status and reward in paid work are affected by childbearing to a greater degree than the man's. Feminist research on childlessness grows out of the social–psychological tradition and uses some of its concepts. So both Marciano and Movius use the term *sex role* without comment or criticism. But because they also bring to bear the perspective that a fundamental (and wrong) inequality exists between men and women, the feminist writers can pose new and useful questions about childlessness.

HOW TO STUDY THE VOLUNTARILY CHILDLESS?

The background to the study influenced my choice of methods. I had decided early on that I wished to know what sort of people the voluntarily childless were and how they got to be that way. My initial 'who and how/why' questions were not particularly amenable to the quantitative techniques used by demographic researchers on childlessness. I wanted to know about the childless more deeply than as a collection of superficial categories of age, education and other social characteristics, and so I decided to use a qualitative rather than a quantitative approach in my research.

As my ideas developed into a theory about ideology, it became even clearer that a 'depth' or qualitative approach would serve me better than a 'breadth' or quantitative one. Research about how people confront ideology is rare; my work is exploratory, and the qualitative method is particularly suitable for exploratory projects. With a new field researchers have no background information that will help them to know whether the questions they are asking bear any resemblance to the ones the researched are answering. So they must attempt to collect in-depth information that will generate such understanding. Moreover, family life is complex, varied and often riddled with conflicts. In some respects, novelists have been more successful than social scientists in generating insights about the family. This suggests that the open-ended narrative style associated with qualitative research might be particularly useful for a study about families.

My own aims, the exploratory nature of some of the research and the demands of the field of study all pushed me towards depth and quality rather than breadth and quantity. At the same time, practical difficulties of obtaining a sample suitable for statistical analysis pulled me away from the quantitative approach. In order to make statistically valid generalisations about childlessness, I would need to have a sample of childless people selected at random from the population rather than a volunteer group. The task of random sampling was simply beyond my resources, as it has been for all other researchers who go 'stalking the invisible minority' (Veevers 1980), so throughout the study, I was concerned with grasping the quality of experience for a small group of childless people rather than making sophisticated numerical statements about a large group.

The qualitative approach permits a variety of possible methods for collecting and analysing data. Collection, for example, may be by interview or observation or based on documents. And those methods may be more or less structured and more or less time-consuming.

Interviews may range from the extremely formal and organised through to purposeful conversations. They may be comparatively brief encounters between researcher and researched or much more sustained attempts to enter the lives of the researched. Once more, there is a trade-off between breadth and depth, and the more depth (the less the formal structure and the more time spent with each respondent) the less breadth (i.e. the fewer respondents). My decision was to focus on a very small number of voluntarily childless couples and to interview them in depth and over time. In other words, I decided to use a case-study approach and to examine a small number of instances in detail, seeking a wide range of information from each instance.

My research began with interviews with eleven couples who met my definition of 'voluntarily childless' by being:
• legally married
• in their first marriage
• childless
• to the best of their knowledge, fertile
• self-defined as not wanting ever to have children.

This definition requires explanation as it is both more restricted than some researchers have used and less restrictive than the definitions of others. I insisted on legally married couples because I assumed that those who marry but remain childless are breaking the marriage–parenthood nexus quite decisively. Given the way 'love and marriage/go together like a horse and carriage' and are supposed to be followed by parenthood, cohabiters are not breaking the nexus in the same way. They uncouple the romantic horse from the marital carriage but can be seen as less odd than those who climb into the carriage hitched to the horse and then refuse to drive off towards parenthood. A subsidiary reason for not considering cohabitees is that there is some evidence that marriers and cohabitees are different sorts of people (Cotton et al. 1983; Sarantakos 1984). Had I included cohabiting childless couples, I would have introduced another variable into an already complicated picture. Similar reasons lay beneath my decision to look only at people in their first marriage. They are most likely to feel the demands of the ideology of parenthood as heavy, and so their refusal to meet them is especially interesting. And second marriages may well be qualitatively very different from first ones. Another reason for my decision to restrict the sample to first marriages and married couples was that since I began the research by wondering if I wanted to 'join the club' of childless people, I naturally thought in terms of people who were in the same situation with regard to marriage.

In some ways, my definition of a childless couple was looser than that used by other researchers. Veevers (1980) and Callan (1985) both argue that a couple should have been married for some time in order to qualify as 'really' voluntarily childless, on the grounds that only those who have lived with the decision for some time are certain about their choice. They allow exceptions for those whose commitment is manifest in one or both partners having been sterilized. I set no such limits, accepting all couples who met my other criteria and who said they did not ever want to have children.

My reasons for this loose definition were that a study stressing 'who, how and why' and concerned with negotiation with ideology has less need of certainty that the respondents are 'genuinely' childless than one stressing 'how many'. In fact some of the couples I studied changed their minds during the course of the research. Their examples suggest that the only way to ensure that a couple is 'truly' voluntarily childless is to study those no longer capable of conceiving or rearing a child. A second reason for relying on the couples' self-definition was my conviction that it is somewhat demeaning to those who volunteer to be part of a study to imply that only those who have been married for a certain length of time really know their own minds.

The other characteristic of my definition—that infertile couples be excluded—is one that most other researchers have used, for the obvious reason that acceptance of infertility is qualitatively very different from a decision not to have children.

My methodology and the origins of the project are discussed in appendix 1. Chapter 2 describes the concept of ideology which is central to the study, and subsequent chapters report on the findings.

2

· ·

ideology:

the

theoretical

context

n this chapter, I will discuss in more detail what I mean by ideology. I will do so in two stages. The first will explore the concept of ideology in general, the second will look in detail at the specific ideology of parenthood.

Ideology is a concept with a long history. It is also a hotly debated concept that 'has given rise to more analytical and conceptual difficulties than almost any other term in the social sciences' (Abercrombie, Hill & Turner 1980). The earliest social scientist to write extensively on the term was Karl Marx and, indeed, almost all writers since Marx have engaged to some degree in debates with his ghost, so it is his work that we will consider in most detail.

MARX ON IDEOLOGY

Marx's views on ideology are not always easy to interpret. His main work on the subject, *The German Ideology* (written in conjunction with Engels), was begun in 1845 and published in incomplete form in 1852. It is clear from later comments that neither author was particularly satisfied with the work, and there are two possible interpretations (a 'strong' and a 'weak' one) of ideology which could be made from this key text. In addition, Marx's later work suggests further alterations to what he meant by the elusive term *ideology*. What follows is my interpretation of Marx, and I am concerned with ideology as a tool for research rather than a philosophical concept.[1]

The ultimate source of ideology, according to Marx, is human practice—the multitude of activities that make them distinctively human and by which people create their material and social existence: 'As individuals express their life, so they are' (Marx & Engels 1852). Practice that develops in a framework of material constraints but is not totally formed by them is the source of all ideas. By our human practice as mothers, farmers or social scientists, we come to see ourselves as such and to view the world around us in terms of its potential and its problems for mothering, farming or the generation of social theory. And as this happens, the social conditions that our human activity has created paradoxically come to be objectified and to seem independent of our creating. To use an example which probably would not have occurred to Marx, mothers do not habitually think in terms of deciding that they will cook the family dinner, change the baby's nappy or sweep the floor. Rather, they think in terms of families needing food, baby needing a change or the house needing a clean. I am not arguing here that cooking, childcare and housework are unnecessary in themselves. What I am pointing out is that they are all taken for granted as part of motherhood. They could, in theory, be done by fathers, children or outsiders, and indeed some mothers do have a sense of this some of the time. For many, however, there is a feeling that because I am a mother it is automatically my job to look after the house, the meals and the nappies. A particular social condition becomes externalized so that it is no longer 'my decision' but simply 'the way things are'.

'The way things are' is not necessarily agreeable to everyone—there is now a vast literature on the discontents of motherhood—but it usually serves the interests of somebody. (Much of the literature on how motherhood is constructed in our society suggests that the interests of capital and the interests of men have been served by the assigning of most childcare to women.) The idea that the fact of having given birth necessarily entails childcare, housework and cooking serves, as it were, to 'paper over' these contradictory cracks between the wants and needs of different individuals. Ideas grow out of human activity but may then constrain some human beings and serve the interests of others.

Practice creates ideas, and ideology is a type of idea. Marx suggests that the ultimate source of ideology is practice but that there is a more immediate source as well. For him, the conditions under which productive practice occurs have, from the first division of labour, included a ruling class and a class which is ruled. The practices of the ruling class create ideas, and these ideas reflect the interests of that class. Precisely because they do rule, and thus have substantial control of the means by which ideas are disseminated, it is their ideas that are likely to dominate. Hence the famous dictum:

> The ideas of the ruling class are in every epoch the ruling ideas; that is, the class which is the ruling *material* force of society is at the same time its ruling *intellectual* force. (Marx & Engels 1852)

Within the ruling class the group that engages in intellectual labour—writers, teachers and so on—are the main creators of ideology:

> The division of labour is expressed also in the ruling class as the division of mental and material labour, so that within this class one part appears as the thinkers of the class (its active, conceptive ideologists who make perfecting the illusion of this class about itself their main source of livelihood) while the others' attitude toward these ideas and illusions is more passive and receptive. (ibid.)

These people give voice to ideas that come from the activities of the ruling group and which reflect its interests. Some of these ideas may in fact reflect truth. (Babies do indeed need to be kept clean if they are to be healthy.) Others do not. (There is no biological reason why fathers cannot change nappies.) Ideology is not totally true but it does not consist of deliberate untruths, nor is it totally divorced from reality. The metaphor used in *The German Ideology* of ideology as inverted images like those found in a camera obscura or on the retina of the eye makes it clear that Marx did not see ideology as the same thing as propaganda. The fact that it serves the interests of the ruling class does not mean that rulers are exempt from the constraining effects of ideology.

The impact of ideology, according to Marx, was to create a state of 'false consciousness' among the population. Both the ruling class and the ruled see the world in terms of ruling-class interests. The ruled are thus prevented from seeing the way things *really* are.

There is considerable debate on just how dominant ideology really is, according to Marx. My perception is that he thought ideology to be dominating but not totally dominant. In *The German Ideology* he emphasizes the power of ruling-class illusions but he also stresses the foolishness of the idealist view that ideas are powerful in and of themselves so that changing consciousness will change the world. Elsewhere, he forecast the growth of a changed consciousness about class among workers as the result of changing material conditions, something which he could not have done had he seen ideology as completely encompassing. He did not, however, regard changing consciousness as a simple matter. Individuals 'undoubtedly make one another physically and mentally, but do not make themselves', he wrote. It will take more than individual effort of will or simple uncovering of a different view to see through an ideology and displace it from individual consciousness. Social conditions must change so that people's practices change and, with *that* change, comes a change of mind. Any woman who set out in the heady early days of 'women's liberation' to change the domestic division of labour or her own habits of fashion will know what I mean. Even if you knew at one level that sweeping the floor was not on your part of the roster or that you did not want to shave your legs, at another level was the knowledge that the floor was too dirty, or hairy legs too daggy to be borne, and that you could not be at peace with yourself until you had done what you rationally did not wish to do. Changing attitudes might take years of gritted teeth and changed behaviour, and in some cases might never happen.

In summary, then, Marx saw ideology as ideas emanating from, and reflecting the interests of, the ruling class that paper over the realities of power and interest and thus distort the truth without being completely divorced from it. These ideas are strong and hard to resist, but they are not necessarily totally dominant and unchanging.

This definition of ideology has useful features but also some weaknesses. One of its strengths is that it helps us to see ideas as important weapons in the struggle for social domination, but not as an irresistible force. In so doing, it avoids the problem of a functionalist explanation of social phenomena, with its inability to account for change.[2] Another is that it avoids the idealist fallacy of taking ideas as a cause rather than a result of social practices. It also offers some guides to the human sources of ideology. Taken together, these points enable us to move some way towards an operationalized definition which would be of use in the empirical study of ideology. Researchers who followed Marx's outline and who wished to study a particular ideology would look for ideas which could be traced back to social experiences but were not simple reflections of reality, which, in their distortion of experience, served the interests of the ruling class and which that class, as well as the rest of society, held to be truthful.

The problems with this definition lie in the definitions of the terms *interest* and *false consciousness* and the question of how transmission occurs.

I have said that Marx defined ideology as ideas that serve the interests of the ruling class. Just how is this phrase to be made specific so that ideology can be studied empirically? Interest could mean those aims perceived by members of the ruling class. In that case, how many of the class need to agree on those aims for an ideology to be present? But, if ideology conceals interests, then maybe the members of the ruling class will not be able to state them. Perhaps interest should be taken to mean what observers in another place or time see as the aims of the ruling class. Is it enough, in this case, to say that it is in the interests of the ruling class that it should continue to rule as a whole or should the interests of individuals, groups and fractions within the ruling class be considered as well? And are we focussing on short-term interests or longer-term ones? Moreover, all these questions imply the need to define the boundaries of the ruling class before its interests can be specified, and there is a long tradition of dispute over the exact nature of the ruling class.

The problem of false consciousness is related to the problem of interest. The idea that people live in false consciousness and are total victims of ideological messages simply does not make sense of everyday life. Where are all those idiots who believe that lemons come tumbling out of washing machines or that a particular bath foam will bring a prince out of the landscape to stand under their window? We have systematic studies that show that people are not simply cultural dupes.[3] I have argued that, for Marx, ideology was dominating but not totally dominant, but this does not really dispose of the problem of defining false consciousness. The question still remains: whose consciousness counts? Surely false consciousness can only be outlined in contrast to the real interests of a subordinate class which they cannot perceive accurately because they are under the veil of ideology? In that case, as I have already suggested, we need to be able to specify those interests, and here we run into the problems which I have already discussed.

A final problem with Marx's notion of ideology is the way it disregards the complexities of the production of ideas. The statement that the intellectuals of the ruling class produce its ideology entails the problem of defining the members of society who make up this group and the further problem of just how ideology is produced and disseminated.

Ideology is transmitted through a series of channels rather than directly from individual makers:

> Group interests and the ideologies supporting them are expressed chiefly through highly bureaucratized institutions ... which are quite capable of establishing their own logic of development in line with their bureaucratic dynamic. (Salter & Tapper 1981)

Thus expressions of ideology in, say, the newspapers are affected not only by the interests and attitudes of the direct 'makers' (the writers) but also by those involved in production (editors, printers), by the commercial and other interests of proprietors as seen by all those others and as directly transmitted by proprietors, the perceived constraints of law (plus those constraints filtered through institutions like press councils), and perceptions of the wider social context expressed in terms like 'Herald readers' or 'the Australian public'. This in turn creates problems for the practical business of studying ideology. Attempts to reconstruct an ideology from official documents cannot easily show what interests lie behind those documents precisely because they have been 'contaminated' in the process of production by all sorts of other ideas and attitudes.

I will return to these problems and offer some (imperfect) solutions later, but will now turn to discussion of how his successors and opponents reacted to Marx's concept of ideology.

IDEOLOGY AFTER MARX

The impact of both the 'positivist' and the 'historicist' followers of Marx in the early years of this century was to broaden the concept of ideology. While for Marx it tended to signify ideas originating in the experience and reflecting the interests of one class (the ruling class), for some later Marxists it came to mean simply the world-view of a particular group. This shift was one that meant that the word 'did not necessarily lose its original negative connotation, but ... displaced its critical aspect to a secondary significance' (Larrain 1983). So it has been argued that Marxism itself was an ideology, and Lenin could speak of the problem of bourgeois ideology being less that it is ideological than that it is bourgeois (this usage clearly 'neutralizes' the concept).

This broadening of the term has unfortunate consequences for researchers trying to examine ideology. If the word includes any form of consciousness based on class experience, there is no difference between ideology and any other set of ideas deriving from lived experience, so that one may as well abandon the word altogether. The 'neutralizing' tendency also has consequences for the debate about distinguishing ideology from truth which has been sketched in the previous discussion of interests and will be discussed in more detail later.

The main Marxist writer on ideology in the first part of this century, Antonio Gramsci, used the word in a broader sense than Marx, thus somewhat weakening its bite. He also, however, stressed the importance of ideology in the struggle for social dominance. For him, ideologies were conceptions of the world that 'create the terrain on which men move, acquire consciousness of their position, struggle, etc' (Gramsci 1976), and the associated term *hegemony* signified ruling-class dominance in the field of ideas, as opposed to dominance based on power over the state. For Gramsci, the hegemony of the ruling class is not complete since the subordinate classes have ideologies or potential ideologies of their own. Ruling-class intellectuals are responsible for refining and presenting to the population the world-view that holds hegemonic sway, and for the subordinate classes this view exists alongside elements of oppositional understanding. These elements are based on experience and constitute 'good sense', by which Gramsci means what we call in everyday speech 'common sense'. This 'good sense' is an inchoate mass, waiting to be given definition and turned into a genuine force for ideological change by the work of intellectuals arising within (or 'organic to') the working class.

It is clear that, for Gramsci, the creation of ideology is an active and at times contradictory process, and the creation and maintenance of hegemony is a process of simultaneous construction and reconstruction of both ideas and intellectuals. In other words, ideology is never static. This emphasis is useful; the broadening and neutralizing of ideology which accompanied it is less so.

Mannheim and ideology

While it can be argued that critics of Marx like Durkheim and Weber make use of the notion of ideology, it is in the work of Karl Mannheim that we find the most detailed consideration of the term from a non-Marxist perspective.

Mannheim's views contrast strongly with those of Marx, though less strongly with some of the early Marxists. He shares with Marx the conviction that social structures determine ideas but, unlike his predecessor, does not see the possibility of a scientific truth which could exist outside such structures. Mannheim describes Marx's notion of ideology as 'relativism' and argues that this concept does not go far enough. What is required is a 'relational' view which assumes that 'there are spheres of thought in which it is impossible to conceive of absolute truth existing independently of the values and position of the subject and unrelated to the social context' (Mannheim 1954). This does not mean that all knowledge is mere illusion, but it does mean that all knowledge must be seen and judged as knowledge within a particular context. In the context of social struggle, some ideas may be described as ideologies.

For Mannheim, ideology emanates from a ruling group which is so 'intensively interest bound' that its members are unaware of 'facts which would undermine their sense of domination'. While the ruling group is obviously in a strong position to spread its ideas throughout society, ideology does not go unopposed. The subordinate groups gradually generate a consciousness of their oppression which Mannheim calls 'utopia'. This kind of thought grows out of the existing social order, as does ideology, but it opposes that order and may even overthrow it. In this case, utopian thought is enshrined as the status quo and so becomes ideology.

There are clear similarities with Marx here, but also vast differences. For Mannheim ideology and utopia are not concepts that can be measured against reality so much as ideas about processes. They supersede each other in endless cycles of dominance and rebellion. While I have argued that for Marx ideology is dominating though not necessarily dominant, for Mannheim it appears to be both inescapable (at a general level) and rather weak in particular instances. We cannot ever reach a 'supertemporarily valid conclusion' about truths and are thus always interestbound to some degree, but specific ideologies seem rather weak, capable of easy overthrow by utopias.

This view of ideology has some useful methodological implications. It offers a critique of the dogmatism of placing too much emphasis on the epistemological privilege of Marxist (or any other) theory. As a researcher in the tradition of 'mild-mannered empiricism' I am sympathetic to this critique. Taken seriously, Mannheim's liberal relativism should lead to a certain humility about one's ideas and methods and to a willingness to outline as far as possible the values underlying research so that they may be taken into account by readers.

Nonetheless, I do not find Mannheim's concept of ideology fruitful as a perspective for two reasons. First, by relativising the notion more comprehensively than any previous writer, Mannheim deprived it of its critical bite, despite his intentions. In his view, ideology on the one hand is balanced by utopia on the other. Utopia will redress the wrongs of ideology and, as it becomes the new ideology, a new utopia will in turn arise to correct it. There is a sense of constant change but little sense either of struggle or of the motor which drives the process. The pluralism inherent in the dichotomy between ideology and utopia in the end undercuts Mannheim's aim of explaining the role of ideas in the maintenance of power.

A second reason for rejecting Mannheim's conception of ideology is that it is extremely difficult to pin down or operationalize for the study of contemporary ideas. Theoretically, the distinction between ideology and utopia is clear, but in specific cases, how are we to determine which sets of ideas are essentially conservative ideologies and which are challenging utopias? (As an example of the difficulty, think about the current debate on in vitro fertilization. Conservative critics regard it as a radical challenge to the traditional notion of parenthood; radical feminist critics view it as upholding the dominance of a masculine medical establishment over women.) Mannheim's own view was that: 'What in a given case appears as utopian and what is ideological is dependent essentially on the stage and degree of reality to which one applies this standard' (Mannheim 1954). In other words, researchers concerned with ideology must confine themselves to the study of the past. Moreover, they should study only those ideas whose realization may be measured in some degree:

Ideas which later turned out to have been only distorted representations of a past or potential social order were ideological, while those which were adequately realised in the succeeding social order were relative utopias. (Mannheim 1954).

Ideas that disappear from an epoch (for example, the notion of the divine right of monarchs) are easily identified as ideology using this notion, but what are we to make of contemporary ideas (such as the belief in an overwhelming 'maternal instinct' in women) which both persist and are under fire?

The 'relationist' view of ideology is thus both less incisive and harder to operationalize than the 'relativist' one proposed by Marx; therefore, it should be abandoned. Rather than directly addressing the work of Mannheim's followers who continue in the relationist vein, I will move on to the work of recent influential Marxists on ideology.

Althusser and ideology

Althusser's conception of ideology shows the influence of several traditions. He is a Marxist, and the impact of Gramsci is clear in his dichotomy of institutions; he has been influenced by French structuralist theory and there are elements of psychoanalytic thought (derived mainly from Lacan) in his work. His ideas have been extensively (and on the whole justifiably) criticized as inconsistent and misleadingly pessimistic, but they have been extremely influential both in reviving interest in ideology and in stimulating later thinkers, including feminists like Mitchell and Barret.

For Althusser, as for Gramsci, ideology is found in all societies and acts as a kind of social cement. It does not, however, function autonomously; rather, it is 'determined in the last instance' by the structure of production (Althusser 1971).

Whatever it may do in other societies, in those with a class structure, ideology is an integral part of the relationships of domination and subordination which are a feature of such societies. For Althusser, as for Marx, ideology serves to misrepresent the real relations between individuals and the relations of production and, because it is made concrete in practice, ideology, while not 'real' in the same sense as paving stones or rifles, nor an autonomous influence, is indeed powerful and real in terms of its consequences.

The sources and main agents of ideology in class societies are the institutions which Althusser (1971) calls ideological state apparatuses (ISAs). These include religious, educational, political, legal and cultural bodies and can be contrasted to the repressive state apparatuses (RSAs) such as the military which belong clearly in the 'public domain' and function explicitly by force. ISAs create and disseminate ideas in a variety of ways and, although repression and force underlie their workings, they are not usually perceived as repressive bodies. None the less, they are institutions of oppression because the content of any given ideology will be ideas reflecting the practices of the ruling class.

Any particular ideology is a set of ideas, joined (though not necessarily in terms of formal logic) under a problematic—the question that commands the form of the answers which will be given to it. And just as any one element within an ideology can only be understood in terms of the rest of the ideas in that ideology, so ideologies can only be understood in relation to each other. Hence, despite the fact that they are varied institutions, the content of the ISA is 'always in fact unified, despite its diversity and its contradictions, *beneath the ruling ideology* which is the ideology of the "ruling class" ' (Althusser 1971).

Ideology works through constituting individual identity. It is in ideology that we recognize what is 'obvious' about ourselves—for instance, that 'of course' I am a woman. But that recognition is also a misrecognition—I am biologically female, but there is no 'of course' about many aspects of my womanliness. I am not 'of course' petty-minded, or maternal, or any of the other things which our society associates with womanhood by natural fiat; if I possess those characteristics they might well have been culturally induced, and there is no necessary connection between them and my femaleness.

In creating our identities, ideology makes us both subjects and subjugated to the dominant order. Along with the (mis)recognition of ourselves as particular kinds of human subject goes the necessity to behave in accordance with the 'obvious' nature of our subjectivity—for example, to behave in a properly feminine way. This is what makes ideology a force for conservatism, since it guarantees that 'everything really is so, and on condition that the subjects recognise what they are and behave accordingly, everything will be all right' (Althusser 1969). Despite this picture of ideology as a strong force, making people subject to ruling definitions as they become human, Althusser follows Gramsci in stressing the contested nature of ideology. He argues that even though the content of a given ideology will represent the ruling class more strongly than any other, there may be contrary representations and the ISAs are 'not only the stake but also the site of class struggle' (Althusser 1971).

Althusser's notion of ideology has been criticized on many grounds. It can be seen as suffering from the weaknesses of a functionalist explanation. The only way in which the formation and dissolution a particular ideology can be understood (if ideology in general is the functional necessity that Althusser claims it to be) is through acceptance a priori that Althusser is correct in his description. And if we accept his view of ideology as social 'cement', what are we to make of the insistence that it is also the site of struggle? There seem to be logical flaws in Althusser's formulation.

In addition, many writers have suggested that his picture of humanity is too deterministic to be useful, especially for those who are trying to create change. Some have suggested that the flaw is an economic determinism while others have focused on the gap between what experience tells us about people as active subjects and Althusser's picture of passive subjugated creatures.

Although I share the critics' reservations on all these points, I find some useful elements in the work of Althusser. The suggestions that ideologies should be seen as overlapping and linked, that they are tied to practice, and that they are part of the process of constituting our individual identities, are all worth pursuing and are influential in the work of later theorists.

CCCS and ideology

In the 1980s the Centre for Contemporary Cultural Studies in Birmingham, UK, has provided some important work (both in the form of empirical studies and in theoretical reflections) on ideology. Two aspects of the work of CCCS are particularly relevant to my study: the emphasis on the importance of language and the concept of negotiation with ideology.

The 'language and ideology' group at CCCS took as starting points the structuralist linguistic tradition represented by, for example, Barthes and the newer 'discourse theory' (represented by Foucault). These led them to see ideology as working through language and to redefine 'interpellation' in terms of entry into the world of ideology through entry into the symbolic world of words. This points towards an emphasis on the analysis of words and images as the technique by which ideology is unmasked. And, indeed, analysis of the content of media such as women's magazines has been a notable product of the CCCS.

It is not, however, this aspect of CCCS' work which is most relevant to my study; content analysis is, after all, a standard technique in several disciplines. The reflections of one writer from CCCS on the notion of interpellation which underlie this technique have been especially useful to me.

The idea of language interpellating us into ideology raises the spectre of ideology as an inescapable force, because language becomes part of our unconscious. If, for example, all language is patriarchal, how can subjects (male or female, feminist or not) ever get far enough outside patriarchy to see the fact and criticize that language (Hall 1980a)? This problem has led some members of CCCS away from a simple focus on language as it is produced in texts towards the ways in which viewers/hearers/readers react to and interpret the text. The emphasis moves from wraith-like subjects existing within ideology towards active humans with some capacity to manoeuvre. This stress underlies some of the empirical studies from CCCS such as Hobson's (1980) work on housewives' responses to media. It has been conceptualised in terms of *negotiation with ideology* (Hall 1980b). While Hall's work refers specifically to the discourse of television, it is clear that his model could be extended to ideology in general.

For Hall, messages are produced and 'encoded' within one social and institutional framework and are read or 'decoded' within other frameworks which may or may not be identical to those surrounding the encoding. Certain codes of meaning, however, are widespread and appear transparent to nearly everybody. They 'constitute a dominant cultural order, though it is neither univocal nor uncontested' (Hall 1980b).

In other words, ideology exists as a dominating force but what the producer of a message—the director of a news broadcast, the writer of a column on childrearing or even the mother handing on folk wisdom to her daughter—means might or might not be what the message means to the recipient. In many instances, ideology will indeed rule, but in others selective decoding of the message might take place. This selective decoding is the result not merely of private eccentricity but of experiences based on social location which lead members of some groups to a particular 'moment' of response to a message. The typology of decoding positions that Hall proposes sets up three possible stances. The first is the 'dominant hegemonic' position. In this

> the viewer takes the connoted meaning from, say, a television newscast or current affairs programme full and straight and decodes the message in terms of the reference code in which it has been encoded. (Hall 1980b)

This is close to the position adopted by devotees of the dominant ideology thesis, although Hall (1980b) points out that, even here, the impact of the 'professional code' of the message-makers (here, broadcasters and journalists) means that conflicts and contradictions may arise.

The second position is that of 'negotiation'. This entails acceptance of hegemonic definitions at an abstract level but does not mean acceptance at a more personal level. Thus, Hall (1980b) suggests, a worker might agree that it is 'in the national interest' for wages to be frozen but might also argue that this should not apply to her/his own industry. The position is one of simultaneous acceptance and rejection.

The final position is the 'oppositional' one where the recipient of a message 'detotalizes the message in the preferred code in order to re-totalize the message within some alternative framework of reference' (Hall 1980b). For example, the reference to 'national interest' in the message about wage freezes might be oppositionally decoded as 'ruling-class interest' or as a typical piece of uncaring and androcentric logic.

This typology seems to me a fruitful device for exploring the relationship between individuals and ideology. It overcomes the problem of having to assume that people are cultural dupes, and it makes clear the possibility of complex chains of interaction in the transmission and reception of ideological messages without recourse to a relationist stance which would deprive the concept of its critical bite.

Ideology and post-modernism

Many of the writers who followed Foucault and the other French intellectuals who set out to 'deconstruct' powerful ideas could be seen as critics of ideology. They tend, however, not to use the word, and it could be argued that the thrust of post-modernism is towards the total relativizing of all knowledge. This undercuts the possibility of distinguishing ideology from any other sort of idea. (The more extreme versions of post-modern theory seem to reject altogether the possibility of truth statements about anything, thereby paradoxically reducing even post-modern writing to empty illusion.) For these reasons, I ignore this body of work entirely.

IDEOLOGY IN THIS STUDY

The foregoing sections have given the ancestry of my own conception of ideology in general and revealed some of the problems involved in reaching a satisfactory definition. In my view, such a definition would have the following characteristics:

1 It would treat ideology as analytically separable from other forms of thought, regardless of any position taken on the ultimate possibility of ever attaining 'true' knowledge. This would avoid the problems entailed in Mannheim's 'relational' definition of ideology and other forms of ideas being inseparable in the present, knowable only in the past. In other words, a satisfactory definition includes the notion that ideology contains false ideas.

2 It would see ideology as bounded by the interests of a ruling group. Despite the problems of definition invoked by the notion of a ruling class, and the problem that interest cannot ever be empirically demonstrated, it is better to work with a notion that limits ideology to those ideas which can be argued to serve the interests of some powerful people than to include as ideology all ideas which are demonstrably false to some degree.

3 It sees those ideas as transmitted from one sector of society (the ruling class) to others. While the proponents of the dominant ideology thesis regard this process of transmission as simple, I think it should be seen as complex and as having some (possibly considerable) impact on the ideas.

4 It would see ideology as operating through language especially, and as having some impact on the identity of the individuals who encounter it—as creators or as receivers.

5 Because of the complexities of interest, transmission and effects, we should define ideology as dominating but not totally dominant. A satisfactory definition would eschew the notion of 'false consciousness' and would stress ideology as a contested product of social experience. This raises the question of how extensively false and interest-laden ideas must be accepted in order to qualify as an ideology. There are two possible answers, one in numerical terms,[4] and one which emphasises qualitative criteria. While it is certainly more

likely that a set of false ideas reflecting dominant interests and agreed to by more than half a population constitutes an ideology than does the same set with only 20% agreement, reducing acceptance to agreement is an oversimplification. It is more convincing, in my view, to say that an ideology exists when the ideas reflecting the ruling interests constitute the only terms for discussion. So a number of people might in fact disobey an ideological injunction without the ideology necessarily disappearing, if the disobedient ones still saw themselves in terms of that injunction. This would hold regardless of whether they thought of themselves as wicked, sick or progressive. It is only when they and others see their action as a simple matter of choice, like buying strawberries rather than peaches, or sending one's child to one kindergarten rather than another, that we can say ideology is overthrown.

6 The definition would also emphasise the potential for ideology to be fragmented and contradictory, because of the complexities of interests it reflects and because it is transmitted by active human beings who might affect the message they are conveying.

7 A satisfactory definition would thus include the potential for individuals to negotiate with ideology. This could mean a range of things. At one extreme, negotiation may mean that there is very little room for movement within the framework provided by a specific ideology. At the other, it might involve direct and self-conscious opposition. In between lie possibilities for more or less dextrous and adventurous appeals to contrary ideas. The form and degree of negotiation that any one person can carry out with any one ideology will vary with the person's social location, since this is what provides access to resources such as contradictory ideas.

In brief, then, I define *ideology* as follows. It consists of sets of ideas that emerge from and reflect the interests of a dominant group and thus tend to distort reality. These ideas are transmitted across society and accepted implicitly or explicitly by the majority of people, in ways which impinge on their identities. Because they have social origins, ideologies are not totally dominant. Any given ideology will be subject to some negotiation.

Operationalizing the concept

The above definition of ideology is still fairly broad and will require some further pinning down before I can claim that there is an ideology of parenthood with which the childless couples I studied are negotiating. I will need to show that there are sets of ideas about parenting, that they do reflect interests, that they are widely held and that they do have a bearing on the sense of self an individual acquires.

This entails two kinds of argument. I can investigate the question of whether ideas exist empirically, either by my own content analysis of texts or by relying on the analysis of others. Similarly, I can carry out, or rely on others' having carried out, attitude studies of various sorts to answer the question about the spread of these ideas. (In doing this, as I indicated earlier, I would find an essentially qualitative approach more illuminating than a strictly quantitative one, and it would be of use in discovering whether these ideas do impinge on how people see themselves.)

It would be difficult but not impossible to use historical sources for answering the question about where the ideas seem to have come from. The difficulty is due to the way in which (especially if we are dealing with long-established ideas) only some kinds of evidence survives. What is impossible to answer in strict empirical terms is the question about interests. This can only be argued for, whether we are talking about current ideas or past ones.

The first half of the chapter has set out the broad definition of ideology with which I am working and looked at some of the problems of pinning it down. Now I will move on to explore the characteristics of the specific ideology in which I am most interested, the one I call the ideology of parenthood.

DEFINING THE IDEOLOGY OF PARENTHOOD

I argued earlier that in order to show that there is an ideology of parenthood I will need to show that there are commonly held ideas about parenting or, in other words, to specify some content for this putative ideology.

Specifying the content of an ideology could be done by focusing on the texts deemed to be transmissions or by relying on the work of others who have done so. Whichever method is adopted, it implies a fairly oppositional reading of the ideology in question, because to those whose stance is hegemonic the ideas will represent nothing but 'the way things are'. Feminists have opposed many of the prevailing notions about parenthood, especially motherhood, for a long time now, and thus it is their work on which I draw most heavily in describing the ideas which make up the ideology of parenthood.

Feminist critics point out three broad statements in the ideology of parenthood, statements which are both descriptions of what parenthood *is* and covert prescriptions of what it *should be*. These are that:

1 Parenthood is natural
2 Parenthood entails commitment and responsibility
3 Parents must therefore make sacrifices, which are rewarded by children.

The idea that there is a 'natural' propensity for women to mother has been sharply criticized by feminists for many years. In 1916 Leta Hollingsworth, a social psychologist and feminist, whose most important work was in challenging the myth that menstruation reduces women's mental capacities, argued cogently that there was little evidence for a biologically based desire for children, or 'maternal urge', but that there was a great deal of evidence for 'social devices' which put pressure on women to become mothers, and 'there has been a consistent social effort to establish as a norm the woman whose vocational proclivities are completely and "naturally" satisfied by child-bearing and child-rearing with related domestic activities' (Hollingsworth 1916, in Peck & Senderowitz 1974). Her comment that maternity is as much a social as a biological construct is typical of many. Although they differed in their views on causation (with the first group tending to see simply historical misfortune, the second blaming the inexorable workings of capitalist interest), both liberal and Marxist feminists tended to accept the case for culture and against nature summarized so briskly by Bernard:

> We do not have to posit a maternal instinct in women that can brook no frustration. The institutional pressures exerted on women to become mothers are more than enough to explain why it is that every little girl automatically replies to the question 'what are you going to be when you grow up?' with a prompt and confident 'mother'. (Bernard 1974)

Psychoanalytically oriented feminists like Chodorow (1978) and Dinnerstein (1977) also began with the premise that there is little biological foundation for the feelings women have about children. But, interestingly enough, their reliance on Freudian theory leaves them in a position where, ultimately, it seems that motherhood does come 'naturally' to women. Because the great bulk of early childcare is done by women and because boys and girls have such different relationships with their parents, grown men and women are different kinds of people. Women are humanly created as nurturers, men are not. Even though the creation is a cultural one rather than the result of any natural law, the outcome is extremely hard to reverse, because the psychic patterns established in infancy are so hard to break.[5]

While feminists have, on the whole, been more interested in mothers than fathers, they have also suggested that there is a prevalent notion of the 'naturalness' of fatherhood which accompanies the notion of natural maternal urges. But when fathers are the focus, *natural* means something closer to 'socially normal'. Russell's comment on assumptions about mothers and fathers makes this clear:

> The traditional assumptions for mothers are that (a) mothers are biologically prepared to care for children, (b) the mother–infant relationship is both unique and necessary, and (c) therefore it is mothers who should care for children. For fathers, the assumptions are that (a) fathers do not have the same capacity for nurturance as mothers do, (b) the father–infant relationship is neither unique nor necessary, (c) fathers need only play an ancillary role in development ... and (d) therefore it is fathers who should be performing an instrumental role in the workforce. (Russell 1979)

Overall, it seems clear that feminist critics have identified a prevailing notion that motherhood at least is natural in a biological sense and that fatherhood is normal behaviour for adult men. They have identified it as an ideological statement and challenged it but, at least some of the time, appear paradoxically to accept it.

As well as identifying and criticising the statement that parenting is in some way 'natural', feminists have pointed out the extent to which we assume that parenthood requires special, overwhelming commitment from mothers and fathers (but especially mothers) and that such commitment is seen in the sacrifices they make. So Hoit (1970) described the expectations of motherhood revealed in Dr Spock's bestselling manuals on childcare: 'Fatherhood ... is still primarily the 8-hour job ... of earning the family's income, while motherhood remains a 24-hour job with no nights or weekends off'. Comer (1974) argues that: 'Caring single-handedly for children in this society deprives women of their own adulthood', and Rich (1977) passionately denounces the institutionalized expectations of motherhood, with its 'insane expectations' that mothers should be completely committed to their children, giving them total and unremitting love which denies the mother's very self. She draws attention to the link between these ideas about responsibility, the sacrifices entailed in living up to them and the violence which she describes as 'the heart of maternal darkness'. Maternal violence against children, she says, breaks out only in extreme cases, but is a constant possibility as a result of the expectations of commitment and sacrifice which all women face. It will become extinct only when men take on equal responsibility with women for the care of children.

In a curious fashion these feminist critics of the ideology of parenthood share with the proponents of that ideology a notion of what motherhood especially entails. They want childrearing to be the equal responsibility of both sexes, so that women are not compelled to make all the sacrifices it entails, but they accept both the sacredness of that responsibility and the need for sacrifice.

It would be ridiculous to expect critics of the ideology of parenthood to argue that children's needs should go unmet, or that parents should deliberately act in what they perceived as the worst rather than the best interests of their children, and I do not hold either position. But I find the acceptance of many feminist critics—especially psychoanalytically oriented ones—that parenthood automatically requires particular kinds of commitment and sacrifice rather surprising. We have considerable evidence that the intense emotional commitment by parents to individual children which we see as the hallmark of the family is in fact a comparatively recent historical phenomenon, and that the modern bourgeois family is very different in emotional climate from any other family form in history.[6] This should, perhaps, alert us to the possibility of going about parenthood very differently, but many feminist critics seem to accept the status quo as a description of the 'real' nature of parenthood and at times to move perilously close to a notion of maternal identity as the 'real' nature of women.

It is not only feminists who have noted ideological statements about commitment and responsibility in families. A survey of a wide range of 'expert' literature on parenthood—clinical reports, scholarly articles, pamphlets handed out by doctors, advice from social workers and so on—found ten basic conceptions which, while not constant and uniform, seem to have been dominant over the last few decades. The first one concerns commitment: 'Conception 1: Children are society's most valuable resource, people's most precious "possessions"—therefore children's needs are paramount, and always take precedence over those of adults' (Rapoport et al. 1977).

Because children's needs are paramount, adults must take responsibility for meeting them in full, including psychological needs. This is the second conception. But responsibility is not identical for both parents. Mothers are responsible for early physical and emotional development, while fathers have the duty of being 'protector and provider of the mother–child couplet'.

Parental responsibilities are heavy and require sacrifices but these are rewarded by the children themselves. The final tenet emerging in the expert literature is that parental responsibility is a total thing:

> Conception 10: No compromises are possible with the totality of dedication that is required to be a good parent—because children's requirements are total and their neglect brings irreversible damage. (Rapoport et al. 1977)

Critics and observers, then, do suggest that there probably is a set of common ideas about parenting. Moreover, the accounts of the psychoanalytic feminists draw links between ideas about parenting and a sense of who one is. I suggested earlier that an ideology will probably enable such links to be made. The critical accounts, however, do not contain very much on the extent to which such ideas dominate. Are they widespread? Can we see evidence that they are believed by ordinary parents?

The short answer is both yes and no. There are now many studies of parents' attitudes to childbearing and rearing, and they certainly suggest that overall most parents have a notion of parenthood as natural and as a matter of commitment. In addition, there is some evidence that these ideas do involve the sense of self. But the same data also suggest that the widespread ideas are not held in quite the form identified by the critics and that they are not held by all parents in the same way.

The feminist critics discussed earlier, for example, tended to focus on the idea that parenthood was a biologically natural urge felt by all decent and ordinary people—especially women. Data from studies of parents, on the other hand, suggest that they think of parenthood as natural but mainly in the sense that it is the normal course taken by all decent and ordinary people. A study of English couples suggested that they had a taken-for-granted assumption that parenthood would follow marriage:

> For most people, the belief that it is essential to have children is so integral

to their way of thinking that when they marry they cannot be said to calculate and weigh up against each other the respective advantages and disadvan-
tages they may gain from having children. Rather, once they marry they
tend to assume that they will have children and plan their lives accordingly.
(Busfield & Paddon 1977)

Lyn Richards' Australian study *Having Families* (1978, 1985), which
focused more directly on the question of how people saw parenthood,
produced similar results. 'Almost all' of the 120 respondents said that
'having children had followed automatically from getting married'. Few
could remember even considering the possibility of remaining childless
after marriage, and most were 'nonplussed' when asked why they had
not considered it. They regarded parenthood as the normal course for
married couples. Moreover, they seemed to see parenthood as 'natural'
in the sense of desirable and right as well as in the sense of usual. Seventy
of the 120 believed that children were 'necessary for a marriage'. There
was a clear association between this belief and occupational status for
wives; the belief was weakest among professionals' wives who were
prepared to work before their children were at school. Parents' comments about the voluntarily childless were disapproving, with *selfish* fea-
turing as a key term. This, too depicts an assumption that parenthood is
both the normal and the correct path for couples who marry.

Both the previous studies can be criticized, as can many similar
works, for being essentially 'wives' family sociology'.[7] A small study of
Welsh males seeking help for infertility shows that men too seem to
regard parenthood as the normal thing to do:

Particularly noticeable among the men interviewed was the extent to which
the desire for children was taken for granted. Indeed, the most noticeable
feature of the reasons the men held for wanting children was the difficulty
they found in articulating any at all. The question of why they wanted children usually met with blank embarrassment ... To want children simply was
not questioned. (Owens 1982)

Clearly, parents do have an idea about parenthood as natural—but it is
not quite the idea that critics have assumed it to be. In the most recent
version, at least, an emphasis on social normality overlays any biological
determinism. There is also evidence, however, that there is a continuum of meanings attached to the idea of natural/normal and that these
meanings vary over time and among classes.

Two studies of family formation demonstrate these points: the 1970s
Family Formation Project, based at the Australian National University,
and the 1980s Institute of Family Studies Family Formation Survey,
which covered similar territory and in some cases exactly replicated
questions.

The ANU study revealed that, overall, there was a tendency to see
parenthood as natural. For instance, in a questionnaire study 68% of
respondents agreed that 'women are only really fulfilled by mother-

hood'—a statement which combines a notion close to biological determinism with one about selfhood. Among the fifty-four Sydney women who took part in small group discussions, there was general agreement that children were an inevitable part of marriage. Attitudes to whether this was a matter of maternal urges varied (with the unmarried middle-class students tending to reject this view) as did attitudes to just how inevitable *inevitable* meant. Working-class women were much more likely than middle-class ones to declare that they could not understand women who did not want children. Similar patterns were found in the interviews with men and women in the Canberra region.

The IFS study, a decade later, also found a general pattern whereby people felt that 'it was natural to have children, that children and marriage went together, or simply that they liked children' (McDonald 1983). But this study, too, found differences within its sample. Views on the importance of motherhood to women and of children to marriage were associated with a set of factors (e.g. education) which are in turn usually associated with social class, although it is important to note that there was no direct connection between occupations and family values. So people rating low on 'social status characteristics' tended to rate high on traditional values and vice versa.

This later study showed how attitudes to the naturalness of parenthood had changed over time. When their respondents were given the statement from the ANU study that 'women are only really fulfilled by motherhood' only 30% agreed—less than half as many as in 1971.

Another recent study strongly suggests that the notion of natural/normal parenthood is not accepted by everybody in the same way. Wearing's (1984) work on the attitudes of 150 Sydney mothers is particularly relevant because it uses the notion of ideology (although a Mannheimian one). Wearing shows that there is substantial agreement that 'motherhood is an essential part of womanhood'—the statement which she describes as the 'first tenet of the ideology of motherhood'. She also shows that not all the women she spoke with regarded motherhood as the only possible normal status for women and that

> ... mothers from middle-class backgrounds, in middle-class family situations or with potential market capacity for professional or managerial occupations do not unreservedly accept the ideology of motherhood, women's place in the home and all the restrictions on participation in the wider society which adherence to such an ideology generates. (Wearing 1984)

Taken together, these data suggest that a simple picture of universally similar subscription to the ideological statement that parenthood is natural is inappropriate. The phrase does evoke agreement but, at the same time, like happiness, it means different things to different people.

The same can be said of the evidence about attitudes to commitment. There is no doubt that parents regard having children as *their* commitment rather than society's and take it for granted that the commitment will lead to sacrifices, but how they define commitment varies.

The couples in Busfield and Paddon's study, for instance, manifested five rather different images of family life (which the authors call 'ideologies', although they mean little more by this term than images). The images—of a 'quiet', a 'collective' and 'active' a 'material' or a 'better' life—varied, as did the decisions about family size and spacing associated with them, but in all cases there was a focus on what parents should do to identify and meet the needs of their children. So, for example, those whose image was of a 'quiet' life thought in terms of doing little more than satisfying the demands of children, but those whose images were concerned with material provision (the 'material' life and the 'better' life respectively) were concerned to provide children with material goods or to give them a chance to move up the social ladder. In all cases, parents are manifesting a notion of an underlying responsibility or commitment.

Similarly, an in-depth study of how a small number of parents actually behave (Backett 1982) shows that the perceived needs of children are the basis on which family routines are negotiated. It is the stage the child is seen to have reached, plus its apparent individual characteristics, that determine things like whether the mother feels able to move into paid work or the parents' pattern of sexual activity. The outcomes of meeting them differ, but the notion that needs count is a constant theme for the twenty-two families, suggesting again that there is indeed a perception of parenthood as commitment to filling them.

A study of the daily experiences of fifty mothers (Boulton 1983) suggests that the strong commitment that these women expressed is based on a notion of children's rights, or what is owed to them, rather than needs. Boulton also found an 'interesting but small' difference in the attitudes of the working-class and middle-class women. The middle-class mothers were most likely to find motherhood meaningful in terms of commitment to children's rights. This suggests that, as we have seen with notions about parenthood as 'natural', the meaning of commitment and responsibility may vary with social class.

The data from the ANU Family Formation study discussed earlier suggest that parents in 1970s Australia had notions of commitment based on both needs and rights. The themes of small families being best because otherwise the economic struggle was too great (i.e. children's needs would go unmet), and because it was parents' duty to provide the best (the child has a right to it), were strong in the interviews with the Canberra subsample especially. In the Sydney subsample, there was a strong focus on maternal responsibility—to use a crèche was seen as 'dereliction of duty' (and presumably as abrogation of the child's rights).

Having Families also provided evidence that commitment is a theme for parents, but that there is not a universal basis for commitment. A 'good' mother was seen as committed to the welfare of her children, and bearing a heavy responsibility, but there were two styles of mothering. The 'old-style' good mother was the woman who willingly put the needs of family first, offering security and love by being 'always there' and 'taking time': 'When asked specifically about "good mothers" most women talked of passive qualities—patience, reliability and willingness to take time' (Richards 1978). 'New' mothers also offered love and security, but in a different fashion:

> Good mothers retain their own personality, for their own sake *and* for the sake of the children ... the new good mother has in many ways a more demanding role than the old. These accounts stressed particularly the mother's responsibility to create and maintain a stimulating environment for the child. (Richards 1978)

Neither image was easy to live up to, and most women felt that they lived in a bit of a muddle, struggling to obey the norms and meet the commitment of being either an old- or a new-style mother. By contrast, the image of fathers was simpler and more static, but it too emphasized commitment and responsibility—especially for discipline. Fathers were depicted as the 'familial authority figure'—ranged in a continuum from 'disciplinary authorities who gave security to loving companions who also earned respect'.

Further evidence about variations in the meanings of *responsibility* links it to social position in a fashion similar to the links explored in the discussion of parenthood as natural. Wearing's mothers overall felt that a good mother was committed to the needs of her children and would make 'every effort' to satisfy them, but differed sharply in how needs were defined. Working-class mothers were much more likely than others to emphasize physical care; feminist mothers (largely middle-class) to stress the importance of meeting the needs of mothers so that they could meet their children's needs. Similarly, the IFS Family Formation Survey revealed links between attitudes to responsibility and social position.

If parents do seem to accept the notion of commitment, then they may well accept also the notion that parenthood is about sacrifice. On this point, evidence suggests that parents, especially mothers, do see themselves as taking on heavy burdens or surrendering valuable attributes for the sake of children and, further, see children as a reward for this sacrifice. They do not, however, see this sacrifice as demanded of them—as an 'ought'. Instead, it is an 'is'—part of what parenting is all about. So in *Having Families* mothers report on being 'tied down', giving up valuable things (including in some cases personal growth or independence) and on the whole report that the sacrifice is worthwhile (Richards 1978). Wearing's respondents note that the 'bad' aspects of motherhood were

> being tied down, constantly in demand, lack of freedom and privacy and inability to plan ahead or complete tasks or even conversations ... on a wider level ... loss of independence and sense of being tied to the home and their inability to pursue former interests outside the home or to participate in

work or other activities outside the home to the extent that they would like to. (Wearing 1984)

The women felt, however, that motherhood was a satisfying occupation bringing with it many rewards, even though they were also aware that it had a low status in society. Again, there is no evidence that the sacrifices or the rewards were things that parents ought to do or had a right to expect; they were simply the nature of the job, flowing automatically from the commitment it demanded.

There is very little material available on fathers' attitudes to sacrifices, but what there is suggests that there is a certain amount of change in the air. It has been argued that in the United States, some men are changing their attitudes to fatherhood, and because of that are beginning to sacrifice pursuits such as friendships with men outside the family, and commitment and success at paid work (Lewis 1984). Again, Lewis' sketchy data suggest only that these new 'equalitarian' fathers see the sacrifices as what one does if one is committed to this type of parenthood, not as a response to an ideological demand.

Overall, then, the statements about parenthood as natural, requiring commitment and sacrifice, are indeed widespread but are not accepted by everybody to the same degree or with the same nuances. This is consistent with the notion that ideology is dominating but not totally dominant and that people negotiate differently with it and within it. We have seen hints in the literature on the spread of these ideas that social location makes a difference to the way ideas are interpreted and accepted. We have also seen suggestions that these ideas do get bound up with a sense of self—at least for mothers. So far, there seems to be evidence that something we could call an ideology of parenthood does indeed exist.

It is also possible to argue that this ideology is linked to and originated from a particular set of interests. Wearing, among others, has pointed out the extent to which an ideology of maternal commitment serves the general interests of capital (in that it enables the reproduction of workers at minimal cost to the ruling class which owns the means of production. This reproduction includes both the daily sense of ensuring that workers arrive at the job fed, clothed and ready to make profit, and the generational sense, of ensuring a continued supply of labour over the long term).

There are some problems with this line of argument. While the notion that parents are the people who should take the majority of the burden of looking after a child probably does serve the generalized interest of that generalized entity, capital, there is no inherent reason why only the parent of one sex should do so. And, indeed, this is in some ways inimical to the principal of efficiency. So in addition to the interests of capital, Wearing invokes the idea of patriarchy—the system of domination and subordination based on sex rather than class. She argues that the interests of individual men are served by having individual women take on almost all the burden of childcare.

I basically agree with this argument and want to explore it a little further. Clearly, there is a kind of fit between the aims of individual capitalists (to amass profit for themselves) and hence between the generalized interests of capital and the kind of family system we have evolved in the West over the last few centuries. Modern families reproduce workers physically and, in a sense, also serve to reproduce the character best suited to the current economic system. As Parsons (1955) from a functionalist perspective and Poster (1978) from a critical one have both noted, the nuclear family structure is one where the intense concentration of emotions produces a certain kind of character—individualistic 'self-starting' and inner-directed rather than collectively oriented and conforming.

While this character might indeed be just what capital requires in one sense, there is another sense in which it causes problems: the latent dangers to capital of a relatively individualized society in which blind obedience to norms is not inevitable are clear. Those who are too much their own people may be hard to persuade as consumers!

The same problem is clear in the argument that the current family structure serves male interests. Although there is abundant evidence (e.g. in rates at which each sex files for divorce) that women are less happy than men with the ways we set up families, it is not necessarily true that men do not have dissatisfactions. In the 1950s, the time when the American nuclear family with strongly segregated sex roles was apparently at its strongest, there is evidence in divorce rates and in popular culture of masculine dissatisfaction with the order of things (Erenreich 1983).

I do not dispute the notion of some functional fit between the interests of capital and patriarchy, and current ideas about parenting, but I do argue that we need to see those interests as complex rather than simple.

Complexity is evident in the history of our current family practices. There is a considerable body of evidence that nuclear families as we think of them—vital, potentially explosive, little centres of emotional energy in which parental love of children is a key element—are a relatively recent phenomenon. The families of the world we have lost, it seems, were characterized by greater parental indifference to children and a less intense relationship between spouses than are ours. Evidence on this point comes from what we know of childrearing practices, marriage and courtship customs, apparent behaviour with regard to the death of spouses and children and so on. There are those who see the family as basically always loving, but they are outnumbered by those who note that childrearing practices which were known to be injurious (e.g wet-nursing, baby-farming) were carried out by upper-class parents who had access to medical knowledge; that marital relations seem to have had an entirely different character from those we prefer; and so on.

The family gradually became the family we know, and family

practices became established as we know them, largely through the efforts of the emergent professional classes—those in the middle rather than the traditional aristocracy. The process took some two hundred years, and the establishment of the practices which flow from the ideas of commitment and sacrifice seems to have been quite recent. In Australia, it was an alliance of groups of professionals that created the current form of motherhood, and this form was indeed commensurate with the interests of an expanding and technologically oriented system of capitalism (Reiger 1982). Housework and childcare practices changed with regard to what parents (especially mothers) did at the turn of this century, and the new style of parenting demanded more intense involvement, commitment and sacrifice than the old. At the same time, the new ideology was not easily accepted. Oral history accounts reveal that at least some working-class mothers managed to disregard the new advice and continue with what the professionals now saw as rather careless and harmful behaviour (such as the use of dummies to stop a baby crying) (Reiger 1982).

However, those who are working to create and transmit ideology are sometimes in an ambivalent position towards it. Dr Vera Scantlebury Brown was an important figure in the movement towards the new 'scientific' childrearing, which demanded on the whole more effort from mothers than the older techniques—babies were to be fed, played with, etc. strictly on schedules, and mothers were to forgo the idea that they could get away with simply responding to their children and letting nature do the rest. As a doctor, Brown attempted to persuade the community of the virtues of the new system. As a mother, she found it hard to practice. On one occasion, she noted that the baby had cried for no reason, and while she should have disregarded this (for fear of injuring his character) she 'broke the rules' and nursed him—following her heart rather than her intellect (Reiger 1982).

Briefly, then, it would appear that the current ideas about parenthood can be seen to have an origin in the interests of capital, although this is not a simple matter, and a more precise point of origin in the actions of middle-class experts who have gradually helped to create a world in which parenthood means a particular conjunction of natural behaviour, commitment and sacrifice. Again, however, there is no simple correspondence between interests and ideas. Rather, the creators of ideology are also negotiating with it and being created by it in turn. Nature, commitment and sacrifice are the characteristics we ascribe to parenthood, but we do not all see these ideas in the same way and so do not invariably act alike as parents.

In chapter 4 I will return to the question of how childless couples negotiate with these ideas. But the next chapter will sketch out what sort of people these couples are.

3

. . . .

voluntarily

childless

couples

C hapters 1 and 2 have been concerned with the ideas behind my study. In this chapter and chapters 4, 5 and 6 I will present the data I collected about the voluntarily childless couples, showing how and why they negotiated their specific position with regard to the ideology of parenthood. My immediate concern is to answer the two questions that arose early in my study: what sort of person becomes voluntarily childless, and how do they reach this state?

TWO COUPLES' STORIES

I first met Gary and Gabrielle (pseudonyms) in Canberra in 1980. A friend whom I had met when I was working in Canberra knew that the Gs were voluntarily childless and arranged for me to interview them.

At that stage, they were both aged 36, a quiet, rather serious pair, who were easy to interview and very hospitable to me. Both were non-religious, ALP voters and eldest children, Gary with one brother and Gabrielle with two sisters.

They both describe their childhoods as happy. Gabrielle says:

We had a very untroubled, happy childhood ... they were very loving parents. And ... I felt I was lucky. We never had much money, because Dad was a teacher, [there were] three kids, and Mum not working ... but ... I never noticed it. I realise now looking back that we were poor; I can remember that we had second-hand furniture, and very few clothes, but plenty of food ...

Gary, also recalls a basically happy childhood in which he had plenty of interests to keep himself occupied. In retrospect, he wishes he had had more company, but otherwise is satisfied with his past.

The parents of both the Gs encouraged them to get a good education, and their most striking characteristic when I first met them was their professional commitment. Both were teachers—Gabrielle in a high school, Gary in a primary—and both seemed very absorbed in their work. All the interviews I did with them were interrupted by phone calls on school business. Gary often took children on weekend camping trips or had students who shared his interest in carpentry visit him at the weekends. Gabrielle organised extracurricular activities for her students and spent many out-of-school hours on school-related activities.

They were clearly fond of the children they worked with and had originally planned to have children. The house in which I first interviewed them had been built to their specifications, which included light-switches set low so that children could reach them. How had they come to change their minds? Their comments, especially Gabrielle's vivid and often insightful remarks, show the flow and ebb of negotiation. Gabrielle says that as an adolescent she never saw herself as a mother, although when she married Gary, they both assumed that they would have children. But:

> *We didn't even think about it ... for years ... Because we just didn't have the finance and we just both needed to work ... we didn't set out not to have children, we set out to have them; this is why we built this house with four bedrooms and everything.*

At the age of 27, she decided that the time had come to have a child:

> *I was going to take my pills to the end of the packet and that was going to be it. So I made the big announcement. 'OK' says Gary. Right. Day came not to take it and I just nearly—oh ... [shudders]. Such cold feet, I'll never forget it! I couldn't do it, and I raced to the doctor to get more ....*

Her commitment to parenthood ebbed back to the taken-for-granted state which had characterized the early part of her marriage, until a visit to a doctor brought the issue up again:

> *I can remember, I was about 28 at the time, I went to the doctor about something else and he said ... 'what is a girl of 28 doing without any children?' And I was a bit insulted. I said to him, 'I don't know, but is there something wrong with me? Because I don't feel like it' ... So I just decided to wait.*

The earlier form of postponement until the couple could afford children gave way to postponement until Gabrielle felt the stirrings of the maternal urge which she was sure would come:

> *And then a lot of friends described to me the feelings for maternity — you know, the urge they had. Some of them had the most extreme urge. They cried and cried when they didn't get pregnant ... And I said, 'Oh well, I'll just wait for this to happen.'*

The urge did not strike when she and Gary moved into their specially built child-centred home or by Gabrielle's thirty-fifth birthday. That event, coinciding with the decision to take a long trip overseas, precipitated new discussion of the issue.

> *I said, 'Look, I just can't go on taking the pill any more, it's just too long,' (I'd been taking it for about eleven years) 'so isn't it about time I had something done, because there's no way I'm going to have children now.' So that's when we finally did talk about it.*

They decided that they would not have children and Gabrielle sought a tubal ligation, but again events altered her attitude:

> *I went to a lady doctor and she said, 'Now, you know, this is a big decision ... You're about to go overseas ... why don't you have your trip and let that be the deciding point?'*

So, in the same spirit in which she had waited for her maternal urge to follow moving into her own house, Gabrielle set off overseas with Gary. She came back sure that she did not want children but, as Gary pointed out, still waited another year before finally being sterilized:

> *It [the trip overseas] made me more sure than ever because I thought 'This travelling bit's the goods; this is what I want to do' and I didn't want anything to stop me ... I certainly gave myself cooling-off time [before being sterilized]. I thought when this idea of overseas trips dwindles into the past I might change my mind.*

She is now sterilized and sees herself as permanently childless and happy with the decision—'I've never regretted anything'.

With two professional incomes, they can afford to indulge in their interest in travel and to live well. By the third interview, they had sold their first house and were in the process of building another one, which was taking up much of their time and meant, they thought, that overseas trips were out of the picture for at least five years.

The Gs' story as I know it ended with their remaining happily childless. John and Judy offer a striking contrast.

They were introduced to me by a mutual friend. Their Melbourne house, on the first interview, seemed large and luxurious but by the second interview they had extended it further. Judy, a nurse, worked for a drug company but by the third interview had returned to hospital and was training in midwifery, where the fact that she had had a tubal ligation and was prepared to say so caused some conflict. But she and John both agreed that in some ways she is unconventional. She would have preferred not to marry, but he wanted to. He is a conventional businessman who had served on the local Liberal Party branch committee; she voted for and belonged to the ALP. This was a potential source of friction in a marriage, which they described as close, happy and tolerant, and in fact they had separated briefly at the time of the dismissal of the Whitlam Labor Government.

They agreed that, because Judy did not want children, John did not want them either. They also agreed that their backgrounds were similar—both the middle child of three and very close to their families. Judy's explanation of why she did not want children was based on her experiences as a child.

She saw her childhood as full of conflict and brought from it clear images of motherhood which she said she did not want to live out. But she insisted that, at the time, she believed she lived in a happy family. Her account wove themes together, shifting from past to present, so that at one stage she complained that 'I don't know where I am'.

JUDY: *I always remember my childhood as being happy ... it's been only in retrospect that ... I've seen conflicts with my sister that I don't think I felt when I was growing up ...*

INT: *Is there anything in your background which is important for your decision about children?*

JUDY: *Yes ... my brother was an asthmatic, and a very bad asthmatic. He was a constant worry to Mum and Dad. And as a child I can remember [him] having attacks, it seemed to me every night ... that's a vivid recollection, of him just gasping for breath and my mother being totally distraught ...*

In addition to the problems of an asthmatic son, her family was thrown into turmoil when Judy's sister attempted suicide. Judy believed that her parents were 'devastated' to discover, when the family went into therapy, that their daughter felt unable to live up to their standards. And the picture of loving parents doing their utmost but still 'failing' remained with her, providing a motive for childlessness:

I think the fact that I had such a good childhood, and felt at the time that my parents were doing everything they possibly could for me—I felt loved, I felt wanted, I felt secure—and yet so many things went wrong with the family situation ... caused so much pain for Mum and Dad, that part of my decision not to have a family was ... a direct result of that.

The themes here are of motherhood as full of problems of coping, of parenthood as in some ways tragic for both parents and children, and of specific events as triggers for later decisions. Did the events cause the desire to avoid parenthood, or had the decision led to the reinterpretation of childhood in a way which justified it? There is, in the end, no way of knowing. Without the events she described as occurring when she was a child, Judy might not have decided that she could not cope with children. But later events may have been equally important. She described an occasion involving her asthmatic brother which took place after she and John got engaged as a turning point in her perceptions of her ability to cope. Her brother had a severe attack of asthma, after years without one, and she had to take him into hospital. She was a qualified nurse but

I couldn't handle it ... I'd always coped very well in crisis situations in the hospital, but when [he] had this attack, all I could do was cry ... We whizzed him into hospital and all I did all the way in was cry ... just holding his hand. And he was gasping for breath, saying, 'It's all right, love', consoling me! And when I got into the hospital, the resident, whom I knew, said, 'What's his pulse?' and I said, 'I dunno'. I was so distraught. And it was then I realised, with people I love and care about, I'm useless, absolutely useless; I just go to pieces. And yet I can detach myself to a certain extent with people I'm not involved with. I might add that I work with asthmatics. So that's had a fairly strong impact on me.

Again, this event, vividly recalled, might have been enough to make

Judy decide against parenthood by itself. Or it might, once the decision had been made, provide telling evidence for the contention that 'I can't have children because I couldn't cope with the traumas they cause'. Certainly, Judy seemed sure that she did not want children because she could not cope with them. And John seemed equally sure that he would never become a parent, because Judy did want children. He said:

> *Judy initiated all my thoughts about that ... I would quite happily have gone along like many other people ... had I not sat down and really thought about it because of Judy.*

The Js seemed to be secure in their identity as a childless couple. Shortly after the third interview, I heard that John, a sales manager for a large insurance company, had been promoted and that he and Judy were moving to New Zealand. Some time later, in the middle of writing up my thesis, I heard that Judy was attempting to have her tubal ligation reversed so that she could have a baby.

As far as I could piece together the story with the help of a mutual acquaintance, events moved like this. In New Zealand, Judy found herself separated from friends and family and unable to get nursing work. She did her best to find interests in handcrafts but was on the whole unhappy with her new situation—so unhappy that her health began to suffer. A therapist suggested that she might want to think again about having children. When she mentioned this to John, he told her that he had always wanted children.

My view is that Judy was searching for an identity that could replace the one she lost when she was forced to give up the job she loved, and that it was this, plus desire to please John, which caused her to change her mind. She returned to Melbourne to have her tubal ligation reversed, but once the operation was complete began to have doubts again. The doubts came too late—she was already pregnant. John's firm moved him to Adelaide, where the baby was born. The person who introduced me to the Js is Judy's best friend; her version of the Js' situation was that while they loved their child, they both rather regretted their decision and were not anxious to have any more children.

But when I was preparing the manuscript for this book, I heard that Judy was pregnant again and shortly afterwards had a chance to speak with her. She said firmly that she was having a second child because she felt that her son needed a companion, that there was a great deal about motherhood which she did not enjoy and that she regretted not being able to return to work as soon as she had planned. This would seem to bear out the view taken by her friend, that parenthood was something of a mistake for the Js, but Judy did not seem especially unhappy with her choices and spoke of her son as a 'lovely little boy'. I think that her rather cool account of motherhood was consistent with her earlier attitudes to it. Her circumstances had changed so she had changed her decision about children, but some of her attitudes remained unchanged.

When I asked her how she thought she was coping with maternity, she said that, as she had suspected, she did not handle crises well, and had a story involving the baby falling out of his pram and her reactions to the incident which echoed the theme of the earlier story about her brother. At the same time, she was clearly managing the daily business of childcare with her normal efficiency.

These two stories show the complexity of negotiation with the ideology of parenthood—how it is affected by events in the distant past and the attitudes formed by such events, as well as by present circumstances and attitudes.

The tale of John and Judy is the one about which I have most knowledge, but the changes I observed during and after the study show the couple not to be unique. During the case study, Bill and Bridget also became parents (of two children). The As, Ds and Is ended their marriages, with Alison becoming a step-parent. (Diane later did likewise, and Isabel subsequently became a mother.) Henry and Heather began to disagree about childlessness, although they remained married and childless. Much later (as I was writing the final draft of this book) Chris and Clare had a son. Above all, these stories show that negotiation is an active process rather than a passive submission to ideology or a simple determination to hold out against it.

The two detailed stories also illustrate some of the characteristics of voluntarily childless couples in general. It is those general characteristics that I will now discuss in order to give a more complete answer to the questions about who and how. I will attempt to place my sample in two sets of contexts; first, in their socioeconomic location (in terms of occupation, income and education) both present and past, and, second, in a more personal location. *Personal location* could be defined as 'where they are at' in terms of religion, politics, family life past and present, lifestyle and personal identity.

THE SOCIAL LOCATION

The bulk of my sample were well educated people in professional occupations. (For details of my methodology, please see appendix 1.) In terms of occupation this volunteer sample is clearly not representative of the Australian population in general. In 1980, when the questionnaire was filled in, more than half of the sample were in professional or managerial occupations (see figure 1; all figures and tables are in appendix 2). In August 1979, 13.2% of the Australian workforce were in the 'professional and technical' category, and a further 8.8% were managers (ABS 1980).[1] At the other end of the scale, only 2.6% of the childless were unskilled workers, while 31.2% of the Australian workforce was made up of 'tradesmen, production process workers and labourers, miners, quarrymen, etc'.

Interestingly, a fairly large proportion of the professionals were found in the one job—teaching. There were thirty-two teachers in the questionnaire group, making up 16.7% of the total and 31.2% of the professional–managerial category. Among the case-study group there were eight who were teachers at the time of the first interview, two former teachers and one who later became a teacher. If it does nothing else, this finding should indicate that the voluntarily childless are not necessarily those who dislike children.

In terms of education, the sampled childless are also very different from the Australian population as a whole. In 1979, more than half the population aged between 25 and 44 did not have any post-secondary education. More than 90% of the questionnaire group fall into that age range, and only 36.9% do not have some tertiary education or training. Degrees or diplomas were held by 55.7% of them, while only 27.8% of the population aged 25–44 had degrees, diplomas or certificates in 1979. Similarly, among the case-study group, there was a high level of education. My first interview for the thesis was with Andrew, who had completed a PhD. (See figure 2.)

The high level of education and occupation among the childless means that their income level is relatively high. Among the questionnaire group, more than 50% of individuals earned between $14 000 and $22 000 per year—a respectable but not luxurious income. Only 16% earned more than $22 000 while about a third of the group earned less than $14 000 in a year.

Male/female differences

As might be expected, the childless men tend to be found in slightly different occupations from the women; all the nine managers in the questionnaire group were men but the bulk of the clerical and sales workers were women. The incomes of the men were markedly higher (19.5% in the lowest category and 27.8% in the highest) than those of the women (46.9% in the lowest income category and only 3.1% in the highest). On the other hand, the women were rather better educated than the men, with 36.4% having degrees or diplomas, compared with 30% of the men. Similar but more pronounced differences exist in the population at large, where the percentage of women aged 25–44 with degrees or diplomas was much higher than that of men in 1979 (30.3% compared to 20.6%), and where the fact that the labour force participation rates of women aged 25–44 are markedly lower than those of men, plus the disparity in wages, based on a variety of factors, leads to marked differences in average incomes. Overall, these voluntarily childless men and women are more similar than might have been expected in terms of occupation, education and income.

Backgrounds

While the childless are now, on the whole, located in the professions or in other relatively high-ranking jobs, they were not all born in higher-status families, as indicated by their parents' occupations. Only 33.1% of the questionnaire group had fathers whose occupation had been professional or managerial. On the other hand, only 5.8% had fathers who had been unskilled workers. The bulk of their mothers (75.5%) had been full-time houseworkers, at least when the childless were living with their parents. Their parents do not seem to have been atypical in terms of education. Of the fathers, 31.6% and 47.4% of the mothers of the childless did not progress beyond year 10, and among the population aged 55–64 in 1979, 33.3% of males and 52.5% of females had left school at age 14 or 15—approximately the same level. In the whole population, 16% of males and 14.7% of females aged 55–64 had degrees, diplomas or non-trade certificates in 1979. Among the parents of the childless, 19.7% of the fathers and 12% of the mothers had some tertiary qualifications.

The childless do not seem to have struggled up from the bottom of the social ladder, but neither were they all born at the top. As figure 3 shows, they seem to have grown up in what might be broadly termed upper-working-class, or lower-middle-class families and made their way into solid middle- and upper-middle class occupations.

The sample compared with others

In terms of social location, this particular group of childless people seem to be similar to almost all those studied elsewhere, whether in Australia, New Zealand, Canada, Britain or the U.S.[2] In studies in all these countries, the childless were shown to be fairly well-educated and high-status workers. While the problem of volunteer samples remains, the general consistency of findings across cultures and over nearly a decade of research suggests that it is probably true that the voluntarily childless are relatively well educated, have middle-class occupations and incomes to match.

COMMITMENTS AND ALLEGIANCES

It is a general finding in other studies that the voluntarily childless are not religiously inclined, and even the two studies that found little difference between parents and the childless found the childless to be significantly less religious than parents.[3] Given the general emphasis placed on family life in most Christian theologies, expressed, for example, in the references to procreation in wedding services, it is unlikely that highly committed church members would find it easy to be voluntarily childless.

While less attention has been paid to the orientations of the childless towards questions about gender than to their religious attitudes, there are suggestions that they tend to less traditional attitudes about sex roles than do parents.[4] This does not appear to mean that they are any more than 'generally sympathetic with the women's liberation movement'

(Veevers 1980). This attitude, however, obviously relates to attitudes to the self (especially identification with a career for women) and to marriage.

It should also be noted that a relatively large study in the demographic tradition found that people who were voluntarily childless tended to be more politically conservative than those who were involuntarily childless (Heller et al. 1986). While this should not be totally disregarded, my own view is that the fact that their definition of voluntarily childless—simply having and expecting no children—means that the authors of this study have no way of excluding from their calculations the possibility that they have tapped attitudes of people who cannot have children. At the very least their results, coming from a random sample from a large American social survey, cannot be taken to disprove the findings of the studies which sample (non-randomly) the population which identifies itself as childless by choice.

Religion

The childless people in my study are, as might be expected, remarkably non-religious. In the case-study group, only Eric and Evelyn attend church regularly, and fourteen of the twenty-two identified themselves as not believing in God. Among the questionnaire group, 87.6% would not describe themselves as religious, only 7.2% would 'often' or 'sometimes' be influenced by religious considerations in making decisions, and 89.2% describe themselves as not belonging to any denomination.

Politics

In political terms, all but three of the case-study group and 58% of the questionnaire group vote for the Australian Labor Party. The rest voted Liberal (20.5%), Democrat (8.9%) or did not vote (7.9%). The low vote for the National Country Party reflects the largely urban location of the couples, although Fiona and Felix, among the case-study couples, were an interesting pair who were involved in National Party politics.

The case-study group as a whole appear to be fairly interested in politics. Four of the twenty-two were current members of a political party, and a further three had been members once. All of them were able to identify a political stance; nobody offered a description of their political position as being 'neutral' or 'not political'. Instead, there were identifications in terms of party or a more general philosophy like these:

FIONA: *Oh, I'm very much a right-wing socialist.*

ERIC: *Oh, left of centre—more precisely, a voluntary socialist or a caviare communist.*

Feminism

The attitude of the childless to what I, following popular terminology at the time, called the 'women's liberation movement' was, broadly speaking, sympathetic. Women were more likely to be very sympathetic to the aims of the movement than men, but both sexes were more likely to be sympathetic than either very sympathetic or unsympathetic. Only 14.4% of the total group were very sympathetic, but a mere 7.2% were either unsympathetic or very unsympathetic. There was a fair-sized group (27.7%) who were indifferent but, overall, the attitude to feminism was favourable.

This sympathy was not reflected in action, since 87.6% of the questionnaire group had had no contact with the women's movement. The case-study individuals were also inclined to be sympathetic to the women's movement, although only one (Diane) had had much to do with it. While they tended not to identify themselves in these terms, they could be described as 'practising feminists'. The men in the case-study group tended to express sympathy (sometimes rather guarded) and leave it at that.

While the lack of comparative data makes it difficult to say whether the attitudes of these childless people to feminism are atypical, in two respects at least the childless couples seemed to be deviating from the social prescriptions for sex-typed behaviour. The identity of both sexes seemed to centre on work rather than home life, and they seemed to see their pattern of activity around the home as highly egalitarian.

Work

The questionnaire group made it clear that work was an important part of their lives, which they enjoyed, and that they put a lot into their work. (See figures 4, 5 and 6.)

There was little difference between the sexes here, since seventy-eight men (81.3%) and seventy-nine women (83.2%) agreed that their job was important to them. While many Australian women now see themselves as workers in addition to being wives and mothers, the notion that a job is central to a woman's life does not sit easily with the tradition that women's identities centre on home and family, which has been a theme in Australian life. This suggests that the childless are different from the bulk of the population in the emphasis the women put on their work.

The responses of the case-study group to the very first question I asked suggests that job is an important part of identity for both sexes. The question 'who are you?' commonly brought a reply that 'I'm a worker of some kind'. For example:

KEVIN: *Oh, I'm a 32-year-old economist who's got a 16-year-old brain.*

KATE: *Oh, oh, I'm just me … Oh, usually I just … tell 'em my job.*

ISABEL: *If it was a work-related matter, I suppose I'd introduce myself in terms of my profession.*

EVELYN: *Important things—where I work. Public servant in a research-type job.*

HEATHER: *I don't know. Sounds like the beginning of an application letter! [After discussion of her career background] I actually have been writing an application letter, which is partly why the job thing looms large. It's not the most important thing in my life.*

Fourteen of the twenty-two childless had made reference to their work early in their replies (or, as in Heather's case, seemed to think in terms of work, despite disclaimers about its importance). Nine women and five men seemed to have identities built around work to a considerable extent, as table 1 suggests. Another four men and one woman responded to the first question in terms of personal qualities, like these:

CHRIS: *Who am I? I would say I'm my own individual self. I don't think I'm affected by people very greatly. That's the first thing. My independence seems to be very important to me ... I don't think I worry too much about the future or things like that.*

Only one of the childless insisted that work was positively not important to identity. Ian, a former public servant who had then done an arts degree and become a teacher, said:

> *How I see myself, perhaps? Well, I don't necessarily see myself in terms of my job; I'm not careerist, I think. I see myself more in terms of my interests—like chess and music.*

Despite this, he made it clear that he found his work quite enjoyable. And he devoted time to thinking about his working life, even though he is not 'careerist'. At the time of the first interview, he was studying horticulture, with a view to working in that field.

His response was unusual. Most of the childless made it clear that they felt very involved in their current jobs:

CLARE: *I'm a nurse ... It's interesting but hard—hard physically. And frustrating working at St. X's because you don't get a lot of patient stimulus ... It's a lot better than a lot of jobs ... I mean, you really feel gratified that you've got a job in this day and age.*

BILL: *[librarian] I love it. It's all the good things about academic history without the hard slog of writing essays and theses. I get up in the morning and look forward to going to work.*

EVELYN: *[public servant] Work tends to be fairly all-consuming ... It's stimulating and at the same time frustrating.*

Overall, identity available to them from work seemed to be important to the childless, and they invested much of their time and energy in work. Researchers have noted that the childless may stress work as a reason not to have children.[5] Certainly, in the group I interviewed, incompatibility between careers and motherhood especially was a common theme.

Marriage

If work is one crucial element in adult identity, which could be used to negotiate with the ideology of parenthood, belonging to a partnership is another. Modern marriage could be seen as 'an almost inevitable step in the transition to adult life' (Busfield & Paddon 1977) that sets the seal of adulthood on individuals. While the necessity to make the partnership legal (i.e. to marry, as opposed to cohabiting) may be declining, it is still true that living with a partner confers status as an adult. It also helps to create a personal identity, refining one's sense of self.

Research on the voluntarily childless suggests that they take their partnerships seriously, whether they are legally married or cohabitees. In one study voluntarily childless women scored higher overall in marital adjustment scales than a precision-matched sample of mothers, largely because they showed a higher level of 'cohesiveness' (Houseknecht 1979). Another study using the same marital adjustment scale found that, according to wives, childless couples worked together more, had more consensus and showed more affection than did a matched sample of parents. They also, however, scored lower on dyadic satisfaction (Callan 1985). Callan analysed differences between husbands and wives on a variety of questions about marriage, and found that both sexes 'expected to have a characteristically open relationship, with an emphasis on individuality, self-disclosure, personal freedom and trust'.

This accords with the description of the marriages of the voluntarily childless as being intensely focused on the partnership (which may lead to a high level either of happiness or of conflict), committed to intimacy, egalitarian and somewhat flexible in terms of sex-role behaviour (Veevers 1980). In contrast, another researcher stresses the dominance of husbands in some childless marriages and suggests that rather than 'oneness', what is important is that the relationship runs 'on an even keel', a course worked out over some time which neither party wants to change and which would be threatened by the arrival of children. This does not, however, preclude the possibility of great intimacy between spouses, or of 'erotico-romantic' relationships lasting well beyond the 'honeymoon phase' (Campbell 1985). While finding no difference in overall marital satisfaction between childless couples and parents, Feldman (1981) found that the childless were significantly more likely than parents to have 'fun' away from home, to exchange ideas and converse on a variety of topics, to work together on projects and to have sex frequently.

It appears from previous research that the marriages of the voluntarily childless are marked by a kind of 'togetherness' which is perceived to be diluted by the arrival of children. This was certainly the view of some of the childless couples in the case-study group. For Gabrielle, it was a major difference between her marriage and those of her friends with children:

> *It's different from people with children, because we rely very heavily on each other for everything; whereas in a marriage with children, children are a third outlet. I just think there is less strain, in one way, in a marriage with children, because the children act as a kind of go-between between parents.*

She sees the focus on each other as a possible source of strain ('You know, I can't go away and talk to somebody else if I'm not talking to him'), but also as a source of strength:

> *I think that I confide in Gary more than anyone else in my life. You know, what you'd call not only a husband but a best friend as well.*

Heather's picture of her marriage to Henry contained a similar thread—they were, she thought, two rather similar people who depended on each other a lot:

> *I mean, I'm fairly dependent, and I tend to think Henry is a bit too ... I mean, we prefer to do things together.*

Felix and Fiona both depicted their marriage as being close, and Fiona's description added to the picture of togetherness, the 'erotico-romantic' element noted by Campbell (1985).

FIONA: *It seems to me that we find it harder being apart even for 24 hours than most other people do ...*

FELIX: *... Well, I couldn't treat Fiona in the same cavalier fashion as I've seen other people do. Just saying, 'Well, I'm going off to A or B, that's it' ... I say, 'I'll discuss it with Fiona first. If she wants to come too, if she minds me going' ... maybe just a much closer personal involvement with each other ...*

FIONA: *We literally fell in love overnight ... We just seemed to sense that we were suited to each other. And so it was a whirlwind romance right from the start.*

Despite nine years of marriage, the Fs seemed to me to be in the 'honeymoon' phase of togetherness, where being apart is a trial and decisions are made on the basis of what the other thinks. This is an extreme of togetherness, but the notion of lives very much shared with a spouse can be seen in the comments of the Gs, Is and Ks as well as in the three couples reported above.

Not all the case-study couples had marriages characterised by 'togetherness', although six of the nine summarized from the second interviews show this characteristic. Two couples described their marriage in terms of separate interests and independence rather than togetherness:

CHRIS: *Well, I think it is the independence that we both lead in what we do. For example, even though I didn't really agree with buying this house [a second house, which Clare had bought with a legacy, just before the second interview], you [Clare] decided that you wanted a house so you went out and bought it. And I was willing to accept that and even help you, but you made the decision about it. We are independent in the way we reach decisions.*

DAVID: *It's different because I believe I give Diane independence which I don't think I have seen practised in a marriage ...*

DIANE: *That's true, but I hate the way you say 'I give you independence' ... we're both fairly independent, I think ...*

The questionnaire couples tended to depict their marriages as fairly free of conflict (more than 70% disagreed with 'we argue a lot') and as having friends in common (nearly 80% agreed with this statement). This implies that 'togetherness' might be more the pattern for them than independence of the sort described by the Cs and the Ds.

The dimensions of togetherness and independence are not mutually exclusive, as the example of the Js given earlier suggests. But both dimensions are likely to be affected by the arrival of children. Parents find less time for the communication and shared activities that make up some of 'togetherness'; they also have less time, less flexibility and often less money for engaging in separate pursuits. It is therefore unclear to what extent the marriages of the voluntarily childless shape their decisions about parenthood and to what extent their marriages are shaped by their decisions.

With the arrival of children, parents are also likely to be 'resocialized' out of any patterns of egalitarian sharing of housework which may have emerged in a dual-career couple with no children.[6] Studies of the division of domestic labour in Australian homes show that mothers bear the brunt of housework, whether or not they also hold paid jobs,[7] and that sharing the domestic tasks fifty–fifty is rare among parents. Half of the questionnaire group agreed that the wife did most of the housework. But another 40% claimed that it was shared, and more than three-quarters claimed that financial decisions were shared—a pattern which is uncommon in Australian families (Edwards 1981). More than 70% also claimed that 'power is shared between us', as table 2 shows.

The picture here is of relatively egalitarian relationships, and the comments of the case-study group support it. They tended to see themselves as dividing tasks and ending up with roughly equal shares of the work:

EVELYN: *I do the vacuuming, the rest of the dusting; Eric does the wet jobs and I do the dry jobs ... We split the housework so that it takes a couple of hours average each, and that's the way we split it up*

FIONA: *Haphazardly ... the nights I'm going out to work he nearly always gets dinner ... I do most of the cooking, most of the washing and ironing unless there's a disaster. But it's always been on a shared basis.*

Seven of the nine couples in the second interview were adamant that they balanced the household chores. And the other two, the Js and Ks, while agreeing that the work was not equally distributed, also made it clear that they were happy with the allocation. Judy, for instance, is very clear, that she does more than John. (She estimated that she does 60% of the domestic work. John thought she did 65%.) But she is also sure that the work is shared, and that, although a few years ago housework might have been an issue, now it is not. Kevin and Kate had a rather similar view; Kevin felt that Kate did the bulk of the housework, but Kate argued that Kevin did work outside the house. In their case, housework was an issue (Kevin regarded himself as fussier about it than Kate), but Kevin said:

It's matters of degree ... We might even get to the stage of raised voices about it, but we are not going to ... dissolve the marriage.

The pictures painted might or might not be entirely realistic; the accounts of 'who had done what' in the third interview suggested that, like many couples, the childless probably slightly exaggerated the equality of their arrangements. The important point is that they perceived their marriages as egalitarian and thought that housework wasn't a big problem, at least while there were no children around:

CLARE: *Housework isn't an issue with us.*

CHRIS: *Well, it isn't really difficult with us ... because there is no one here during the day most of the time and there's no kids, and we are not messy.*

Overall, then, the personal location of these childless people seems to be mildly to the left in political terms, non-religious, committed to identities as workers and oriented towards marital equality and 'togetherness'. The next section of the chapter will look at another aspect of the 'who' question: the family experiences of the voluntarily childless.

LITTLE MOTHERS AND FRIGHTENED ONLIES?

The social–psychological literature on voluntary childlessness in particular has attempted to explain why some people become voluntarily childless in terms of early experiences. This invokes the question of 'how' as well as 'who'. Research has focused on two broad areas: the impact of one's position in the family of origin and the images of parenthood (and especially motherhood) acquired in the family.

Some studies suggest that only children and eldest children are over-represented among the voluntarily childless.[8] While there is disagreement over details (for instance, over whether small or large families are most likely to produce voluntarily childless adults) there is a general tendency to argue that the eldest child is likely to be a victim of the 'little mother' syndrome and be disenchanted with parenthood through the experience of looking after siblings, while only children may be fearful of becoming parents because they have not had the chance to observe parents other than in relation to themselves.

Is there such a relationship between position in family and childlessness in my sample? Just 9.3% of the questionnaire group were only children, while 38.4% were eldests. Family size was not large; 89.1% of the group came from families of three or fewer children. The questionnaire group data seems to contradict the assumption that only children are led to childlessness by fear that they will not make good parents (through having no objective picture of what parenting entails) (Veevers 1980).

First, only children seem no more likely than those with siblings to be certain that they do not want children. In the questionnaire group, 66.7% of the only children were absolutely certain that they did not want children, and 16.7% were 'not quite sure'. Among those with siblings, 63.4% were absolutely certain, and 14.9% were not quite sure, and it was siblings rather than onlies who were likely to be sterilized (33.3% compared to 16.7%). Second, only children seem to be marginally less likely than siblings to give as a reason for childlessness the statement that 'I would make a bad parent'. The difference is slight (33.3% to 36.8%) when we focus only on the 'important' reason column but increases a little (50% to 58%) if we take into account the 'unimportant reason' category as well.

None of the comments from the only children in the case study (Clare, Eric, Fiona) make direct reference to lack of experience with children or clear pictures of parenthood as a reason for childlessness, though Clare notes that 'I think if I'd had more to do with children I might have had different views'. She also feels that being an only child has left her unsuited to parenthood because:

> ... if you've been an only child, you're used to having a lot of time to yourself and you've always been able to amuse yourself and find things to do, and I think I'd react badly to not having time to myself.

This is consistent with the picture of an only child growing up into an adult who cannot be bothered with childish things (Callan 1985), but not with the picture of lack of training for parenthood (Veevers 1980). Overall, the connection between childlessness and an only childhood seems to be weaker and less clear-cut than some of the literature suggests.

The same is true of the connection between being an eldest child and childlessness. The thirty-three respondents from the questionnaire group who had more than four siblings were examined in some detail and, on a variety of dimensions, they seemed to contradict the thesis about 'little mothers' growing up to be childless.

Table 3 shows that it is non-eldest children who seem likely to be certain that they do not want children and to be sterilized to ensure that they cannot have them, regardless of sex. Eldest men seem a little more likely than non-eldest to decide about childlessness rather than drifting into it, but the opposite is true of eldest women. Eldest women seem slightly more likely than non-eldest to make an early decision, which is consistent with the notion of 'little motherhood' putting them off having children of their own, but the opposite is true of men—non-eldests seem to reach a decision earlier. Eldest men seem likely to consider that they would be bad parents, which is not consistent with the 'little mother' notion, but this is not true of women. Overall, the support for the 'little mother' hypothesis is mixed. None of the differences between eldest and non-eldest children are statistically significant, and the differences between the sexes suggest that women might be influenced by the experience of being an eldest rather more than men. This might account for previous findings where sex has not been taken into account as a variable.

Among the case-study group, there is only one account of the 'little mother' experience, but it is a particularly clear and vivid one. Isabel recalls her first seven years as 'pretty calm' but, with the arrival of her brother, things changed:

> My sister and I, because of the big age-gap, were really put in the role of surrogate parents at times ... I remember at the age of 10—I'm not trying to make this out as terrible, but I remember hanging loads of washing before I went to school. And I remember my sister ... Because my mother unfortunately damaged her hand, she needed someone to help ... So my brother was put into my sister's bedroom and my sister was the one who was involved in getting him up and feeding him bottles and what-not during the night. She was only 11 then ... So I don't have the most positive feeling about the impact that children make.

This account is consistent with the 'little mother' thesis. But it comes from a second rather than an eldest child and concerns observed experiences (of her sister) as much as Isabel's own direct experience as a 'surrogate mother'. Her sister, incidentally, is now a mother of two, as is Isabel.

The ambiguous evidence from the questionnaire group and the scarcity of comment from the case-study people need not be taken as evidence that the 'little mother' hypothesis is totally wrong. Rather, it suggests that the connection between position in family and childlessness is complex. I suggest that it is the consequences of occupying a position, rather than the position per se, which is important as an antecedent to childlessness. That is, it is being put into the role of 'little mother' or some other role which leads to a negative picture of parenthood that is important, rather than being an eldest child. Of course, eldests (and especially eldest girls) are probably more likely than others to find themselves co-opted into parenthood while still children. But the notion that it is position in family which somehow creates childlessness is misleading; it is the interaction of events which happen to people in their positions which counts.

For Isabel, factors that she shares with others (being a second child, growing up in a particular town at a particular time, being a girl, belonging to a middle-class family), together with factors unique to her family (her mother's damaged hand when the last child was born, her mother's history of a career sacrificed and at least two children born against her wishes, etc.), began the process of her becoming voluntarily childless. Reconstructing what happened in the light of her later decisions, she said in the first interview that her childhood had made her feel defensive about children:

> *I suppose really by the time I left home at the age of 19 to go and live in college ... I had a pretty negative view about the impact of children on a happy family life.*

Position in the family may lead some people to voluntary childlessness by giving them an unsatisfactory image of family life based on childhood experiences. Research suggests that such an image is indeed a factor associated with becoming childless. Campbell (1983) offers accounts of 'unconventional' family situations such as marital breakdown, having a handicapped sibling, being taken into care or having an anti-natalist or career-oriented mother as leading some men and women to avoid parenthood. Veevers (1980) states that 'almost all' the voluntarily childless people interviewed in her study thought that their parents (especially their mothers) would have had different and possibly happier lives if they had not had children. Callan (1985) describes families where parents 'demonstrated that not everyone was suited to raising children' (for example, where fathers could not cope with the financial demands of family life) as leading to 'anti-natalistic' attitudes in adulthood. He suggests that an image of unhappy or unsuccessful motherhood haunts women particularly.

Kaltreider and Margolis (1977) record some instances of harsh treatment in childhood among a small group of voluntarily childless women and suggest that a 'common theme' among them was fear of becoming like their own mothers if they had children. Houseknecht (1978) found that voluntarily childless single women were significantly more likely than single women desiring children to come from 'mother-dominated' families and to have grown away from their families during adolescence—a fact that she relates to their developing a non-traditional sex-role concept, which might in turn contribute to voluntary childlessness. Feldman (1981), however, found no difference between parents and voluntarily childless couples with regard to mother dominance, and the last section of this chapter shows that the childless women do not seem to be particularly committed to feminism. So the decision to learn 'lessons from our mothers' lives' and not to repeat their mistakes is not necessarily one made only by women with non-traditional ideas about femaleness.

Overall, it would appear that images, based on a variety of experiences of parenthood as a problematic status, do form some kind of 'motive antecedent' (Veevers 1980) for some of the childless at least. There is no way of telling how closely the images reflect experience (Callan 1985); the important thing is that the images exist as a basis for decisions about parenthood.

The images of family life found among the case-study group in my own research are varied. The question 'tell me about your background' evoked long and complex biographies, out of which several themes emerged. For two or three, the basic theme was 'I had an unhappy childhood'. Only Andrew was really emphatic about this and prepared to relate his feelings about parenthood directly to his experiences as a child:

> *As far as the entire family situation goes … this must have … a bearing … on my having children in that I did not have a happy childhood. It was miserable.*

He is an adopted child who now feels that he was misplaced. An academic boy, he grew up in a house where academic pursuits were not valued and among people with whom he felt temperamentally incompatible. And now he fears that if he had a child of his own the same incompatibility might exist and make for the same kind of childhood he experienced:

> *You can muff it, although obviously with your own children there's … less chance of a child which is incompatible, but it's possible; it's possible that the child will be miserable as a result of it.*

It is worth noting that Andrew at one stage after the end of his marriage to Alison contemplated marrying a woman with three children, but nonetheless his attitude here is clearly compatible with the idea that unhappy childhood circumstances of some kind may predispose adults against parenthood.

Two other husbands, David and Henry, are less extreme, but also seem to be describing their childhoods as unhappy. David says he 'didn't really enjoy' his childhood and in explaining why he does not want children, he evokes an image that suggests a perception of his father as a failure at parenting:

> *I don't think I'd have it, that definite consistency where I could be rational all the time … I think that goes back to my childhood, though. My parents were never too rational, and they'd never think. The old man used to give you a clout around the ear and say, 'Don't do that again'. I think that goes back a long way.*

For Henry, the youngest by many years and, in effect, an only child, his childhood was 'probably fairly lonely'. As an adult, he definitely does not want children. If he had a child:

> *I'd feel responsible not just for its welfare ... but also for its entertainment. And I object to that responsibility. I mean, I don't want to spend that sort of time.*

For these three men there is fear of replicating in a child the unhappiness experienced in the past or a feeling of inability to provide what is necessary for happiness.

For another three people, childhood was an ambiguous state, which does not seem to be linked directly to decisions about parenthood. Clare described her childhood as 'mediocre'. Both Heather and Bill saw theirs as mixed. The most common perception of childhood, however, was that it had been happy but in a qualified sense.

The qualification might be that a basically happy childhood contained some unhappy elements or that, from an adult perspective, childhood was a trying time for either parents or children. Thirteen people held such qualified views and, in some cases, the qualifications related directly to the desire not to have children.

The unhappy elements might be minor, compared to the overall impression. Eric, for example, is enthusiastic about his childhood. It was

> *excellent; couldn't be better. Lots of relos to go and visit, lots of cousins my age, and they all lived out of [town] so I could go away for school holidays ... very stable.*

So for him childhood was good. But he was always aware that it might not have been as good for his mother:

> *My mother had a bung hip and she took a gigantic risk to have me.*

Bridget (at that stage childless but by the end of the research a mother of two) emphasized the problems that children can cause for parents. For herself, as for Eric, childhood was good ('essentially a happy one') but her eldest brother, who 'very much went off the rails', caused great pain to her parents, and she worried that the same might happen to her if she had children:

> *Now it's wrong that I'm emphasizing the one as against the five that they didn't have to go through it with, but the thought of bringing a child into the world and then having the life they had with him for eighteen to twenty years is pretty awful ... So while there's a possibility of having a child who would do that to you, it's easier not to take the step. You might end up with six of them!*

Two of the childless give particularly dramatic accounts of how an adult view qualifies the notion of a happy childhood and how this relates to childlessness. Judy's account has already been quoted. Kevin's story raises some similar themes and has the same air of childhood re-evaluated:

> *My sister's six years older, so ... apart from being a girl, being six years older put her on a different plane. So there's only me and my brother, and we spent our entire life as kids trying to kill each other. Which we didn't think was particularly abnormal until we grew up. At that time we both had totally opposing views of our childhood. He was always regarded as me Mum's favourite; I was always regarded as me father's favourite. And so we were always played off against each other ... We've decided since that there was a distinct—not animosity—but there was certainly opposition from time to time, and the kids used to get dragged in. We now reckon that there was a conscious effort to play each other off. As I said, we used to spend the entire time trying—we didn't think it strange to take to each other with knives or forks or whatever was at hand, until you talk to other kids and find out that that wasn't normal family life ... It was something we learned from our parents. My mother in particular was rather unstable. Which we didn't know at the time, of course; it's something you find out for yourself later on ... We don't think she could cope with the sort of pressure that motherhood brings ... They're the sort of things that stand out ... those things you remember more than the other.*

Despite this, Kevin regards his childhood as comparatively happy.

> *... yeah, it was a happy childhood. I mean, I think other kids probably had happier childhoods. But I wasn't so depressed that I had to run away from home or anything like that.*

So his adult view is that his childhood, which at the time he saw as normal, was odd and, unlike Judy, he tends to blame his parents for that. But, like Judy, he sees parenthood as having caused problems for his mother. And, like Judy, he fears replicating the problems. He sees himself as too unstable to be a good parent—too short-tempered and too like his mother. As a student, he attempted suicide and is unsure that he will never be depressed again:

> *... despite the fact that you go around saying, 'Oh well, it's never going to happen to me blah blah blah' I'm reasonably intelligent enough to assume that it could happen. And once again, I don't think that's ... the right environment to start having kids in. Given that— yeah, well—see, my mother was the same. I told you she was unstable; she's also tried to commit suicide on two or three occasions. She's also made a miserable attempt at it. So we have an unstable background somewhere along the family line. I don't plan to propagate that.*

In both Kevin and Judy's autobiography, links are drawn between childhood events and the desire not to have children. Did the events cause the desire to avoid parenthood, or has the decision led to the re-interpretation of childhood in a way which justifies it? There is, in the end, no way of knowing. Kevin raises the issue of how to treat his own evidence when he says:

> *I often wonder if I'm hiding behind my own psychiatric disadvantages ... You know, I mean I make a conscious decision not to have kids, then when people ask why, you run around looking for reasons to justify [the decision].*

The fact that Judy has changed her mind about childlessness suggests that childhood events are used in her account to rationalize her position. But would she have thought of childlessness if those events had not taken place? And would she have changed her mind had she and John stayed in Australia, where she could have continued to work as a nurse?

I do not think that the childless people are using their autobiographies to 'justify' their actions, but neither do I think that there is a simple straight line between childhood experience and later childlessness. Rather, I think that childhood events might start some people on a path that leads to questioning the value of parenthood, but that they are also later reinterpreted as part of the process of negotiation with ideology. This reinterpretation includes the possible re-evaluation of the image of motherhood. The feminist movement of the 1960s and 1970s undoubtedly helped to make people conscious both of the strains of motherhood itself and of the tensions between motherhood and careers in the workforce.

On the whole, the theme of motherhood as a problem was a feminine one, although Kevin's comments on his mother 'not coping' and Eric's perceptions of the risk his mother took to have him have already been noted. In addition, five women made comments about problems of motherhood. Judy's long description of the tensions caused for her mother by an asthmatic son has already been cited. Fiona offers a different picture with no hint of tension over coping but a clear understanding that her mother's life would have been happier without her:

> *I think my mother was a very important part, yes. Well, she never wanted children anyway. And I was an accident. And as much as she loved me dearly and was very, very good to me, I always knew and understood that if she'd have had her way, there'd have been no children ... And I think that was the sort of thing that influenced me— the way my mother felt about children ... And I think I probably just took most of my mother's ideas; the only differences between the two of us being that I live in an age where it's much easier to avoid having them.*

Diane sees her mother as now 'worried' by children she does not understand and as having been oppressed by her condition. She describes it as having affected her own decision:

My mother's role was hideous enough for me never to want to follow in those same footsteps, so initially it was only a reaction against her ... one of the things that could keep me from being like my mother was not to have children.

So the image of one's mother as less than happy may be a potent warning to some women about the dangers of having children.

There is little from the questionnaire group on images of childhood or parenthood. The group as a whole regard childhood as having been happy rather than unhappy, suggesting that accounts like Andrew's are exceptions, but there is some suggestion from the questionnaire data that perceptions of one's childhood as bad rather than good may be associated with feelings that one would make an inadequate parent. This fits the assertion about the childless having learned that parenthood does not suit everyone (Callan 1985). A rough scale was constructed for my data by adding the responses which might be taken to mean that childhood was perceived as unhappy. An individual who circled up to 2 of the words (like *cold, insecure, unhappy, unfree, stormy*) which I took to indicate a 'bad childhood' was classed as having a happy childhood. One with a score of 3 to 8 was classified as not having a happy childhood.[9] When scaled responses were cross-tabulated with the statement 'I would make a bad parent' as a reason for not having children, it did seem that there was an association between an unhappy childhood and fears about performance as a parent. Of those who saw childhood as happy, only 31.1% thought that 'I would make a bad parent' was an important reason for their childless state, but among the few people who saw childhoods as unhappy, 72% thought that they would make bad parents. (See table 4.)

While this association was very significant, it should not be taken too seriously because of the small size of the group with unhappy childhoods and the problems of the sample (discussed in appendix 1). It should also be noted that while there seemed to be some (non-significant) association between unhappy childhood and certainty about childlessness (63% of the individuals with a happy childhood and 75% with an unhappy childhood were 'absolutely certain' that they didn't want children), there was no such association between unhappy childhood and sterilization. In addition, the questionnaire group does not seem to be much influenced now by family. Their family was stated to have had either 'very little' or 'no' influence on 91.1% of them. This, however, refers to the present and does not mean that the sorts of experiences and feelings recounted by the case-study group are absent from the lives of the questionnaire people. The questionnaire data seem to support the broad contention of a relationship between the childless couples' images of family life and their late parenthood decisions, and to suggest that those whose early experiences in families have been unhappy are perhaps provided with the means of 'seeing through' parts of the ideology of parenthood.

These data provide some possible answers to the 'how' question as well as the 'who' one. For some people at least, childhood experiences do provide some basis for later decisions. But we have seen that there is no straightforward link between early images of parenthood and later decisions. The same complexity is evident in the data on the timing of these decisions.

EARLY DECISIONS AND POSTPONING PARENTHOOD

Many researchers have followed Veevers' (1974, 1980) lead in classifying the childless as either 'early articulators', who come into marriage already committed to childlessness, or as 'postponers', who enter marriage expecting to become parents and gradually drift into childlessness. The dichotomy is well established, as is the predominance of postponement as a way of entering the childless state.

Undoubtedly there are childless people who decide early and irrevocably, and others who drift imperceptibly into permanent non-parenthood, but the existence of a dichotomy should not obscure the fact that all the voluntarily childless are, to some extent, becoming rather than being. In other words: 'Intentions are not fixed; the meanings that inform reproductive commitment may be suspended, modified, subsequently reinstated, or subverted in the course of an unfolding life history' (Campbell 1985).

The process of becoming can be seen in Gabrielle's account which opened this chapter. She is in a sense both a decider (who did not see herself as a potential mother when she was an adolescent) and a postponer. But she does not drift in a straight progression towards childlessness; rather she moves actively, forwards and back. The accounts of the others, both postponers and deciders, confirm this kind of pattern:

DAVID: *It was sort of a slow process. I just didn't get up one morning and say, you know, 'no kids'.*

DIANE: *Look, I have procrastinated all my life about them. I've never got around to making a decision.*

DIANE: *After the abortion, I sort of got a bit thing and said—oh, you know, 'Let's have kids.' And he said, 'Oh, we'll wait for a while.' That's about as far as we got, wasn't it?*

DAVID: *Yeah, that's it, I don't think it was [anything more than a reaction to the abortion] ... I just backed off, let the thing calm down ...*

FELIX: *It was something we discussed even before we were married ... maybe we were in the process of making the decision about three or four years ago, and I think ever since then ... that's been it, decision's been made, sort of thing, doesn't really come up. It's just understood.*

Fiona claimed that she had never been attracted by children but had assumed she would have them, until a precise date:

By that stage I'd been married about eighteen months, and we had begun to collect antique furniture. And we'd had a child come round to visit us, and I'd had hell's own trouble controlling that particular child—it was inclined to put everything down on anything. That afternoon I rang Felix up ... and said, 'Well, love, I think at this stage we've got to make a choice—antiques or kids, which is it going to be?' And without hesitation he said, 'Antiques'. And I said, 'Great'. And that was the decision ... I've wavered, both times in connection with my mother. When I thought I was going to lose her in July, with a stroke, and then after she died in March there was a short period in which I felt possibly I should have children.

KEVIN: *When we got to the stage of getting married—no, before then, because we didn't know we were going to get married ... we chatted about having kids before then. In detail. Obviously not to the extent that Kate had the sterilization operation, because at that stage we didn't know what plans we'd make in that direction ... I'm never totally certain of anything, I've always got an idea that things can change, but we were 90% certain that unless there was going to be a wholesale change of attitude on both of our viewpoints, not just one, that it isn't likely.*

Kevin sounds closest to a decider, but even he shows signs of indecision. He and Kate agreed that when they came to consider sterilization, it was decided that he would have a vasectomy. He backed out at the last minute, put off by the nature of the operation, and Kate was sterilized instead.

The picture of an inconstant flow of decision is confirmed by the questionnaire group. While a clear majority (72.9%) saw themselves as having decided not to have children rather than drifting into childlessness or still being in the process of deciding, they also indicated that the matter had been discussed both before and after marriage (76.2%) rather than simply before (6.7%) or after (17.1%). The majority had made an individual decision before marriage, as table 5 shows, but it cannot be assumed that they were early deciders for whom the matter was fixed and simple, if the detailed data from the case studies are relevant.

So progress towards childlessness is uneven—a matter of two steps forward and one back which may entail sudden about-turns. Specific events can raise issues and changes of direction. Moreover, the couples do not always dance in tune; one may see a fairly steady progress, while the other is aware of checks. An interesting feature of the case-study data is the way in which the husbands see a fairly smooth process of drifting, while wives recall a more difficult and involved passage. This is shown in the accounts of Diane and David, and Fiona and Felix given above. (Felix noted that now his wife's mother was dead, the issue might be re-evaluated; Fiona has already been quoted as having 'wavered' in connection with her mother.) The contrast between

Gabrielle and Gary is more dramatic. Gabrielle's tale of their shift from taking parenthood for granted to conscious denial is, as we have seen, long and complex; Gary's is short and vague:

> I'm not particularly conscious of any milestones along that way. I suppose when we first got married like everybody else we thought we'd buy a house; once we got a bit of furniture or something, well, they'd come along and that'd be that. We didn't feel financially secure for a long time and I think I would have been reluctant [to have children without security] ... We became selfish and wanted to go overseas ....

He went on to say that he would never push Gabrielle into having children but that if she wanted them, he would be agreeable. He regards her as having made the decision and, perhaps because of this, cannot recall any of the 'milestones' which she perceives.

Eric and Evelyn also offer accounts that suggest that he sees the process as having been simple and she does not. For Eric, they

> ... never talked about it to any degree. It was a very easily arrived-at decision or situation. Scarcely a decision, sort of 'no, not now' and as you get more engrossed in your career and things like that ... It just drifts further and further on; you get fixed in your ways.

But for his wife:

> It's something I had to think about fairly closely initially when we were married, because I think that initially, Eric, being an only child himself ... was reasonably keen ... I've had to think about it more deeply since I got married because there are two people involved in it. It's not just my wishes.

She and Eric are agreed that they don't want children yet. But for Eric the agreement was a matter of drifting; for her one of deciding. In other words, for Evelyn (and the other women quoted) the issue of whether to have children had greater salience than it did for Eric and the other husbands. This is reflected in an exchange between the Es that took place during the second interview, where Evelyn suggested that Eric may have wanted children initially, but he insisted that he didn't particularly and that the issue was 'a bit of a bore'. Whether or not he wanted children, it was clear from that exchange that she took the issue more seriously than he and wanted to set the record straight. As far as she is concerned, they did not drift into childlessness, nor did they both come in determined not to parent. She sees herself as having convinced Eric and as having more stake in the issue ('I don't think he ever really thought about what was involved'). Eric agrees with this by implication ('she had lots of experience and I haven't') and insists that he wasn't in particular need of converting; his attitude when they married was much the same as it is now. The impression is that Eric would have been happy one way or the other and that Evelyn was the one on whom the decision weighed heavily.

Gabrielle and Gary in the second interview came to exactly this conclusion—somewhat to Gary's surprise.

GABRIELLE: *You never even particularly wanted to talk about it. But [to Gary] it was me who was going to have the baby so—*

GARY: *It was a decision I was certainly not opposed to. I mean [to interviewer] I think that Gabrielle did a lot more thinking about it than I did.*

And later Gabrielle told Gary:

It was all on me really. I don't think you realize what I really did go through ... To you it was fairly clear-cut, wasn't it? I don't think you ever agonized over it.

GARY: *No, I never agonized, that's true.*

GABRIELLE: *I did—a bit.*

While the last phrase qualifies the depths of Gabrielle's agony, it is clear that she sees herself as having given more thought to the question than Gary did, and she persuades Gary that this is so.

The issue seemed to be more salient to seven women (Bridget, Diane, Evelyn, Fiona, Gabrielle, Isabel, Judy) and three men (Andrew, Chris and maybe Kevin). Because Henry and Heather were in dispute over parenthood by the final interview, it is impossible to determine which of them gave more weight to the issue. This does not mean that husbands will not determine the outcomes of discussion. It has been argued that where there is dispute over not having children and the couple stay together, the husband who prefers childlessness will win (Marciano 1978). This seems to be the case with Henry and Heather. The case studies show that the process of becoming childless should be seen as consisting of 'his' and 'her' journey. On the whole, his is less difficult; the consequences of having children are less dramatic for him than for her, and the ideology of parenthood lays heavier obligations on her.

This might be the reason for a significant difference in the questionnaire group's reasons for not having children. Women were markedly more likely than men to say that 'I don't think I'd make a good parent' and that 'I don't want the responsibility of having children' were important reasons for childlessness (see table 6). They were slightly more likely to see children not fitting career and travel plans, while men were much more likely to say that the spouse not wanting children was an important reason for childlessness. This reflects the differential impact of ideology on the sexes, but we should note that the statement most often checked as an important reason ('I would like to be free of the constraints children impose') was one where there was little difference between the sexes. This presumably shows that both men and women are taught in our society to put a high value on independence and freedom but that they are taught different things about what parenthood entails. For women, maternity is seen as bringing constraints that paternity does not impose on men.

SUMMARY

This chapter has explored the backgrounds of the childless couples and found that the people in this survey do not differ enormously from the childless people surveyed elsewhere. It has shown that the process of becoming childless is complex and might more accurately be described as a journey that can be interrupted or even abandoned than as a simple movement towards a goal. And it has shown that the process might be more salient for wives than husbands. The last two points suggest that the phenomenon of childlessness needs to be treated as one where people actively negotiate within the social constraints they inhabit—a view that I outlined in chapter 2. Chapter 4 picks up that theme and continues to explore the reasons given for not having children as I examine the response of the childless to the ideology of parenthood.

4

. . . .

the

childless

and

ideas

about

parenthood

n chapter 2 I identified three themes about parenthood: that it is seen as natural, that it entails commitment and responsibility and that it requires sacrifice. These themes were shown to be present in the real world, although not necessarily in the universal and static form ascribed to them by feminist critics. Against this background, I now examine the perceptions of the voluntarily childless couples about parenthood. By doing so, I can begin to describe the ways they negotiate with the ideology of parenthood.

If the voluntarily childless accepted completely the ideological propositions about parenthood, then they could be seen as totally engulfed by the ideology of parenthood, and my assumptions about negotiation would need to be questioned. If they reject all the propositions, then my assumption that ideology is dominating would be called into question. And if the propositions about nature, commitment and sacrifice are completely without meaning to the childless, then my assumptions about ideology will be shown to be quite incorrect.

If my assumptions are correct, the childless will take up a position within the ideology of parenthood but not totally dominated by it. Of course, in the sense that they are disobeying its implied prescriptions, they are defying ideology, but that does not necessarily mean that they will stand outside it. Rather, they will make use of devices such as the exemption clause technique suggested by Hall (1980b) to explain and excuse their conduct. The following three sections take the themes of naturalness, commitment and sacrifice, and examine the views of the childless couples on each. (The data come mainly from the case-study group because the questionnaire was constructed before the concept of ideology emerged as central to the study.)

IS PARENTHOOD NATURAL?

As we saw in chapter 2, feminists have identified *natural* as meaning 'biologically based' or 'innate' while sociological research has tended to show that parents see parenthood as an 'inevitable' or 'normal' identity (especially for women). While the two meanings may well come together in a phrase like 'it's natural, innit?', they are not identical. Some of the childless made use of both senses. David, for example, late in the first interview said:

> *I think if you want kids you should have them … I think it's just a matter of a thing that happens. You'll know when you want them. I think you have a yearning or a craving, or they fulfil something that's missing out of your life.*

Here, parenthood is 'natural' in a sense similar to that used by the feminist critics of ideology. But it is not, David implies, 'natural' to the entire species, as an instinct is. Instead, it is 'natural' in the same way that eye colour is—inborn, but not the same for everyone.[1] And it is prescriptive, since, if you naturally want children, then you should have them. But early in the first interview, he offered an explanation of why people have children that relied on social pressure and the idea of normality:

> *I think probably that too many people have children to meet ... social pressure.*

Kate describes parenthood as biologically natural—for some:

> *... some people are just natural parents and the nurturing role is just so appropriate to them that there is never any question of them not having children. And in those cases I don't think that it is an invalid reason.*

In other words, if you are a natural parent, then you are right to have children.

The corollary to the idea of some people being biologically ordained as parents is the declaration of exception—that 'I am not that sort of person, so count me out of parenthood'. Moreover, exempt me from criticism, since, if parenthood is something which, like blue eyes, one either has or hasn't by nature, it would be as wrong for me, who could not do the job properly, to have a child as it would for those with the innate wish to ignore the promptings of nature:

> FELIX: *My brother went out at the earliest age and populated ... I suppose he's the fatherly type, the sort of person who looks right with three children round him, and good luck to him ... I don't see myself with three kids hanging on to my shirt-tails ... I just don't have the desire.*

> EVELYN: *I think ... good luck to the people, the genuine cases who have a real maternal instinct, who want to have children and ... have some reason for having children. But I think it's crazy to keep perpetuating the race on the basis of 'everybody does it'.*

The theme of parenthood's biological basis, or of 'innate' tendencies, ran in a complex fashion through the interviews with the childless. It is explored in more detail in chapter 5, where it becomes clear that, for the childless, the notion that not having children is an 'innate' tendency plays a part in explaining and defending their state. But this theme is, on the whole, subordinate to the version of parenthood as socially normal—or the inevitable step which follows from marriage. The picture of parenthood as the proper path emerged clearly from the accounts of why people have or do not have children offered in the third interviews, with interesting overtones.

The adjective *proper* implies both good and bad qualities. On the one hand, it can mean 'genuine, real; normal' (for example, 'sociology proper' is distinguished from spurious activity calling itself sociology) or 'fit, apt, suitable, fitting, befitting'. Both these senses are benign—what is proper is usual as well as right. But a subordinate usage is slightly pejorative. *Proper* may also mean 'in conformity with the demands or usages of society; decent, decorous, respectable, "correct" '. In this last sense 'proper' can be used as a snide put-down. If I am described as 'a very proper sort of person', then I am at best stiff and formal though worthy, and at worst positively dull and stodgy. The childless couples see parenthood as a 'proper' consequence of marriage, both in the approving and the pejorative sense of the word. Ten of the sixteen who completed the three interviews described marriage followed by parenthood as the normal course of events. And of those ten, six depicted normality in derisory tones. Chris, for example, said of parenthood:

> I guess it's a decision they make, and they make it on the grounds that maybe they've reached that stage in life. There seems to be a pattern in everything they do, that other people do and they think perhaps they should be fitting into that pattern. They think it's a normal stage.

The thrust of this comment is that most people follow a normal path into parenthood without sufficient thought, and its implication is that some parents are timid conventionalists who feel that they should do what everybody else does. Diane, too, presented a picture of unadventurous parents, who acquiesce to the (faintly ridiculous) business of the 'big tummy' stage:

> There's a whole lot of them with these big [pregnant] tummies and your tummy is only a little tummy. So I think [there is] the pressure of other people having children and you have sort of, at this stage, already acquiesced to the pressure of being in the relationship and then getting married, and then finally the next stage is this big tummy business.

Isabel was anxious not to judge parents harshly, but she too saw them as being 'proper' in the sense of rather blindly walking along the normal path:

> ... they all assumed that they will have children ... [a] sort of lack of questioning ... I suppose I had the idea ... that some of them might have been better off if they'd had the opportunity to look a bit more carefully at why they were doing things, but I wouldn't want to be judgemental and say they were lesser beings because they hadn't questioned it.

Overall, the 'proper path' was the normal one, and at times that meant the boring or foolish one. Again, the complexities of this notion are explored in more detail in chapter 5. For the moment, it is clear that the childless couples do make some use of the notion that parenthood is 'natural' and that they invoke both the biological and the social connotations of that term. But they are able to side-step the implication that, since parenthood is natural, then they should become parents. They seem to do this in two ways. By adding the notion that non-parenthood is also natural to the concept of biologically natural drives to reproduce, they can make use of exemption clauses for themselves. And by deriding the notion of parenthood as a 'proper' thing to do, they can make their childless state more attractive and defensible.

DOES PARENTHOOD REQUIRE COMMITMENT AND RESPONSIBILITY?

I argued in chapter 2 that the ideology of parenthood clearly describes and prescribes parenthood as a matter of total commitment. The evidence about attitudes to parenthood showed that while ideas about what parental responsibility meant in action varied more than the critics of ideology believed, the general notion that parents owed their children total commitment was very strong.

The elements of commitment and responsibility are visible in the statements of the case-study couples, frequently in those words (and in the notion of 'owing' to children). Twelve of the twenty-two individuals produced explicit statements about the moral basis of parenthood, and the views of the others can be inferred from their comments on parenthood. (See table 7.) Bridget's summary was crisp and characterizes the view of parental responsibility:

> If I'm bringing a child into the world, then I owe it ... We would have decided to have them, so we would owe them more than they owe us, because they didn't ask to be born.

While her views on what was owed changed over time, her perceptions that, as a parent, she would face obligations to her child did not. In the first interview, when she regarded herself as voluntarily childless, she seemed fairly sure that a proper commitment to a child should entail giving up paid work, at least for a time, but that she would not want to do that. Therefore she would be a 'bad' mother:

> Because I enjoy this job so much I wouldn't be prepared, I think, to give it away, therefore ... I couldn't be, I think, a very good mother ... Everybody that I know, every girl who is a working mother is fairly frustrated ... and so my observations have led me to think that you might be opening a hornet's nest that isn't fair, ultimately to the child or to yourself.

But shortly after the first interview (and, they later told me, perhaps in part because of it) Bill and Bridget changed their minds about children, and Bridget became pregnant. Since her first child was born, Bridget's pattern of activity has been rather different from the one suggested in the interview. She took maternity leave and then study leave, and was thus technically free to be at home for the early period of her son's life, which she saw as important:

I feel that those first five years of a child's life are extremely important. I don't think the mother has to be there full time for that, but I think there's certainly got to be a strong bond and relationship, which I think I would owe the child having brought it into the world.

But during her leave, she spent much of her time away from the baby, either in research for her doctorate or in part-time teaching. The baby was minded either by Bill or by paid minders. This was both more consistent with the 'new style' of mothering than with the 'old style' which Bridget thought she should adopt and much less difficult than she had anticipated. What had changed was her notion of just what commitment and 'owing' entailed. Before becoming a mother, she visualized a situation where she either worked for pay or gave her child what it was owed. When her son was small, she and Bill visited me, bringing the baby with them. Bridget apologized for this, saying that she had originally planned to leave him with a sitter, but that she'd been away from him several times that week, and it 'didn't seem fair' to leave him behind. Obligation now seemed to mean a strict accounting of time and 'fair shares' for all.

When her second (unplanned) child was born, Bridget appeared to have moved well away from the position she had depicted in the first interview. She took an extremely demanding job, requiring interstate travel, and continued to juggle timetables so that she could be both worker and mother. I met her, for instance, at an airport, shortly after the third round of interviews. She was off to a conference, leaving Bill to mind the children for a week. Then she had some business in Tasmania; Bill and the children were to fly there, they would have a family weekend, and then Bridget and the children would return home while Bill flew on to a conference of his own. Bridget looked successful, organized and not at all guilty about this. She was committed to her children, as she had known she should be; all that had changed was her notion of how this commitment should be manifested.

Judy's story, told in the last chapter, also provides evidence for the idea of commitment providing a basis for actions by both the childless and parents. When she was sure that she should be childless, she argued that she would have to sacrifice her identity as a worker for the sake of a child and that she did not want to do this. Once her son was born, she decided to return to work when he was a year old. This could be taken to mean that she had abandoned the idea of commitment and was prepared to be a 'bad' mother. But she decided to have a second child and put off a return to work, and told me that she did so because she thought that children needed companions. Again, what she is prepared and able to do in the name of commitment is not what she had envisaged as a childless woman, but the commitment is still present and strong.

While the form of commitment may change, it is seen as irrevocable—at least for the foreseeable future:

ALISON: *That long-term commitment ... of really having to organise your life around someone who's going to be dependent on you for ten or twenty years is a commitment I'm not all that anxious to make.*

Since it is taken to be impossible to give away a child once it is there, commitment also involves the acceptance of whatever sort of child you get:

BILL: *I mean, having a blind child or a mongol ... [the child] has got to fit in just as much, and you've got to want to have a child like that just as much as you'd want to have someone who is a genius and a Brownlow medal footballer.*

The commitment needed for parenthood is invoked as a reason for not having children:

ANDREW: *The idea of playing God really frightens me ... I've never been a really self-confident person who felt that I want to have the moral responsibility of educating and bringing up another human being.*

CLARE: *I guess I might be afraid of responsibility, I don't know. But the idea of a little human life being totally dependent on me doesn't appeal to me.*

The theme at work for Andrew and Clare is that they believe in commitment but cannot offer it in this case. They agree with the statements in the ideology of parenthood about the demands of the job but seek exemption on the grounds that they could not fulfil them. This could be seen as a claim that 'my allegiance to the standards set by ideology are so strong that I cannot obey the demands of that ideology', or as a form of negotiation which turns one element of an ideology against the whole. This kind of negotiation is visible in Bridget's claims from the first interview about not being able to be a good parent, because good parenting probably required her to stay home with a child. Gabrielle made similar comments:

> *Now to me, there's no point in having a child if somebody else is raising it. And I wouldn't trust—I know I'm wrong but I wouldn't trust another person to do it the way I wanted it. So for me there was no compromise, it was going to have to be 'give up work' ... it would hurt a little bit now to do that ... And I don't feel that I have the stamina to run a family and run a teaching job, both well. One or both of them would've suffered, because I just feel now that I put everything into it, and I don't think there's anything left much in me to come home to kids and give them something.*

Besides the appeal to the notion of commitment which means that if you bear a child you must raise it, Gabrielle covertly appeals to a tenet of another possible ideology—that a profession like teaching demands full-time dedication.

The childless women's perceptions of what the commitment to parenthood would require of them is curiously old-fashioned. Alison, Diane, Fiona, Gabrielle and Kate all stated firmly that children require a parent (usually a mother) at home if they are to be properly brought up. Clare, Evelyn and Heather all implied that motherhood would involve their staying at home, although it is unclear whether they saw it as a necessary part of parental responsibility. The attitudes of Bridget and Judy differ from their eventual practices, as has been noted, but for both of them maternal commitment was initially seen as incompatible with paid work outside the home. (See table 8.)

The case-study women believed that they could not easily combine work and motherhood despite the fact that they (as professional workers, whose incomes would enable them to purchase high-quality childcare) are among the group who would have the best chance of doing just that. Their statements indicate a close adherence to the ideological prescription for commitment which can be turned against the prescription for parenthood by simply adding 'but I couldn't cope', as Kate and Evelyn, for example, imply. Kate believes that mothers should stay at home, but:

> *I hate staying home. You know, I barely make it through the Christmas holidays … I'm very career-oriented … and I don't think children fit very well into that sort of framework.*

> EVELYN: *I just don't think I'm suited at this stage, anyway, to doing the right thing … by kids that I'm trying to bring up … having to stay at home, not being able to go to work.*

As indicated in chapter 3, the women in the questionnaire group were significantly more likely than the men to focus on not wanting responsibility or fearing that they would make a bad parent (i.e. they 'couldn't cope'). While among the case studies the pattern is similar, men did sometimes offer comments suggesting that they could not live up to their responsibilities, as Andrew's remark about playing God suggests. David gave another example when he said that he hasn't the necessary 'patience, persistence, nor the responsible attitude'. If they discussed commitment, the men were likely to see it as involving a moral obligation that they could find difficult, boring or unpleasant to fulfil:

> HENRY: *Parents have a full-time, uh, responsibility's the wrong word … I suppose I'd feel obliged to entertain children because it's my fault …*

He likened the responsibility to the obligation he feels (and resents) to take his dog for walks. He doesn't always do what he should for the dog, and if it were children to whom he had responsibility, the burden of obligation and guilt would be even heavier. In other words, parenthood imposes obligations as part of responsibility which Henry feels and dislikes. To avoid them, he avoids parenthood.

The childless seem to accept the ideological imperative about responsibility without question and to make positive use of it in explaining and defending their state. For women especially, this involved invoking the notion that they could not cope, or declaring an exemption for themselves by comparing the prescription about responsibility with the one about having children.

DOES PARENTHOOD REQUIRE SACRIFICE?

In chapter 2 I argued that critics of the ideology of parenthood saw a moral imperative pressing on parents that their commitment result in sacrifices for their children and that parents saw sacrifices as what parenthood was all about rather than as moral imperatives. The childless couples all offered comments on what unpleasant consequences would flow from their commitment or on what sacrifices they would be called on to make in the name of parenthood. Sometimes the comments were linked to the theme of commitment, so that sacrifice became a moral imperative or obligation of the sort Henry described in his comment on responsibility. Sometimes they were simple descriptions of parenthood. So the childless share the views both of critics of parenthood and of parents in this respect. Exactly what was to be sacrificed varied but can be grouped under five headings: time and trouble, money, freedom and spontaneity, emotional energy and dyadic intensity, and (for women) the sacrifice of self.

Time and trouble

At a superficial level, children were seen as entailing a certain amount of trouble and creating a degree of havoc in daily life. This is, of course, a staple theme about parenthood, especially in comedy. Although the trouble and mess caused by children are epitomised in the image of the dirty nappy, only one person (Fiona) made any reference to this symbol of domestic hardship. Instead, images of children making adult conversation impossible, or causing havoc with treasured possessions predominated. Chris, for example, 'hated' children 'becoming the centre of attention':

> *I really object to that, when I go to people's places and the kid's sitting there and you just can't communicate properly.*

Isabel commented on the effect of giving priority to infants' needs:

> *I mean, if I had a child here now and it was screaming in the bedroom*

*as I was talking to you, we couldn't as fellow human beings just sit
here and ignore it!*

(When she became a parent, Isabel showed the commitment to her
child at which this statement hints. While I was working on this book,
I heard from a mutual friend that her baby was difficult to settle at night
and that she sometimes took three hours to get him to sleep. From this,
I infer that she has a totally child-centred parenting style.)

Isabel also noted that children can be destructive of property. Ian had
a similar view, although he was a little more accepting of it:

> *... the usual mess and untidiness and that sort of stuff. But I don't
> think they matter very much.*

Fiona's account of how she had been impelled into childlessness by a
trying time with a child who menaced her antique furniture ('it was
inclined to put everything down on anything') has already been noted
in chapter 3. The sacrifice of order, pleasure or property may be seen as
trivial or as important. It may be based on the moral imperative of commitment (as Isabel's comment shows) or it may simply be the way things
are (as with Fiona's notion that one may have either children or antiques
but not both). But there is no doubt that it is there for the childless and
provides a comprehensible reason for not wanting to have children.

Money

The image of children as entailing financial sacrifice emerged in a total
of ten comments and usually at a superficial level, perhaps because (as
some of the childless noted) sacrifice is comparative and most of the
couples could well afford children. Certainly, in the questionnaire
group it was not an important reason for childlessness. It possibly serves
as a throw-away answer to queries.

DAVID: *[Earlier] I don't think we could have afforded it ... but certainly now it's more selfish in monetary terms. We just wouldn't live
the good life that we do now ...*

GABRIELLE: *Well one friend suggested that it was money that was stop-
ping me ... When she ... brought the subject up I realised, oh yes,
our salaries would go down horribly. But then I could see everybody
around me doing it, and we've got a lovely house. We would have
been fine.*

Freedom and spontaneity

If the sacrifices of time and trouble and of money were regarded fairly
lightly on the whole, the notion that children (especially babies) curtail
freedom was taken more seriously.

'Freedom' may mean capacities to go out on a whim or to indulge in
what Veevers (1980) describes as 'disreputable pleasures for adults only'.
For some of the childless, the capacity to act in accord with their whims

was a valued part of their lifestyle that would disappear if they became parents:

ANDREW: *[In response to question 'Why don't you want children?']* I enjoy my lifestyle ... I enjoyed being a student ... enormous amounts of freedom. You can do all sorts of things and your social life is completely uninhibited.

DAVID: See, I wouldn't go out on the piss if a bloody son and daughter were home.

FIONA: ... we're the sort of people who're quite liable to make love on the loungeroom floor at midnight ... and with kids you don't do that sort of thing.

GARY: *[Asked why he didn't want children.]* I suppose the restrictions ... certainly they tie you down as to what you can do, where you can go.

KATE: Also we love travelling and kids don't really fit in with that, either.

At a deeper level, there were expressions of fear that children would mean a need to sacrifice personal autonomy:

CHRIS: It's not the work. It's just the fact that the things you've always taken for granted as a part of your life are no longer viable because you've got so many responsibilities. Your life becomes the child's life rather than life standing up on its own.

ISABEL: I can see that people can do a lot with childcare and all the rest of it, but—you know—that sort of lets go of rights ... you don't have that sort of personal freedom.

This view of freedom is much broader than the notion that it involves the ability to stay out late, behave irresponsibly or travel. It has obvious connections with the notion of a sacrifice of self (and so shows up more often in women's comments than in men's). This dimension will be explored in a later section of this chapter. In the meantime it is clear that the childless couples think that freedom in some form or other is lost when people become parents. Among the questionnaire group, 80% of the men and 76% of the women thought that children would constrain them. In this sense, as Alison phrased it:

A lot of people, I realise, see a baby as something added to [life]. I see it as an infringement.

Emotional energy and dyadic intensity

Chapter 3 showed that the couples in this study, like the ones in several others[2] tended to have marriages characterized by a high degree of 'togetherness'—although this did not prevent some of the marriages ending during the period of the study. Given the 'dyadic intensity' of the marriages, it is not surprising that nine people gave as a reason for not having children the idea that their marriages would be changed for the worse or that all nine couples in the second interview felt that having children would drastically change their marriage, probably in undesirable ways. Some of the imagined changes were to routines and lifestyle, involving time and trouble, or freedom. Others had to do with a dilution of commitment to each other that the childless did not desire:

FIONA: *I think it would spoil our relationship. I feel that once children arrive there'd be a distance between Felix and me.*

GABRIELLE: *[If you are childless] ... I think you demand very high standards of one another ... in your relationship. [Children] would dissipate that closeness ... I do think that all my friends who have children do have a different relationship with their husbands ... They don't appear as interested, or they'd probably say they are not as obsessed, whereas I am. But I would say they appear to have lost a certain amount of romance out of it, which of course is natural. They just don't seem as close, to me.*

ISABEL: *[If we had children] I think that communication time would be certainly eroded very substantially.*

IAN: *Yeah, it'd be—we'd still have it, but it would ... become more technical ... Instead of talking about the things that we wish to discuss, we would instead be talking about the things that we had to discuss such as ... baby-minding and caring-for arrangements.*

For some of the childless, having children could cause discord, even if it did not reduce marital intensity:

KATE: *[Kevin's] a very possessive person and I think it'd create conflict in our marriage.*

DAVID: *[Having children] would put untold pressure on the marriage ... I'm sure everybody has caused their parents to fight, you know, even over things like discipline. You know, one parent thinks the kid should get a smack for something and the other doesn't ...*

The theme of potential disruption to the marriage could be summed up as a fear of sacrificing what is felt to be good for what may not be better:

KATE: *... people say to me, 'Oh, you don't know what you're missing, they add so much to a marriage'. But we feel our marriage doesn't seem to be lacking anything for not having children, and we don't really feel they're going to add much to it ... maybe take something away.*

Mothering and the sacrifice of self

I have already noted that the theme of sacrificing a crucial part of identity was connected with the theme of sacrificing freedom. For the case-study women, this meant sacrificing work in order to be a mother—and the comparatively old-fashioned view that the two things are incompatible has already been discussed. Given that work identity is important to the childless (see chapter 3), this is an important sacrifice:

JUDY: *I need to work ... and I feel for me to be an adequate mother I would need to give up work. And I feel ... it's a vicious circle. Because if I gave up my work I would feel as though I was being cheated.*

GABRIELLE: *I don't think a great deal would change for Gary [if we had children] but I would see a horrendous upheaval for me [to Gary] ... See, you've got other interests and you would always have those other interests and I would've had the children.*

Gabrielle and Judy seem to be saying that much of their being is tied to their work and that motherhood, by taking away the opportunity to work, would diminish their being. Similar comments about work came from Alison, Bridget, Clare (who described the mothers she worked with as 'desperate' to communicate with people outside the household), Diane, Evelyn, Fiona (who says 'I first and foremost have always wanted to have a career' and that children would prevent that) and Kate, whose problem with surviving the holidays at home has already been noted.

In addition to comments implying that motherhood demanded a sacrifice of one's identity as a worker, a sprinkling of comments suggested that it affected other elements of the self by removing time for being a wife (as when Isabel's observation of her parents led her to suggest that having children left them little time 'for themselves' as a couple) or that it trapped women in a 'role'. Diane described this last as a 'horror'. It implies that she fears that motherhood would make her a puppet rather than a person. This is, of course, the standard feminist critique of the sacrifice of self in motherhood, but it appears to be less important to the childless women than the notion that one would have to sacrifice working identity to motherhood. The questionnaire group women did not, on the whole, give commitment to a job as a reason for childlessness. Only 26.8% said that 'children don't fit with my career plans' was an important reason for not having them. This may, however, be a response either to the phrasing of the question (which suggests definite arrangements rather than identity as either a worker or a mother) or a response to the term *career*.

It is possible, of course, that these women would adopt different positions if they were at home with children. It seems likely that Judy, who saw herself as one who 'needs to work', did this. And Bridget shows that motherhood is by no means incompatible with a strong commitment to a working identity. So there is evidence that the duties of motherhood are seen as requiring sacrifice of the mother's self, but there is also evidence that, as with the perceptions of commitment, the ramifications of sacrifice vary according to circumstances.

Sacrifice as moral demand or just part of the job?

In chapter 2 I showed that while those critical of the ideology of parenthood assumed that it contained a moral demand for parents to sacrifice, parents themselves were more likely to see sacrifices as simply part of the job than as abstract moral imperatives. The comments of the voluntarily childless are ambiguous in this respect. Sometimes sacrifice is portrayed as a moral obligation imposed on parents; for instance, in the comments of mothers' having to give up their identities as workers for their children's sakes. At other times—when the focus is on time and trouble, for example—it is portrayed as simply part of the condition of parenthood.

One way to sort out whether the childless think that sacrifice is imposed on parents, or whether it is just what parents do, is to look at how they react to the accusation of selfishness. There is certainly evidence that parents are willing to label the voluntarily childless as selfish.[3] If sacrifice is a moral requirement of parenthood, then it might be expected that the voluntarily childless, who refuse to make such sacrifices, would fight the label of selfishness. If, on the other hand, sacrifice is simply the natural condition of parenthood, then the childless might see themselves as merely making a choice between alternatives, without any moral connotations.

On the whole, the couples were more likely to apply the label of selfishness to themselves (as David does in his comment about sacrificing money) than to agree with its application by others. So Kevin can say of himself:

> In cold hard terms, it's because I'm bloody selfish. I don't want 'em imposing on things I like to do.

But when I put the question of whether he was selfish in a later interview he refused the label:

> Actually the other day somebody asked me [why I have no children] and I just said that they didn't fit into our lifestyle. In fact, I might have even said to them at the time, 'That might sound terribly selfish but then we don't have to apologize for that either. We are mature enough to have worked our way through that argument' … that is their definition of selfish. Our definition of selfish is how we see ourselves.

Judy's comments on selfishness show that she had worked hard to fight off the label:

> Probably the hardest thing I found to come to terms with was the fact

that I was continually telling people that I was basically a selfish person ... no, that's the wrong way round. People were telling me: 'Gee, that's selfish' ... And the more I thought about it, the more I thought I don't have to make excuses; it was a decision that we made that I'm happy with, and I resent having to say that I'm selfish because basically I feel that it's not a selfish move.

Kate suggests something similar. She argues that many parents have children for what she considers the wrong reasons:

... because they will be there to support them in their old age, or because the family says you should, or because it is the done thing ... I see them as far more selfish ... because they are making choices that do affect other people and for the wrong reasons ... I will not accept the label of selfish ... nobody misses out by the fact that I don't have children. If anybody misses out, it is us.

The idea that many parents were actually the selfish ones is a counter to the label being applied to oneself, as is the redefinition of selfishness. Table 8 suggests that the couples do feel some need to fight the label, which suggests in turn that there is, for them, a moral aura around sacrifice which is not necessarily there for parents. The aura may not, however, be as strong as the critics of ideology suggest; much of the material on selfishness is the reaction to my direct question, and there is comparatively little to suggest that the couples often encounter suggestions that they are selfish. (See chapter 6 on the comparatively benign climate of the couples' networks.)[4]

Are the sacrifices rewarded?

The critics of the ideology of parenthood argue that sacrifices are believed to be rendered worthwhile by the presence of children, and there is much evidence that parents find children rewarding. Do the childless see recompense from parenthood which would make the sacrifices worthwhile? Their responses to questions about the rewards of parenthood[5] suggest that they think there are indeed rewards from contact with children, but that it is not only parents who can have such rewards and that, in general, the impact of parenthood on their own lives would be disturbing rather than rewarding:

INT: *... what do you think you are missing out on?*

DIANE: *... those gorgeous cuddles that you get from kids, the total acceptance. But then I get that from [my niece], from [a friend's] kids, get it from [another niece and nephew].*

FIONA: *Nothing. Absolutely nothing. I get as much love out of animals as I can out of children. And as much laughter.*

KEVIN: *... the development ... but can't say that I miss it ... It must be sort of scaring [the] influence that you have on the development of* *a human baby ... For the right person it must be wonderful. For me, it frightens the hell out of me.*

CLARE: *Grey hairs ...*

CHRIS: *It's an experience of life, isn't it? If you have no children you just never experience it.*

For Diane and Fiona the rewards of children can be obtained from sources other than parenthood. For Kevin, the rewards are equivocal and 'scaring' and for Chris, while the rewards are there, you don't miss what you don't experience.

In a minority of cases, one of the 'bad things' was a straightforward dislike of children. This was a motive for Andrew, Clare and Fiona— although it was not a pronounced theme for any of them. For a larger group, however, the opposite was true. Bridget, Bill, Diane, Eric, Gabrielle, Gary, Isabel, John, Judy and Kate made it clear that they enjoyed children in various ways and at various stages, and so could be seen as getting rewards from contact with them.

GARY: *I enjoy their company enormously. I've had a lot of kids over here for the weekend to potter around the place with me.*

JOHN: *I get a great delight in seeing my nephew and niece ... whenever they're around I'm always the one playing the games ...*

KATE: *Well, it depends what you mean by children ... I like adolescents. That's why I teach them. You know, I feel I like to be able to help them and see them develop ... that's really good.*

For most of the couples, then, there are rewards to be had from contact with children, but they are not big enough to outweigh the sacrifices required by parenting.

The material so far has indicated that the voluntarily childless couples do not reject the ideology of parenthood, the content of which was outlined in chapter 2. They see it as socially normal (and at times as biologically natural), but evade the corollary that they should go ahead and do what comes naturally by invoking the notion of childlessness as also 'natural' or by implying that normality is a little boring. They accept without question the statement about commitment and responsibility and use it in fact to defend themselves by arguing that they could not cope with the burdens of parenthood. In this way, they turn their adherence to one element of the ideology of parenthood against another element—invoking the responsibility prescription against the one which enjoins parenthood on married couples. They perceive a variety of sacrifices associated with parenthood, some of which flow from the prescription of responsibility (especially the sacrifice of self for women). These, too, are invoked as defences for not having children, while the rewards which go with them are seen as inapplicable or inadequate.

A theme I have not yet addressed is the way in which the childless make use of words which have come to have a multiplicity of associations as part of their negotiation with ideology. Terms like *natural* and *responsibility* are given meanings that flow from their meanings in the ideology of parenthood, but which can be used against it. So, for the childless, being 'responsible' need not mean playing the grown-up part of a parent—a meaning implied in the ideology of parenthood. The 'responsible' course of action might be to refrain from having children with whom, in Fiona's terms, one 'could not cope'. Similarly, in one context 'natural' progress may mean the move from marriage and 'getting set up' into parenthood and being 'tied down'. But to the childless, it may refer to an essential element in character that makes one totally unfit to be a parent.

The ways in which the voluntarily childless negotiate with the ideology of parenthood are explored in chapter 5. It addresses the question of where they stand in the continuum of negotiation, from hegemony to opposition, and explores their perceptions of and explanations for their childless state.

5

. . . .

negotiating

with

ideology

The idea that people actively negotiate with the ideological frameworks they inhabit, rather than being either imprisoned within them or totally free agents in the world of ideas, has already been introduced, along with the ideas of hegemonic, oppositional and negotiated positions towards ideology. In chapter 2 I argued that ideology prescribes parenthood as the proper path for married adults to follow. This means that those married couples who decide not to have children might develop some special negotiating techniques in order to defend themselves. Chapter 4 focused on the childless couples' perceptions of parenthood and showed that, rather than being total opponents of the ideology of parenthood, they accept some key premises about what parenthood entails and use them as part of their defence of childlessness. This, I claim, is an example of negotiation with ideology.

The focus in this chapter is on how the voluntarily childless experience the ideology of parenthood. I am concerned to know how they view the world, whether they perceive an ideology about children with which they must deal and, if so, how they perceive its sources, transmission and impact. The bulk of the data come from the third interview, which was designed to expose their approach to ideology.

I am looking at three sets of data. The first concerns the world-views of the couples. I asked: 'Do you think there are different sets of values about adult lifestyles in Australia? If so, what are they? Can you draw me a rough diagram showing how you think people are divided?'

Although these questions probably forced more categorization than people usually use, the answers to them and to my subsequent questions about the values of parents versus the childless can be examined for ideas about ideology. Examining the world-views of the childless can give clues about how salient the issue of parenthood is for them and whether or not they see it as an issue involving conflict.

The second set of data comes from the ways the childless explain (formally in response to my direct questions and informally as part of answers to other questions) how some people choose to be parents and others to remain childless. In analysing these explanations, I am asking to what extent the comments of the childless imply that ideology exists.

The third set focuses directly on ideology—whether the childless see an ideology of parenthood at all and, if they do see it, where it comes from and how it works.

PICTURES OF THE SOCIAL WORLD

How do the voluntarily childless see the social world? And how salient to them are the differences between themselves and people who become parents?

My expectations when I came to look at these data were that the couples would see the world as divided into childless 'us' versus 'them' the parents and to regard parents somewhat negatively. If the ideas about marriage and parenthood that were described in chapter 2 have any power, then the childless, because they are not following the pre-scribed path, must see a significant difference between parents and themselves. If they do not, then ideas about parenthood are probably not powerful enough to be called an ideology.

To what extent were these expectations fulfilled? While each individual had a unique world-view, enough common themes ran through some responses for me to group them into three broad types (see table 9).

The first type I labelled the *social location* view. This implied that people's lives and values differed according to where they are placed in a stratification scheme, usually an economic one. Phrases like 'haves and have nots' typified this scheme. While individual responses differ in detail, they have in common a sense that it is where you are born in a social structure (and especially the economic position to which you are born) that is significant in explaining your life. Five of the sixteen people who took part in the third interview had such a view of the world.

For another five the world was divided by factors of *character* rather than by factors of circumstance. There were no shared phrases here—distinctions included the division between the 'intelligent' and 'idiots', the 'inner directed' and the 'other directed' and the 'Type A' and 'Type B' personality. Whether they divide the world in terms of intel-lect, psychological traits or characteristic outlooks; they all see personal attributes as the items that sort the sheep from the goats.

The third scheme was based on the idea of *lifestyles*. For the other six childless people, the world was divided not by where people were born in the social order, or what sort of characters they had, but simply by how they lived, especially with regard to paid work and family style. These world-views are less concerned with what people are (in terms of character) or where they fit into a social structure than with what, in the twin spheres of work and home, people do.

What are the links between these world-views and ideas about par-enthood? At one level, there seems to be little connection, since none of the interviewees referred to a distinction between parents and child-less people as a key division in values. Even Isabel, whose world-view included series of family types, did not mention childlessness—and was very amused when I pointed this out.

But although they did not build typologies of the world in terms of parents and children, all the childless could fit choices about children into their schemes. After they had drawn their pictures of adult lifestyles, I asked, 'Is there one set of values held by people who choose not to have children?' and 'What about parents?' Thus prompted, fif-teen of the sixteen indicated that parents and the childless were indeed different types of people. Furthermore, the general tendency was to see the childless as a more *specialized* group than parents. Eleven of the childless people saw parents as spread through a number of categories and people without children clustered in one or only a few. In other words, for them, the childless are a less diverse group in terms of their values than are parents.

That parents and the childless are seen as differentially distributed within types, and that the childless are seen as more concentrated in distribution, is evidence that ideas about parenthood are a force that the childless must reckon with. Even though the division between parents and the childless is not salient enough to be a direct part of their world-views, they see clear differences between the sorts of people who have children and those who do not, and do not dismiss the issue as a simple matter of personal taste.

As well as presenting themselves as a more specialized group than parents, the childless also tend to present themselves as clustered in the groups with connotations which are agreeable. For Gary, for example, the childless were 'thinkers' while parents could be 'thinkers' or could come from any of the conservative and individually oriented types which he despised. Parents, in other words, may be nice or nasty people; the childless are always nice.

Later discussion will show how complex the links between world-views and explanations of parenthood decisions can be, but it is clear that the world-views already discussed could offer possibilities for explaining why some people have children and others decide not to do so. The location-based views provide a background for pictures stressing social constraint on individuals. The character-based views suggest that decisions about parenthood are the result of individual tendencies (which may, of course, be based on some innate capacity or urge, and are thus not completely amenable to human will) rather than social forces. Both these world-views suggest a notion of some determining structure while the third view is a classification at a simpler level of individual preference and choice.

These are examples of one form of negotiation at work. The association of childlessness with agreeable characteristics (found in eleven of the sixteen cases in the third interview) enables the childless to avoid the disagreeable consequences of disobeying an ideological prescript. This is compatible with the idea that they are under pressure from the ideology of parenthood which they must counter—to me and to themselves. But the extent to which they are aware of ideology and how they think it operates are both unclear. The following section begins to explore those perceptions by looking at how the childless explain parents and themselves.

EXPLAINING CHILDLESSNESS

If an ideology of parenthood exists and is powerful, there should be some evidence of this in the explanations given by the childless for why some married people become parents while others deliberately remain childless. If the explanations posit parenthood as the normal course in the social as well as the statistical sense, and childlessness as the option in need of explanation, then they suggest that ideas about parenthood are a force to be reckoned with. But if childlessness is taken for granted as simply a personal choice or parenthood is seen as the option which needs a special explanation, then it would seem that there is not an ideology of parenthood requiring negotiation.

The explanations should also provide evidence about forms of negotiation with the ideology of parenthood. I would expect that childless people who negotiated from a more-or-less hegemonic stance would be respectful towards parenthood and that those who were closer to the oppositional end of the continuum would be equivocal about parenthood and more positive about childlessness.

This section examines the explanations of parenthood offered by the childless couples. Do they see parenthood as normal and childlessness as the state which requires explanation? Are they wrestling with the implications of their explanations? The data come from many sources. The final interview sought a formal and explicit account in words and pictures of 'what happens to turn out some people as parents and some as like you'. But implicit or informal explanations of fertility behaviour occurred throughout the three interviews. The explicit and implicit explanations could be very similar or quite different—even contradictory, suggesting that negotiation is a matter of fragmented responses rather than self-conscious justifications. The themes from the worldviews ran through explanations of fertility behaviour in various ways. Almost always there was an assumption that the normal path led from marriage to parenthood, as I noted in chapter 4.

Ten out of the sixteen accounts contained this theme. But *normal*, like *proper*, is a slightly ambiguous word, and the normal course was portrayed in a slightly derisory fashion by six of the ten. Comments about parents suggested that, at best, they were following expectations without much thought and, at worst, they were being careless in making important decisions. Normality was portrayed as somewhat boring or stuffy, or the path into parenthood was seen as the 'default option' (something like the decision you make when you're not making a decision).

There were two variations on the theme of parenthood as the normal route. Both tend to show those who follow the normal course as foolish (and, by implication, those who deviate from the course as more sensible). Four people added the variation that some couples have children because they are dissatisfied with their marriage as it is. This behaviour is condemned explicitly, either because it is intrinsically wrong or because it does not work:

CHRIS. *I can also see people having children as a way of reinforcing their relationship or keeping what they've got together, giving them a common interest to keep their relationship going. I really think that's bad.*

JUDY: *Because, without exception, in all three cases of friends who have done it [i.e. had a child in an attempt to improve their marriage], it didn't do it … so they have been left with another child. It doesn't work.*

Chris and Judy also condemned those people whose marriage requires stimulation from children, by implying that they are shallow and materialistic, so that children represent nothing more than new toys:

CLARE: *… half my theory on why people have children is because they get bored with each other and it is a new dimension.*

CHRIS: *That goes with new acquisitions, too. Like buying things … They are just about on the skids and they go out and buy a car or they go out and buy a house … and they seem to patch it up for a while.*

In this variation, having children for a specific reason becomes positively wicked. While there is evidence that parents, too, condemn the idea of using children to save a marriage, the childless people seem to be particularly harsh in their definition.

In the second variation, those who followed the normal course were seen as being led up the garden path—not really understanding what they were in for. These implications surfaced in remarks on the lives of ageing parents which arose during discussions of the reasons for not having children. They were sometimes unprompted, sometimes the result of a direct question. They referred to the belief that children provided security for their parents in old age. Seven of the childless mentioned this, all cynically. Fiona and Felix had cared for Fiona's mother until her death and, in spite of having an example to the contrary, were pessimistic about children being a source of comfort and care for their parents:

FIONA: *I've seen so many elderly people shoved into old people's homes, anyway.*

FELIX: *Yes, seeing the way that children react these days to old-aged parents, there's no guarantee that if you did have a child they would look after you.*

Comments like these suggest that those who follow the proper path are not merely a bit unadventurous, they are positively silly. They cannot see that the path does not lead necessarily to a secure marriage and old age, and they have no idea that they could follow any other way through life. These explanations also imply that all parents have pretty much the same experiences. The childless see only one proper path—it leads from marriage to parenthood, and it is walked in the same way by all parents. This is especially noticeable with regard to gender. Although both men and women quite often mentioned the impact of children on women's lives as a reason why they did not want children, when the childless couples explained parenthood, they presented parents as sexless beings, who came to their status by the same route and experienced it in the same way.[1]

As well as presenting parents as androgynous, the childless tended to present them as socially homogeneous. Only Isabel and Kevin make any reference to the possibility that people may reach parenthood in different ways according to their social location. For most of the childless, parenthood is taken for granted as the normal thing for married couples and assumed to be the same for all parents.

It is clear that the childless see having children as the normal course of events for married people—the default option—as might be expected where the ideology of parenthood is still powerful. But they negotiate with this idea of parenthood as normal by comments which slightly disparage the normal course as a little too 'proper' and imply that the people who follow it are a bit short-sighted if they think they are heading for stable marriages and contented old ages.

This stance, slightly anti-parent though not overtly defensive of the childless, is what I would expect from people who were negotiating with ideology from a somewhat oppositional position. So, while the data on world-views showed the difficulty of immediately identifying the couples in this study as either opponents or hegemonists, the data in this section suggest that some of them at least are oppositionally inclined.

The perceptions of the childless about the proper path are not all that different from the perceptions of parents. Richards (1978, 1985) reports that among her sample 'the assumption had almost always been that there would be children'. Wearing's Sydney mothers had a similar attitude, and Busfield and Paddon (1977) make the same point about the respondents in their English study.

So there is evidence that parents and the childless share a perception of the proper path. Where they differ is in the tone in which that path is described. As we have seen, for the voluntarily childless *proper* is not necessarily a complimentary term. For parents, however, *proper* has overtones of moral rightness. At least some of the childless questioned the wisdom of the adage that 'children make a marriage'. The parents in Busfield and Paddon's (1977) study, however, expounded a theme of children as 'important, if not essential to the survival and success of marriage'. Richards (1978) also found that marriage was seen as 'a fixed thing, entered with finite potential, threatened with boredom, filled with children to stop it going flat'.

Further evidence that parents and the childless agree on the notion of a proper path but disagree in their evaluation of it comes from the tendency of parents to describe the voluntarily childless as 'selfish'.[2] Parents appear to stereotype the childless and thus confirm themselves as doing what is right, while the childless, through their reactions to the term *selfish* and stereotype of the sheep-like parents, imply that their unusual position is really an acceptable one.

Subtle negotiation with the image of normality is evident among parents as well as the childless. While some of the childless dealt with the problem of being 'abnormal' by implying that normality was a somewhat negative quality anyway, parents might deal with the problem of being 'ordinary' (rather than 'special') by making a joke of their normality. A young father in *Having Families* epitomizes this technique, as he sums up his life, with 'amused consideration' of its predictability:

> You graduate, you put on a certain tie and off you go to find a nice young lady and get married and you have children and O.K. the whole circle goes on again. (Richards 1978)

His view is similar in content to the views expressed by some of the childless people I interviewed. The difference is that he can be gently amused at the thought that his life is so predictable while they negotiate with their abnormality by denigrating the normal. The words are similar, but their meanings are very different.

WHO MOVES OFF THE PROPER PATH?

In terms of explaining parenthood decisions as a whole, the notion of a proper path is of limited use. If parenthood is the usual way, those who take the deviant course must still be explained. It is only if there were no ideology facing them that the childless would reply to my request for an explanation, 'Don't be silly, it's just an individual preference'. There should be further evidence of negotiation in the explanations of childlessness. A more-or-less oppositional position would mean a tendency to denigrate parents, while hegemonic negotiators might be defensive of their position but not aggressive about it. Moreover, it should be possible to see at least some consistency between the accounts of childlessness and of parenthood. Those who were most vehement in their denunciation of parenthood as a proper path should also be those who are anti-parent in their explanations of childlessness. They may also be those who have the clearest picture of another possible path besides the parenthood one.

There were three major themes in the accounts of childlessness, which could be related to two of the themes in the world-views. All three explained why some people did not stay on the proper path. One explanation was that some people are able to choose a different path because they are standing at a particular point in the social structure where other paths are visible to them. In other words, voluntary childlessness is explained or partially explained in terms of the social location of the childless. Another theme is that the childless have a particular sort of character that enables them to resist pressure to stick to the beaten track. And a third theme is another variation on the idea of character— the idea that some people are just naturally inclined not to have children. The following sections will explore these three themes in detail.

The childless have choice: Social location as an explanation of childlessness

The world-views that were based on the idea of social location stressed the difference between those who 'have' and those who 'have not', usually in terms of economics and the educational and emotional resources which are unequally available to rich and poor. Seven of the childless people used a similar distinction to explain the difference between parents and the childless. The basic message here was that the rich have options but 'the poor get children'.

Chris and Clare both described the world in general as divided into the fortunate haves and the unfortunate have-nots. Their account of why some people become parents and others do not uses a similar division:

CLARE: *Well, what I've observed ... is, because of unemployment, girls leave school early, they can't get a job, so they might as well get a bit more money and be a mother because [as] a lot of them have said to me, 'It is something to do'.*

This explanation focuses on only one group of parents: young, single mothers. It is an overgeneralization and it is fairly judgemental—Clare remarks later that 'they are so short-sighted that they can't see that a baby is going to cost money'—but it answers my question about why some people are parents and some childless by focusing on the socio-economic circumstances that deny some people the chance to be childless.

Gabrielle's first comment in her formal explanation suggests that she has an idea about social location as a factor in fertility choices. She links education and jobs to progress through life stages:

The ones without [children] tend to have longer education, I think, interesting and challenging work. They tend to get married just the same, resist pressure. Very busy, need more money ... to travel, etc. Things like that. United life. As a result of that, there are no children.

There are a great many factors compressed into this explanation, but the two that are basic are the longer education and the interesting and challenging jobs, which presumably give the childless the capacity to resist pressure, enjoy an exciting lifestyle and stay away from parenthood. And, since education and jobs are closely related to economic location, this can be classed as a locational explanation of childlessness. Evelyn, like Gabrielle, focused on jobs and education. Earlier, in her world-view description, she had mentioned education as the thing that enabled some people to escape what she called the 'poverty trap'. In her formal explanation, she linked education and career as helping some people to escape the parenthood trap:

EVELYN: *Most people drift into it [having children] ... unless there is some physical problem, the people who remain childless have taken a conscious decision to do it.*

INT: *What makes some people drift and some people deciders?*

EVELYN: *Education. But why they decide that way—I suppose with females it is generally their career orientation. I suppose this is my case, a lot of my case ... I'm sure this is the main motivating force with females. With males who are married to those females, I suppose it is a case that they have agreed with that thought process and that decision.*

At a more general level than situation in terms of money, job or education, 'social location' refers to vague but powerful cultural influences. Isabel and Kevin focused on these in their formal explanations of parenthood choices and were the only people for whom social location was the sole explanation of childlessness.

Isabel noted a strong contrast between her middle-class friends, who made planned choices, and the young girls in the outback town she had lived in recently. Her account is similar in outline to the one Clare gave, though more sympathetic:

> *Young girls, faced with the prospect of too little to do and all those sorts of problems, and very little knowledge about contraception or knowledge about parenthood, find themselves pregnant. 'Cos it's a town where you've got a Catholic priest who dominates, they're often advised against abortion; early marriage is encouraged. So that's a very different process operating there.*

Kevin sees three background factors at work that differentiate parents and the childless. They are class, religion and ethnicity. For him, certain groups ('Catholics, working-class and Italians') have no consciousness of options about parenthood. For them, it's 'just a process' from marriage to parenthood. But other groups may have more options. Either they are aware of choices which 'socialization' had denied to Italians, Catholics and the working class or they have protection against social pressures:

KEVIN: *Childless couples fit into some sort of category about coming from middle-class backgrounds, Anglo-Saxons and Protestant or something like that, which would generally reflect ... that they would be more capable of putting up with, or perhaps be less susceptible to, pressure.*

The theme of social location is comparatively weak, especially with regard to explaining 'why we are childless'. Kevin was the only person to apply comments on socialization to himself as well as others. He said:

*I think everybody has got choices, but I think by a process of social-
ization a lot of their choices are eliminated for them and they no
longer question them. The choices are still there, but they are not
brought to the forefront ... I think that occurs with us too, but in different areas. I'm quite sure there are a number of choices that we've
been deprived of, if you like, or not had the exposure to due to our
socialization processes, whatever they might be.*

But even Kevin is silent about why the childless are all WASPs but not
all WASPs are childless. Perhaps this reflects the fact that the childless
were defending as well as explaining themselves and that the sociological view is not a useful defence in ordinary conversation about
childlessness. Certainly in terms of numbers and strength of conviction,
the theme of social location as an explanation for parenthood decisions
is markedly subordinate to the two themes of character, which will now
be explored.

The childless are resisters: Character as an explanation of childlessness

Nearly all the childless made at least some use of the idea of individual
variations in character as an explanation for those people who did not
follow the normal course from marriage to parenthood. It was the
major element in explanation for eight of them (see table 10).
'Character' took two distinct forms. The first was the idea that some
people are more resistant than others to social pressure and so are less
likely to be pushed on to the proper path.

Clare, for example, sees herself as facing pressure but resistant to it,
just because that is the sort of person she is. There is 'a lot' of pressure
on her:

CLARE: *But then it depends whether you react to it.*

INT: *Do you?*

CLARE: *No, because I don't care ... I don't care what people think ...
I can appreciate that what is right for them is not right for me ...*

Chris also makes resistance the key element in his picture of why some
people become parents and others do not. In the first interview, he had
described himself as 'not responsive to social pressure'. Asked, in the
third session, to draw a diagram of his explanation, he said:

*... couldn't have just one person. I would have to draw a whole range
of people and show that each person's process would be different ...
And then you would have resistance—some would be more resistant
than others.*

His diagram represents differences in resistance to pressure through
what the stick-figures are saying. Apart from their words, the figures are

identical. So, for Chris, the key to explaining voluntary childlessness is people's capacity to think for themselves and not to give in to what others say.

Diane's formal explanation for childlessness resembled Chris's on the surface. She invoked a notion of people, herself included, who had 'internal check-points' that made them question social conventions— rather like the third figure in Chris's diagram insisting on the need to stop and think carefully about a decision. But she went on to speculate about the origins of the internal check-points of the resisters—were they biological or environmental? She explored the sources of resistance by talking about her own family. On the one hand, Diane had already argued that the reason she did not fall in with others' opinions about having children was the environment she grew up in and, especially, the example of her mother's life:

> ... my mother's role was hideous enough for me never to want to follow in those footsteps.

But, she argued, there must be other factors at work, because her sister had the same role model as she did but did not become a resister: Diane eventually decided that biological factors must play some part in creating resistance, since 'we do have a phenomenally radical family right through'. The radicalism shows in her father's 'independent mind' and is perhaps inherited genetically:

> I think it must have something to do with genes as well—[what] you inherit as well as your environmental factors.

Gabrielle and Gary both saw themselves as people who were childless because they were resistant to social pressure to have children.

GARY: *It's peer pressure I think ... [that creates parents]*

GABRIELLE: *That's another thing. I never responded to peer pressure groups at all. I didn't smoke when the other kids tried to make me. Even at university I refused to drink ... I just never ever responded to peer pressure. [To Gary] And you wouldn't have! I couldn't see them pushing you to do anything.*

The themes for Gabrielle are that she has always been one to enjoy being different, or at least to wear her difference without rue and that neither she nor Gary are turned off a course once they have chosen it. The flavour here is of an admirably tenacious character as a basis for childlessness.

John's picture of resistance to pressure stigmatised parents rather than depicting the childless as heroic. His drawing of the process by which some remain childless and some become parents has three charming sheep saying 'baa baa baa' under the figure 75%. He explained that he thought that 75% of the population were just sheep and that 'I just think it [having children] is the norm—most people do it'. Like Gabrielle and

Gary, he is prepared to account for his decision in terms of character but, unlike them, it is not his own resistance to pressure that counts but Judy's. Until she persuaded him that she did not want children, he says, he could have seen himself:

> *Merely as a sheep, yes. Going along with the crowd or going along with the norm.*

The implication here is that his character is sheepishly non-resistant but because he is married to a resister, he is childless. Character and resistance are still the key elements in his explanation.

The negotiating technique displayed in all these comments is a variation on the one called 'rejecting the rejectors' (Veevers 1981)—defining childlessness as the property of positively valued groups.[3] The people who used the idea of resistance are presenting a message like this: 'You thought I was an odd, selfish person, didn't you? Well, I might be odd, but I'm not so much selfish as resistant to pressure.' This enables them both to agree that normal married people have children and to present themselves in a favourable light as individualists.

The technique of redefining childlessness in terms of a desirable attribute might be especially useful to those negotiating with the ideology of parenthood, simply because they live in a world where they frequently encounter parents. The 'selective perception' of parenthood that Veevers (1981) describes may reinforce the self-images of the childless but it is difficult, in conversation with parents, to insist that parenthood 'does not reflect any special talent ... precludes other activities ... and is itself of minimal significance'. It is easier in face-to-face situations to abandon the stereotype of the 'sheepish' parent and to include specific parents in the category of 'resisters' than it is to explain that, while parenthood is an insignificant state, particular parents are not worthless people.

This became clear to me when, at the end of the third interview, I explained to the couples that I was now convinced that I wanted a child. There were no reactions of obvious disapproval, but there was an assumption that (presumably because I had done research on the topic) I must have thought about the matter. Indeed, most people reacted warmly. Evelyn said:

> *That's fine. If that's what you want to do, then that's great.*

John asked why I had changed my mind, explaining that he had assumed that I, too, was voluntarily childless. I replied that carrying out the research had clarified my feelings, and he then approved of my decision:

> *Well, you've thought about it and that's fine. You've chosen it because it is the track you want to go. What gets to me is that so many people go along and have their kids and think, 'Gee whizz, what are we doing with these?'*

Judy had a similar reaction, and the exchange that followed shows clearly that she will not go as far as John in accommodating parents.

INT: *If I had just said, 'I dunno, I just want children', what would you have been?*

JUDY: *Angry!*

INT: *Angry?*

JOHN: *I don't get angry with that sort of thinking, that's just—because the majority of people do it ... that doesn't make it wrong ... It would be natural, I guess, to follow that same line. But you've obviously thought about it or you wouldn't have gone into it as thoroughly as you have.*

Here, he is making it clear that he does not disapprove of all parents and that he can even understand those who simply follow the herd without thought. So his comments on the resistant nature of the childless (in spite of the picture of parents as sheep) should be seen as *supporting the childless* rather than *condemning parents.* And faced with a live prospective parent, his emphasis on revaluing the childless enables him to avoid social unpleasantness. He declares that I'd 'obviously thought about it' and thus moves me out of the category of 'sheep'. Those who become parents because they have really decided to do so are not sheep—they're merely wearing sheepskins! This stance is consistent with the hegemonic end of the continuum since, while it redefines childlessness as acceptable, it does not challenge the ideology of parenthood directly. Moreover, the technique of exempting particular individuals from the stereotype of unthinking followers of the normal path, while making interaction with parents easier, means that the childless do not often appear as opponents of the ideology of parenthood.

Some of us are naturally childless: Another form of character as an explanation

The technique of redefining the childless as acceptable because of their resistance to pressure is one of the ways the notion of character is used to explain childlessness. A second use of that notion is the idea of 'natural' childlessness.

Diane, for instance, saw the difference between the childless and parents as a matter of their possessing or lacking those 'internal checkpoints' which would enable them to think for themselves. Here, her view of character stressed the element of resistance. But she went on to speculate about the causes of resistance and ended up by suggesting that some people might be more resistant than others because of their genetic make-up. This implies that childlessness might be literally 'natural'—determined by innate physical forces within the individual.

This is a common sense of the word *natural* and has links with the notion of biological determinism. Some people are born sheep who will follow the herd while others are born individualists who will think for themselves and resist pressure to be like the rest. And what is 'natural' is virtually immutable. Unless you can alter biology, you cannot turn a natural sheep into a resister or vice versa. An allied sense of the word refers to deeply ingrained habits and characteristics that may not be caused directly by biological forces but have become part of an individual's very essence or 'second nature' and, by implication, this is as difficult to alter as nature proper. Both senses of *nature* are visible in Judy's formal explanation of parents and the childless:

> *I think there are two groups again. There are people—it's genetic factors that influence them—and in that group there can be childless people as well as non-childless. The same in this group, people who can think and make the conscious decision to have children or not to have children.*

INT: *So for most people ... it's really genetics?*

JUDY: *Yes, maternal instinct and hereditary factors. And I mean by that, their mothers had it so they have them, that sort of thing. Just a logical progression where they are not thinking about it, it is just that they think it is expected of them.*

She illustrated her two groups by sketching a genetic family tree for the first and a human brain for the second. Her explanation combines the idea of 'biological nature' and 'second nature'. There are some people who are, by virtue of biology, likely to have children (they have 'maternal instinct') and others who lack it. Others, both parents and childless, seem to be less affected by biological impulses; they 'can think and make the conscious decision' rather than being driven by their natures in one direction or another. But, in her second comment, she slides into talking about 'second nature'. Having children, she says, is an unreflected action; 'they are not thinking about it' but simply doing what they feel is expected of them. This explanation leaves open many questions about the people who are not the victims of biological nature, but it offers Judy a potentially useful tool for negotiation about her childlessness. She accepts the ideological statement that 'parenthood is natural', but her rider that non-parenthood is also 'natural' avoids the consequences of having to deal with the idea that she is an 'unnatural' being.

Clare's idea of maternal instinct is similar to Judy's idea of nature in that, for her, the desire to mother is traceable both to biology and to cultural factors. Clare's diagram explaining parenthood choices contains the heading 'yourself' (as one source of pressure on people) and, under that heading, the term *maternal instinct*. This is connected by lines to both 'heredity' and 'family upbringing'. So, for her, 'maternal instinct' is both biologically based 'first nature' and unreflected, socially ingrained 'second nature'. Clare took the idea of the naturalness of not having children a step further than Judy when she described herself as lacking maternal instincts. In the first interview, she made it clear that she saw herself as 'unmaternal':

CLARE: *Some people would really love it [having children], and that's their natural maternal instinct. But it's not mine. I guess I lack maternal instinct …*

INT: *Is maternal instinct inborn?*

CLARE: *Probably your childhood would have something to do with it, but I think basically it's an inherent characteristic, like some people say, 'Oh, she's a born nurse'. You know, it's just something that comes really easily and is a natural development of the person, just as some people are kind or some people are emotional.*

Here, although she seems a little more inclined to give weight to a biological basis of nature than Judy did, Clare too slips between the notions of 'first' and 'second nature'. But whatever its roots, her 'unmaternal' character is deep-seated and unalterable. In the third interview, she responded to Chris's remarks about her needing support for childlessness by telling him that she did not need support because childlessness was in effect her nature:

I disagree because even you don't understand how much I dislike children.

I lost contact with Chris and Clare after the research was done and so have no way of knowing what is Clare's current view, as a new mother, of her 'maternal instinct'.

Fiona and Kevin have rather simpler ideas about a natural urge towards parenthood. Fiona began to explain parents and the childless with an example:

Again I think you come back to physiology in some sense. If you take two sisters. One sister says that the only time she has ever been really happy in her life is when she has a baby in her arms, and she had eight. And yet the other one had one and didn't want any more. So there are obviously people for whom motherhood is a very great satisfaction fulfilment.

This implies some notion of a physically based instinct to have children. It is amplified in Fiona's next comments. Felix responded to her tale of two sisters with a comment about two men in his own network which suggested that they were 'born fathers' full of 'paternal instinct'. Fiona agreed in one case but not another:

There is a big difference in them—Bob gets away from his as much as he can … Ron is a man who is a real father.

Fiona has a concept of 'natural' parental instinct that is 'genuine' and will determine the lives of those who have it, giving them no option but to be parents.

Kevin, too, had a notion of 'real' parents, although most of his explanation for parenthood choices was based on social location. In the second interview, he distinguished between people who 'genuinely want' children and those who only want them 'to make you feel good'.

So, for both Kevin and Fiona, there are 'real'/'natural' parents and, presumably, those who lack the natural capacity to look after children. Some of the latter will be childless, but others will become, as it were, 'false parents', of whom they disapprove.

Eric also had a simple view of biological nature. The idea that some people were instinctively inclined to be parents and others were not was the most noticeable feature of his formal explanation of parenthood decisions. He declined to diagram the process, saying that the only person whose motives he understood was himself, but his comments reveal that he has a clear notion of the childless as lacking the instinct to become parents:

> There is a certain innate—well, it's an instinctive thing really. It's the second ... procreation, second instinct after self-preservation, isn't it? So there's a fair element in there, I suspect. But there's always been childless people.

There is no element of 'second nature' in this comment and no notion of people who are parents but not 'real' ones. Parenthood and childlessness are simple outcomes of possession or lack of the procreative instinct. And he and Evelyn lack it.

Eric is the most ardent believer in a relatively simple kind of 'first nature'. Gabrielle's explanation of parenthood and childlessness involves the clearest vision of 'second nature'. She had observed friends who apparently had deeply felt urges towards maternity but did not see these urges as the result of biological processes. Her formal explanation of parenthood decisions makes this clear. She described a theory that a friend had reported to her, suggesting that the kind of parenting an individual received was what determined how she/he would approach parenthood. While Gabrielle doubted the logic of this with reference to couples, she saw some relevance in it for her own feelings:

> My mother was a person who made me feel I could never be like her ... I always wanted to be a mother when I was young [in early childhood]. But my mother is ... anti-social, resistant to change, completely lacking in self-confidence, no outside interests ... Did I grow up with this absolute abhorrence of this thought of children holding you back that much, even though I know it's not true? ... I was determined that when I got married I would never do what Mum had done. I think there is something in it.

This exploration of her own background is rather like the one given by Diane. But Diane comes to the conclusion that it is heredity that creates resistance and resistance that creates childlessness, while Gabrielle is moving towards accepting a notion of 'abhorrence' of the consequences of motherhood as part of her (environmentally created) character. Although she is saying, in effect, that her mother rather than biological nature made her childless, she is certain that the result of her socialization is as immutable as the result of biological forces. While she explains childlessness in terms of both social location and 'second' rather than 'first' nature, it is clear that Gabrielle sees herself as deeply 'naturally' childless—if she was a parent, she would not be the person she feels herself to be; she would have to change her very essence.

Diane, as has been shown, worked with ideas of childlessness as due to natural resistance. But a brief comment suggests that she may also have a notion of 'natural forces' affecting women. She explained in the first interview that she had been pregnant fairly early in her marriage and had had an abortion. Because she had been on medication that might have resulted in a deformed child, she felt that she had no real choice but to terminate the pregnancy and, in that sense, 'the abortion itself went off very smoothly' but afterwards:

> ... very maternal instincts came out ... and I had to be very careful that I wasn't just reacting on unnatural maternal instincts, if you like.

Here, desire for children is an 'instinct' and, in one sense, 'natural' but, when it is a reaction to previous circumstances, it can be seen as 'unnatural' and, had Diane then decided to have a child, she would have been acting against her own preference for asking questions and acting logically. Parenthood here is both 'natural' and 'unnatural'.

Obviously the idea of 'natural' tendencies can be very complex. It seems to be, however, a useful concept for the childless, perhaps because of the link so frequently made between the natural and the good. It is arguable that the sense of 'unnatural' as 'monstrous, abnormal ... outraging natural feelings or moral standards' (according to the *Shorter Oxford*) applies particularly strongly to women who move outside the conventions of feminine behaviour of their world. Think of the use of the expression *unnatural woman* as a term of deep reproach in Victorian novels and the pop song that extols the virtues of a man who can 'make me feel like a natural woman'. If Ortner (1974) is right, and 'femininity' is universally equated with 'nature' while masculinity is allied with the concept of culture, then women who behave in 'unnatural' ways will be in special need of techniques to negotiate the term.

Unlike the explanations involving resistance, which redefined childlessness in terms of a desirable attribute, the explanations that stress natural childlessness do not redefine either parenthood or childlessness; they accept as given the ideological statement that 'parenthood is natural' and simply extend the scope of 'nature' to allow inclusion of childlessness.

On the whole, what is 'natural' is equated with what is good or, at least, what it is wise to accept. Like the gay liberationists who claim that homosexuals are born not made, the childless who insist on their naturalness are saying, in effect, 'You can't blame me for my state, I simply am what I am'. This sort of fatalism is reflected in Felix's comment about parents:

> You know, it depends on the person ... If you are content to let things go it will happen and, whether consciously or subconsciously you want to have children, you will have them.

This form of negotiation, with its acceptance of naturalness, is distinctly hegemonic in tone. But in the comments about 'second nature', it is possible to see a thread that prefigures a more oppositional outlook. If 'maternal instinct' has a social basis, then perhaps powerful ideas are involved in the making of each individual's 'nature'. The recognition of 'second nature' is not the same as a recognition of ideology but is an essential antecedent to it.

The theme of 'natural' childlessness thus contains the potential for oppositionally oriented negotiations but frequently denies it. When 'nature' means 'biology' the negotiation is distinctly hegemonic.

THE EXPLANATIONS AS A WHOLE

The foregoing analysis has separated themes from the explanations, beginning with the idea of parenthood as the 'proper path' and then examining the factors which cause some people to stray from the path. It is clear that most of the childless perceive parenthood as the proper path for married couples and that deviation from the path is attributed more to character (mentioned by thirteen people, heavily stressed by eight) than to social location (mentioned by seven people, heavily stressed by two).

But taking each theme in isolation oversimplifies the data. Each explanation was an intricate whole, a pattern into which the themes were woven. Sometimes one theme would dominate the pattern, sometimes they combined. At times, themes would contradict each other (as with Diane's dual use of a 'character' explanation).

Table 10 attempts to summarise the explanations offered by the sixteen people in the third interview set. A glance across the columns 'proper path', 'social location', 'resistance' and 'nature' will show how complex each explanation might be. Comparison with the first column will also show that there is no necessary connection between the essence of an individual's world-view and her/his explanation of parenthood decisions. All five of the 'location' world-views give way to a variety of 'character' explanation for parenthood choices, although 'character' world-views seem to be reflected in the explanations of parenthood decisions. Males seem slightly more likely to offer a fairly simple explanation for choices than females and to opt for 'character' as the single major element.

I suggest that this complexity reflects the impact of negotiating techniques on the eventual stance taken towards the ideology of parenthood. If the notion of childlessness as due to innate 'character' is a particularly useful tool for dealing with the unpleasant possibilities that one may be sick or wicked for not wanting children, then it is hardly surprising that even those whose overall view of the world stresses social location should fall back on character to explain their own conduct. And, in a society where the ideology of parenthood lays particular stress on motherhood, it is not surprising that childless women should require more complex explanations of their choice.

Individual situations may require special negotiating techniques that in turn influence explanations. Henry and Heather both insisted that parenthood choices were not, in the end, explicable. Although Henry spoke of 'some factors' that might affect decisions, he declined to commit himself any further as to the nature of those factors. Heather mentioned social locational elements ('the circumstances, which include income and job') and 'predispositions' (both biological nature and 'accidents' of biography) as part of the process by which people become either parents or childless. But she insisted that, in the end, there is no order or sequence and thus no possible explanation for the process. It is

fatalistic. A mixture of temperament shaped by inherited characteristics, predisposition, which also means accidents of meeting at a particular time in circumstances. And that is not a process because ... someone might have looked as though they were settling down to have a family, but then they wouldn't for some reason ...

Moreover, my demand for her explanation struck her as foolish. Her factors can *describe* childlessness, but not *explain* it and, anyhow, she says, 'I don't believe in theories'.

That last statement seems unusual, coming from a trained social policy researcher. My view of what Heather means is not that she has no faith in theories but that she finds this area too difficult to attempt to apply any theories to it. She and Henry were, by the third interview, in disagreement over childlessness, and she wanted to have children. To explain parenthood decisions in terms of social location might be painful because it would require taking a clinical and detached attitude to her own deeply felt problem. To explain them in terms of character might be dangerous, since it could simply be that she and Henry were fundamentally different sorts of people who could never resolve their situation. So it was better to attribute cause to 'fate' and avoid possible recriminations.

The explanations offered by the childless show a variety of negotiating techniques at work. Six people clearly applied negative stereotypes of parents as a way of defending themselves, while nine clearly redefined childlessness in terms of a valued attribute like individualism. The use of a concept of 'nature' to defend childlessness as a valid identity of equal status to parenthood is visible in varying degrees in nine accounts and could be described as a technique of turning one tenet of ideology against another tenet. It also illustrates the importance of the ambiguous use of words, since the childless people who rely on an idea of innate tendencies away from parenthood have as much chance as parents to defend themselves by saying 'it's natural'. The complexity of the explanations reflects the variety and complexity of techniques used by the childless to negotiate with ideas and with people. The question of dealing with people is explored in chapter 6. The remainder of this chapter asks whether the childless couples can be described as seeing an ideology of parenthood.

FOCUSING ON IDEOLOGY

The chapter so far has shown that certain themes recur in the explanations of their state offered by the childless and are, on the whole, consistent with a 'negotiating' stance towards the ideology of parenthood. Now I will explore the question of whether the childless see the ideology of parenthood with which they are so actively negotiating. Chapter 2 argued that negotiation goes on both with and within the framework of ideology which surrounds us and that there is a continuum of negotiating positions from the pole of hegemonic unawareness and acceptance through to oppositional activity. This naturally raises the question of how much people can see of the framework around them at any time. To what extent are we aware of ideology as a force in our lives?

If the theory of negotiation is correct, the answer to the question should be that while different people will have different levels of awareness of different ideologies, on the whole they will be neither completely unaware nor totally and self-consciously aware of the power of ideas on a given topic. I would also argue that there are many ways of being 'aware' of ideology, and the forms and degrees of an individual's awareness of a particular ideology will depend on the circumstances in which negotiation takes place. Forms of awareness might embrace any combination of awareness of *sources* of an ideology, awareness of the *interests* served by the ideology and awareness of *channels* by which it is transmitted. Degrees of awareness could range from vague feelings that false ideas are floating around and somehow affect one's life to explicit theories about the origins and impact of an ideology and a pervasive awareness of its effect. Awareness, however, does not guarantee successful opposition in practice to ideology, as feminists who have tried to break away from the tyranny of fashion know. So another dimension relevant to awareness, though not part of it, is *action* vis-à-vis ideology. This dimension may, at times, obscure from an observer the extent and form of an individual's awareness of any given ideology (the aware feminist with shaved legs might have given in to what she sees as the ideology of fashion, but she is not identical with the woman who shaves her legs because 'everyone knows that hairy legs are horrid and unfeminine'). The variations in extent and form, and the possible masking effects of action, mean that gauging anyone's awareness of ideology is extremely difficult. This is true of the childless and the ideology of parenthood, as the example of Diane shows.

DIANE AND THE IDEOLOGY OF PARENTHOOD

Diane is more aware of the ideology of parenthood *as an ideology* than anyone else I spoke to, but her awareness is not uniform or easy to pin down. She is, for example, aware of interests underlying ideas about motherhood and of the effect of those ideas on others, but sees herself as having escaped from the ideas. When I showed her the three cartoons (figures 7–9 in appendix 2) and asked for her interpretations of each one, her response to the first one (which I had christened 'the big black ball'; figure 7) was an account of how the institution of motherhood oppressed women:

> *I suppose it gets back to the patriarchy as I see it … I think it wants to perpetuate that hold. I mean, it keeps women powerless, pregnant in the kitchen, and they are less likely to be able to make demands— too busy breeding … I mean, if you've got babies and all that … shelter and caring, and all that stuff… to cover you won't be getting into abortion issues and nuclear disarmament and checking out the world and what is happening.*

She is not implying a simple conspiracy of all men against all women, as she later made clear. She is, however, identifying a set of ideas (that it is women who have 'shelter and caring, and all that stuff ... to cover') with a set of interests ('the patriarchy'). She seems to be identifying the interests as the source of the ideology ('it gets back to the patriarchy ... it wants to perpetuate that hold').

This awareness of interests behind ideas and of a source of ideas is what might be expected of a self-defined feminist (the only person in the case-study group to have had much actual contact with the women's movement) and suggests that Diane is oppositionally aware of the force of the ideology of parenthood. But her explanations of parenthood decisions rely on the notion of 'character' in the form of resistance to social pressure and are therefore more consistent with a hegemonic-style belief in the capacity of individuals to make up their own minds than an oppositional-style awareness of ideology. When I asked her to choose the cartoon which best fitted her own situation, she did not pick the big black ball of ideology (figure 7). Instead, she chose the picture of the balloonists (figure 8)—although with reservations:

None of them appeal to me. Perhaps this one with the knife [figure 8] but then I would hope that I haven't got that far. I certainly have in my own personal life, but not in relation to having children. That looks like it has gone a bit far before ... working out what you want. It looks like the balloon is going to take you away. It's up to you to sever that cord so you can come down again and work it out but at the moment the pressure is taking you off on a path that you don't nec- essarily want to follow. So I don't see that that happened to me in terms of having children ... that was one aspect and one area where I could rebel.

Her reservation is that she has more control over her decision not to have children than the balloonists seem to have. They are in danger of being 'carried away with the weight of other people's opinions' and can only land on the ground of their choice by taking drastic action and cut- ting the ropes to their balloons. Diane implies that she is not at the mercy of the winds of opinion and that she need not resort to desperate measures in this matter. In other words, in the area of parenthood deci- sions she has had control. This view is consistent with her explanations of parenthood decisions, her general character-based world-view and her reported actions in her own life (she had one abortion during her marriage and later a tubal ligation). It is less consistent with her picture of a dominant ideology that reflects the interests of patriarchy and oppresses women who mother. But she returns to this gloomy larger picture in response to my question about her explanations of parent- hood decisions:

INT: *Would you say it is a question of ideology, in a sense, people accepting having children?*

DIANE: *Lack of ideology! ... they are just living out society's ideal ... I think that most people get sucked into that ... whole Cinderella syn- drome [i.e. the belief in romantic love as a solution to personal prob- lems]. Yes, I probably think that most people haven't thought it through.*

And the same oppositional tone can be heard in her comment on the impact on people of media images of family life:

I think a lot of it gets back to that old sexism, not giving people the choices, not allowing them to see that there are other options.

Here, the ideas are false but powerful and by implication should be opposed. Diane's use of the actual word *ideology* is very different from mine. She means it to stand for the explicit political orientation that would *oppose* false and oppressive ideas about romance and the family. Diane says that she talks to people about the tubal ligation and that, while she does not try to influence people against having children, she does try to influence them to think about the issue ('I will question them why they are having them'). She comments on arguments between her mother and herself about feminism ('Mum blames Germaine Greer but I said, "Germaine Greer is just the trigger, Mum"...'). There is no doubt that she *acts*, at least in some ways, as an opponent of the ideology of parenthood, but her awareness of ideology is not totally oppositional. The duality in her explanations of parenthood choices is paralleled by the duality in her awareness of the ideology of parenthood. On the one hand, it is a real and powerful force, reflecting the interests of some and oppressing others. On the other hand, it isn't able to influence Diane at all.

And Diane is another of the people whose life changed dramatically during the course of the study. She and David split up, and after some years Diane married a man who was a divorcee with children. At the time of her remarriage, she assumed that she would be playing the role of wife to an access parent, but soon after that I heard that she would have an adolescent stepchild living permanently with her.

AWARENESS OF THE IDEOLOGY OF PARENTHOOD

Diane's case is atypical as she is more aware than the other childless people of the ideology of parenthood. But the uneven texture of her awareness is a characteristic Diane shares with the others.

Some of the childless women were, like Diane, very certain that there exist *false ideas* about the family. For Diane, as has been shown, such ideas function to oppress women. For Judy, wrong ideas about the nature of motherhood have a bad effect, but they cause distress (such as 'third-day blues' for new mothers) rather than oppression:

> *Those incredible advertisements for the perfect mothers—how lovely it is with these beautiful babies who are never sick, and who only wet and never poo, so you don't have to change grotty nappies ... I think that is an incredibly subtle pressure to place on women, to make the whole thing look so wonderful ... They talk about women going through 'third-day blues' in hospital ... so much of that could be taken away from them by educating people properly into what motherhood is all about ...*

For Kate, the false ideas hurt children rather than women by setting up false expectations of family life, while, for Heather, there is a link between the limited self-image encouraged in girls and the idea that motherhood is female destiny:

> *... if young girls are taught to feel that they've got no control over their lives and themselves, well, that may mean that the option of taking [motherhood] on seems the only possibility.*

These statements have an oppositional flavour and certainly suggest that there are incorrect ideas about motherhood in the air. There were no comparable explicit remarks from men about motherhood or, indeed, parenthood in general. This might be because the debate that has taken place about images of the family has been closely bound up with debates about images of women, making it easier to see false ideas about mothers' roles than any other aspect of family life. Or it may be a reflection of the greater salience of the whole issue of childlessness for women.

Although some childless women shared Diane's dislike of the ideas which they labelled false, none of them (and none of the men either) shared her perception of interests at work behind the false ideas or of interests as a source of an ideology. Instead there was a tendency to see the means by which an ideology was transmitted as identical with its origin. This tendency was especially marked among the six people who focused on socialization as a channel through which the ideology of parenthood was transmitted. Evelyn, for example, said that ideology meant:

> The society, probably. As I was saying before, people drifting into having children. Also the pressure of society, because it is the done thing.

In other words, the source of the ideology of parenthood is 'society', and the transmission is through 'social pressure' to do the done thing. Eric, asked if any group or institution was responsible for setting our choices about children (that is, if there is a source of ideology), replied that it was a matter of 'conditioning' (that is, of transmission); Henry and Heather agreed that religion was an ideology and Heather suggested that there had once been religious pressure to have children. Implied in both comments is a notion that religion is or was both a source of ideology and the channel for it, through socialization. Chris completely merged sources of the false ideas about parenthood with the channels of transmission when he said simply that having children is not a matter of ideology but of 'culture'.

Kevin agreed that having children 'can be' a matter of ideology. Asked how people got it, he described a process that perpetuates ideas within a group. So for him, too, the source of the ideology of parenthood is the same as the means of its perpetuation:

> Inculcating from the family and peer group influences, and getting back to the sorts of exposure you get in those situations.

Kevin is aware that he, too, has been affected by socialization—that ideas 'inculcated' by family and peers have limited his options in ways which he cannot know about:

> I think everybody has got choices, but I think by a process of social-ization a lot of their choices are eliminated for them and they no longer question them. The choices are still there, but they are not brought to the forefront ... I think that occurs with us too, but in different areas. I'm quite sure there are a number of choices that we've been deprived of, if you like, or not had the exposure to, due to our

socialization processes, whatever they might be.

In this he is atypical. None of the other respondents showed such clear awareness that they might be victims or partial victims of any ideology. While he has no awareness of the dimension of interests behind ideology, and makes no comments about its oppressive effects, Kevin is more aware of the power of ideology in this respect than is Diane.

The impression that awareness of the ideology of parenthood is partial and patchy is reinforced by analysis of comments about the media as a channel for its transmission. Here, as in comments on socialization, the implication is often made that 'we' are immune to an ideology but 'they' succumb.

Five of the childless made explicit claims that media images of the family did not influence them. Fiona and Felix, who worried about the influence of Princess Di on teenagers, found the media powerless as far as they themselves were concerned:

FIONA: ... *the influence on teenagers. Look at the media interest in Princess Diana.*

FELIX: *If she had had twins or something, the whole world would have stopped.*

INT: ... *How do you react to that?*

FIONA: *With a bit of a giggle ... Oh, some of the ads are enough to ...*

FELIX: *Well, we don't often watch commercial television.*

FIONA: *We hate the ads.*

FELIX: *So it doesn't really get to us in that sense.*

John, too, argued that he was not influenced by what he saw on TV, and Eric and Evelyn said that since, like most childless people, they were ABC viewers and didn't watch 'family' shows or ads, they were unaffected by images of families.

These comments, like the ones on socialization, imply that the childless are immune to infection with the ideology of parenthood which strikes all others. And, by implication, all others have the same symptoms. (So for Fiona and Felix, all teenagers are vulnerable to media images, without qualifications.) This dichotomized view of ideology—that it exists and hits some people but not others—is what Diane displayed, and is similar to the character-based explanations of parenthood which focused on 'resistance'. But, since awareness of ideology is a complex state, there is no automatic correlation between explanations for parenthood decisions and comments on ideology. Of the five people who explain parenthood decisions mainly in terms of resistance, it is only John and Diane who clearly make the assumption that the ideology of parenthood hits others but not them.

Three people implied that the ideology of parenthood might be complex and that images about the family might not strike all others in the same fashion. Gary and Isabel argued that the media might have helped to encourage childlessness. For Isabel (who explained parenthood decisions in terms of social location), this was because the media showed a variety of family styles. For Gary, whose explanation focused on resistance, it was due to what others have called the 'revolution of rising expectations' (Runciman 1966):

> *Communications have certainly created perhaps the desire to want to see distant places ... I certainly think you've got to ask the question why there has been a lower birth rate. I think it is probably related. Simplistic as it might perhaps be, explained by 'the more you've got the more you want' ...*

And for Gabrielle, the portrayal of childless women on TV as unusual ('an extremely dominant, witty, clever, brilliant, proud sort of woman—and very bitchy ... never a normal sort of everyday person') is incorrect, but not unattractive.

Although the examples just given show that it is not automatically linked to an oppositional stance, sensitivity to the possibly double-edged impact of the media as a channel for ideology is more characteristic of an oppositional outlook than is the simple perception that silly people are affected by false images but I am not.

The childless couples saw the media as a source of false instruction but reacted to it in a variety of ways. The same variety was evident in their reactions to the three cartoons (figures 7–9). The cartoon chosen by the largest number as 'closest to your situation' was the one I called 'the balloonists' (figure 8). Eight people felt it applied to them. While I had seen it as representing a drift into childlessness with a degree of control, most of the comments suggested that the couples saw more control than drift. Evelyn, for instance, suggested that, to resemble them, the couple should have steering wheels attached. Responses to this drawing showed little awareness of an ideology that influenced decisions, which was not quite what I had expected.

Responses to the picture that I called 'the thinkers' (figure 9) were closer to my expectation, stressing the capacity of the childless to choose freely between options. This is a picture consistent with a hegemonic outlook and was chosen by three people.

While I had expected that the picture of the 'big black ball' (figure 7) would evoke an oppositional response, the comment from Clare (the only person to think it resembled her situation) made it clear that she saw looming ideas threatening others rather than her. This interpretation is consistent with her insistence on her capacity to resist pressure.

There is, then, a range of awareness about the ideology of parenthood as an ideology. But, overall, there is not much sign of the explicit awareness that would accompany the oppositional stance towards it. This is reflected in the absence of the word *ideology* itself from the vocabularies of the childless. No one used the term of their own accord, and when I asked after the discussion about the cartoons, if the word was applicable, eight of the sixteen rejected it. Their own definitions of *ideology* varied greatly, as table 10 shows. The noticeable feature of their reaction to the word, apart from a tendency to dismiss it as not relevant to their situation, is the absence of any connotation of interests behind ideas and the presence of 'society' or allied terms in their descriptions of ideology. The problem is not the interests of some; it is the impact of 'society' on their lives. It is hardly surprising that none of the childless explained parenthood decisions by saying 'Well, it's all a matter of ideology isn't it?' since, when the word is used in everyday conversation, it usually refers to 'isms' which smack of the dogmatic and the extreme and are likely to be rejected as wrong and silly. But the vagueness of the childless people's perceptions about the ideology they are disobeying is striking. They see false ideas to which other people are susceptible and may see some social factors increasing susceptibility or resistance, but they are more likely to see 'natural' or character-based vulnerability or resistance. Thus the ideology of parenthood, if it is seen at all, is seen by the childless as something out in the middle distance, lying like a fog over the heads of other people. There is little evidence that they see themselves as negotiating their way within the mist that they discern affecting others.

But they are not blind to the impact of ideology on their own lives. They see it as 'pressure' from other people—which they may relate back to 'society'. Their awareness of pressure is, in fact, sometimes more subtle and acute than that of researchers on childlessness. This is the theme of chapter 6, which studies the ways in which the childless negotiate not with ideology but with other people.

6

. . . .

negotiating

with

people

C hapter 5 established that, while the voluntarily childless people do not respond hegemonically to the ideology of parenthood, they lack the awareness that would characterize an oppositional stance. When they are asked about the forces that create parents and the childless, they do not answer like people who have a clear perception of ideology around them, although they may have some picture of ideology surrounding others.

It was apparent from early in the study, however, that the voluntarily childless were very aware of pressure in their surroundings. Not all of them felt that they were under pressure, but most of them agreed that they had encountered, in some form or other, forces suggesting that they should become parents. This chapter is concerned with the sorts of pressures that the childless meet and how they react to them. Thus it deals more with interaction with people than with reactions to ideas.

Of course, not all pressure is the outcome of ideology, but, if ideologies are packages of interest-based ideas that include statements about what *ought* to be, then it is probably true that all ideologies result in a certain amount of pressure on individuals to behave 'correctly' or 'normally'. The impact of a particular ideology at a mundane level may well be feeling that some people (teachers, preachers, parents, etc.) are pressuring us to do something.

We may be able to discern an individual's stance towards an ideology by exploring their feelings about pressure. For example, a woman whose stance towards the ideology of parenthood is hegemonic might know that there are expectations that married people have children and might have encountered comments suggesting that she should do so, but might not feel that she is under pressure—or at least *external* pressure. Comments that it was time she started breeding might strike her as reflections of what was usual and 'correct' rather than as any kind of social pressure. She might, however, have a sense of internal pressure—of 'need' or 'natural impulse' to have a baby, or of promptings of conscience to do her social duty. At the other end of the negotiating continuum, a woman with an oppositional stance towards the ideology of parenthood might feel that comments, questions and even trivial gestures and glances all constituted 'pressure from outside'.

Similarly, the two women might have very different views on the circumstances under which pressure was applied to them—with the opponent being more keenly aware of how pressure varied than the hegemonist.

How much pressure do childless couples face, how do they perceive its forms and how do they react to it? Much of the literature on voluntary childlessness refers to pronatalist pressure as a feature of modern Western society. Certainly, expectations about parenthood do exist, and there is no doubt that in a very vague sense 'pronatalist pressure' is a force in people's lives. There is, however, comparatively little detailed and systematic investigation of direct pressure (as opposed to the amorphous 'pronatalism') on the voluntarily childless.

The bulk of the literature suggests that 'pressure from parents and close friends to "start a family" ' (Schapiro 1980) is the most common example of pressure in action. But there is little hard evidence for this, and the sole study that goes into detail comes up with a different finding. Barnett and MacDonald (1976) found no single major source of pressure for their respondents. The source most often ranked as 'most important' was the media (16%) closely followed by friends (14%), mothers and co-workers (13% each). This would suggest that family is a less important source than many think and that the question of sources of pressure is not a simple one.

Similarly, there is a tendency to assume that pressure always takes the same forms and is always strongly felt by the childless. Studies that focus in more detail on the question (e.g Cooper et al. 1978) again suggest that the matter is more complex than other researchers have suggested.

If the literature on childlessness is unclear and oversimple on the issues of where pressure comes from and what it is, it does reveal something of the complexities of differential impact of pressure and its relation to other characteristics of the childless. Some studies, for example, have suggested that wives encounter heavier pressure to become parents than husbands.[1] Similarly, there is some support for the idea that commitment to childlessness and the length of the marriage both affect pressure. Nason and Paloma (1976) state that for their thirty couples, pressure was more likely to be felt by those who were 'reasonably committed' than those who were 'irrevocably' committed via sterilization or 'strongly committed', with no doubts about their future. Similarly, Veevers (1980) argues that the people most vulnerable to pronatalist pressure are women who are deciding whether to have children, having been married for four or five years, especially if they are approaching 30. More recently, however, Callan (1982, 1985) has argued that confrontations by the parents of the childless, which might be seen as a form of pressure, are more common for 'early deciders' than postponers. This tends to contradict the picture of pressure on the undecided but is not necessarily incompatible with it. Rather, it suggests that as well as the factors of being in the process of deciding versus having decided, and of the length of marriage, there is a factor about publicizing the decision that affects pressure. The young couple who, early in their marriage, announce their intention to remain childless, might be strenuously advised to wait or firmly told that maturity will change their minds for them. The couple who are 'putting off' childbearing and who explain their childlessness in those terms may be treated differently.

The literature is gradually moving away from a notion of pressure hitting all couples equally towards the realization that it might be a matter, like childlessness, of 'different things to different people'. My data confirm this view.

HOW MUCH PRESSURE IS THERE?

The findings from both the questionnaire group and the case studies suggest that pronatalist pressure does exist but does not have a uniform impact on voluntarily childless people. Among the questionnaire group, for example, two-thirds of the respondents identified at least one source of pressure to have children, but only half agreed that they were under any kind of pressure. Tables 11 and 12 show the responses (and indicate, incidentally, that men and women are astonishingly similar in their feelings). Some comments from the questionnaire group show how pressure might be seen as a very real force or as an insubstantial element which is recognized but not felt. A male secondary teacher, aged 32, coded as 'no pressure', is sure that pressure exists but that he does not feel it. So in effect it does not exist:

> *There is pressure but I don't let it affect me. So I feel there isn't pressure.*

On the other hand, a 33-year-old itinerant worker has felt pressure but never encountered it. He wrote that:

> *I have never had any pressure from anyone in this regard, except maybe once from myself when I saw a grandfather with his grandchild in a park and I must admit it confused me for some time after.*

The case-study group produced some similar comments, showing how perceptions of pressure vary. Only six of the twenty-two people used the term *pressure* to describe the reactions of others to their childlessness, but all of them described reactions that could have been labelled 'pressure', and all but three agreed that they had encountered pressures of some sort. But, as with the questionnaire, encountering pressure and feeling it were not necessarily the same thing. For Isabel, like the teacher quoted above, comments from friends constituted pressure only if she let them:

> *Ian didn't really feel pressure in the way that I was feeling pressured. I remember after having a holiday with some friends ... they were really putting the hard word on us ... I remember driving back with Ian to Melbourne after that and I said to him, 'I'm not going to feel pressured about kids one bit more. As far as I'm concerned, I'm going to enjoy my life for what it is now. If we decide to have children later on, so be it. But I'm not going to get about the next four or five years feeling like a prospective parent' ... And I found that gave me strength having made that decision, it really did. I mean, it probably sounds a bit childish but, since then, I've found things easier.*

Heather, who by the third interview wanted children, is a contrasting example, closer to the itinerant worker whose pressure came 'from himself'. She reported instances that might be labelled pressure, but in the third interview stated that she could not calculate how much pressure to have children anyone she knew experienced because the only sort of interaction that was real pressure was with one's spouse. Thus Henry was under pressure to have children—from her. But she was not under pressure, except 'internally' from her own desires.

An indicator of how complex and varied the perceptions of pressure may be is the range of sources of pressure listed in table 12. While the sources of pressure perceived by the childless can be categorized roughly as 'family', 'peers/friends' and 'general social pressure', there is no clear pattern of a single important source. Family members were mentioned as a source of pressure by 13.4% of the questionnaire group and eleven case-study interviewees; friends, peers or workmates by thirteen interviewees and 9.8% of the questionnaire group; and the nebulous 'social pressures' by seven interviewees and 13.4% of questionnaire respondents.

There is some evidence that the childless feel the pressure of their own parents' desires to be grandparents (and, in some cases, the desires of their grandparents to be great-grandparents). Seven interviewees mentioned parents as a source of pressure and three mentioned grandparents. But the extent to which they could be seen as 'special pressures' is limited since the pressure was often a matter of what parents were seen as wanting rather than what they demanded. It did not seem to be a heavy pressure.

ANDREW: *They [Alison's parents] are very anxious to become grandparents again, and I think there's a fair bit of gentle pressure from that side.*

ALISON: *Mum was rather concerned ... all her contemporaries have grandchildren and she was kind of out of it. She's quite happy now that she's got one.*

In all cases, pressure from parents seems to be manageable. It is indirect or gentle rather than outright and angry. Even the more direct manifestations are felt as gentle rather than brutal. Diane described an example of her mother-in-law saying that she didn't know how people lived without children that I would have thought was pretty direct pressure, and which she called 'pointed', but when she summed up the pressures she had met she said they were 'very subtle, subtle, subtle'.

This generally benign view of pressure from parents might not be typical of voluntarily childless couples. Perhaps only those who had maintained placid relationships with their families felt secure enough to volunteer for interviews, and for the majority 'would-be grandparents' do constitute a source of heavy pressure. But the picture of network support for childlessness given later suggests that in fact this is not so.

Among the case-study group (although not the questionnaire couples) friends, peers or workmates were very slightly more likely than families to be mentioned as a source of pressure. But, once more, there were variations in the extent to which there were *feelings* of pressure.

Fiona and Felix, for example, (both speaking during the first interview) saw their situations rather differently:

FIONA: *Some of our friends have tormented hell out of us ... The continual thing 'When are you going to breed?' got us both very, very irritated.*

FELIX: *No strong pressures apart from the mere social one of being the odd one out.*

Felix added that friends who knew the number of pets they owned would probably not expect them to increase the size of their household by adding a child. The Fs had a dog, several large cats, a bird and a pet sheep.

The degree of pressure felt might vary and so might the perceptions of what constitutes pressure. While for Fiona, questions from friends and peers about when she intended to have children are a form of pressure, Eric regards a similar kind of question as mere banter:

Oh, it [pressure] happens occasionally ... At work, there's two of us childless ... Occasionally there's comments or little suggestions ... 'Come on, Colin, Eric, what are you doing for Australia?'—facetious comments like this, but obviously [meaning] 'I've got kids, why don't you?'

Andrew's comments suggest yet another perspective on pressure from friends and peers. He says that there is no pressure on him from his own family, from whom he is both geographically and emotionally distant, but with friends:

It's difficult to hold up our wicket, as it were, for several reasons. It's not just because all one's friends have kids and hence one feels left out—that's a minor thing. The major thing is that you can lose friends because they have kids.

The strains placed on friendship once Andrew's friends settle into parenthood are seen by him as a source of pressure. Evelyn also sees a kind of pressure in the simple fact that numbers of her friends have children, but her reaction to that fact is different from his—she is, on the whole, dismissive of it. There is no sense that she finds it hard to 'hold up her wicket' in the face of her peers:

I think there's always peer group pressure ... in not a positive sense—I mean the fact that everybody is having children at about the same time. All your friends are having children. Certainly none of them placed any positive pressure on me.

She notes that 'peer group pressure' often has an 'opposite effect' on her, making her obstinate in defying the norm, which suggests that she might even find being the odd one out quite enjoyable.

Overall, the case-study couples do not seem to find pressure from friends, workmates or peers any more troublesome than that from families. Their ways of dealing with any pressure that they feel range from placing those who do create pressure in the category of 'acquaintance' rather than friend (David) to deciding simply to ignore comments, as Isabel did.

The same tends to be true of pressure from the broader category of 'society' into which pressure from peers might shade. Seven people described general social pressure to have children, one of whom (John) felt it was the only pressure on him. This kind of pressure was usually seen as light and not particularly troublesome, although it might be irritating:

JOHN: *I felt the pressure that when you get married you buy your triple-fronted brick veneer house ... and the kids follow along with your mortgage ... When we got married ... twelve to eighteen months or so after, I guess, there were people making suggestions ... it seemed to be the norm around the time ... I would say I got upset with that sort of thing and I still do ... but I don't recall or I can't recall any specific cases.*

GARY: *I think there's just so much societal pressure ... to have kids that you're considered to be something strange if you don't. In fact I think there's a certain feeling about in society that people who don't have children are to be pitied ... I think that our society does tend to merge the family with children.*

The impression given by these remarks is that social pressure varies but does not, on the whole, weigh heavily on the childless. What are the factors that make for differences in felt pressure? The childless couples I studied were not blind to the possibility that what they felt was different from what other childless people might feel or to changes over time in the pressures they encountered.

Sex

For Ian, Isabel and Eric, sex made a difference to the amount of pressure one faced, and they felt that a wife probably faced more than her husband:

IAN: *I wasn't aware of it [pressure] to begin with. I notice Isabel tended to be more aware of it than I was. I saw it after a while, I began to see it.*

But the majority of the case-study group made no reference to pressure differing by sex and did not consider that women were under particularly heavy pressure. While this suggests (like table 11) that there is no noticeable difference in felt pressure related to sex, later comments on techniques for negotiation will suggest that circumstances related to sex, such as being in a particular job, might relate to feelings of pressure.

Time

There were stronger suggestions that time made a difference to the amount of pressure one faced and to how one felt about it. Heather described a kind of pressure from friends that disappeared over time:

> ... when some of our friends had the first child, they were full of the job and, without exactly applying pressure ... they'd say, 'Oh, it's terrific, you really should'. And it was quite interesting to notice how they shut up immediately after their second [laughs]. You know, it vanished, this great world of propaganda for having a baby, just went.

It is possible, given Heather's change of mind, that she ceased to see pressure rather than that it vanished. But Isabel suggested that she had seen a similar process. For Felix and Henry, too, time brought change in that as everyone became more used to the idea of the childless Fs or Hs, comments simply fell away or became less noticeable.

FELIX: *For the first three years we were married I suppose there was more pressure ... Just a sort of social thing ... But that sort of pressure has either dropped or I've become immune to it.*

Alison's remark about her mother's concern that she did not have a grandchild suggests that this is another area where time might bring changes and lessen pressure on the childless.

One of the very few older respondents in the questionnaire group, a self-employed typist, added another dimension to the ways in which pressure may vary over time by referring to the broader social climate. She had been under pressure:

> ... only in the past tense; now they have all given up, even agree we were ahead of our time; but pressure was intense and continuous in the 1950s and 1960s.

None of these comments is incompatible with the ideas that length of marriage and early or later decisions about childlessness are related to pressure, since both these factors occur over time. But they do suggest that feeling pressure is in itself a complex process and that it should not be reduced simply to the presence or absence of other factors.

Geographic location

There is one brief suggestion that pressure must be understood in terms of geographic location as well as gender and time. A couple of school teachers in their late twenties in the questionnaire group write of their situation:

> Having lived in a small country community for five years and taught at the same school as my husband, it is painfully evident that we have not followed the accepted pattern of the community, i.e. buying a house and having kids.

In a small country community, the pressure is great! Mainly on my wife. Most families have children and you are left out of many social ... events. Individuals put a great deal of pressure on you after there has been a birth in our circle of acquaintances.

Theirs is the only comment that stresses geographic location. But, as the sections on networks and negotiation with people show, the pressures encountered by childless individuals and the degree to which they are felt vary with where one is socially—in terms of jobs, encounters with others and norms about such encounters. Fairly clearly, the artist associating with childless and bohemian peers and friends is going to face very different pressures from the stockbroker who lives in a suburb which is experiencing a baby boom, and any account of the pronatalist pressures on the childless must take such differences into account.

The foregoing section suggested that the factors influencing pressure are rather more complex than previous researchers have realized. There are differences between 'external' pressure—which may be 'seen'—and internalized or 'felt' pressure that should be taken into account. And the dimensions of gender, time and location interact in complex ways to create situations in which there are varieties of pressure, seen and felt.

This does not mean that there is no pressure on the childless or that pronatalist pressure is not an expression of the ideology of parenthood. But it suggests once more that ideology works in complex ways and is not irresistible. People in particular social locations might be able to escape pressure for a time, and time itself might wear down pressure, so that eventually some individuals appear to have escaped from some of the prescriptions of an ideology.

The couples in this study *feel* comparatively little pressure, although they might see rather more. This leaves them somewhere between the hegemonic position of ignorance of any ideologically based pressure (and hence no feelings of pressure) and oppositional awareness that it exists. I explain this as the result of techniques that the childless couples have used to maximize their comfort and minimize strain in interaction with other people about childlessness. These techniques are explored in the following sections of this chapter.

DEALING WITH PRESSURE THROUGH DEALING WITH PEOPLE

It is clear that pressure is seen by most of the childless people in this study but is not felt by nearly as many and is felt heavily by very few. Variations in pressure relate to factors of time, location and sex. But variations in pressure alone cannot account for the comparative ease felt by the couples—they must use techniques for dealing with whatever pressures they do encounter. The two concepts that are relevant here are those of *network* and *reference group*.

The concept of human networks did not become prominent in

sociology until the 1960s. While the exact definition of the term *network* varies, it always implies linkages or a 'web of affiliations' between people (Simmel 1955). The web may cover a larger or smaller part of the 'social field' of an individual and thus the idea of a network links the 'micro' perspective on interaction between a small number of people and the macro-level analysis of an entire social structure. Networks are the connection between individuals and whole societies.

They are also social sites in which both action and constraint are visible. They are, to some extent, 'given' to us by virtue of our location in particular social categories of age, class, sex etc, but they are also our chosen creations, as we set out to make new friends or to break loose from old ties. They can be supportive and burdensome simultaneously.[2] Within our networks and the constraints they provide, we exercise our capacity for making our own history:

> A person's network ... forms a social environment from and through which pressure is exerted to influence his [sic] behaviour, but it is also an environment through which he can exert pressure to affect the behaviour of others ... His interaction with this social environment is neither wholly self-determined nor wholly predetermined. He is not only constrained and manipulated by his environment, he also manipulates it to suit his interests. (Boissevain 1974)

Networks have been studied as sources of emotional and material support for individuals and families and as reinforcers of value positions for mothers.[3] Two aspects to network support are of particular interest to me: the kind of people who come to make up the network of a voluntarily childless individual, and the kind of interaction that goes on over childlessness.

The eventual pattern of a network is the result of what has been called 'network management' (Richards 1983). It should be possible to see strategies of management in the comments of childless couples about their networks. An analytic distinction could be drawn between management strategies that affect the shape of the network, and those that relate to the style of interaction within it, although in reality, of course, strategies affecting style must also affect shape, as particular exchanges realign members, drawing some closer to the network, pushing others out.

THE NETWORKS OF THE CHILDLESS
Most of the data for this section come from the final interview with the case-study couples. After I had persuaded or cajoled people into setting out their personal typologies of the world as described in chapter 5, I had them draw their own networks, using the types they had nominated as a basis. The highly coloured results showed me something of the shape and density of the 'inner zone' of the networks since I asked for 'people who are reasonably important to you and you are pretty

close to'. It also showed me how similar the network was in terms of marital and parental status and (by the use of coloured stickers) how similar the childless people thought their networks were in terms of values.

Analysis of the diagrams is restricted by the fact that they do not cover more than a small portion of the networks of the respondents, and I am not concerned with measures of density, multiplexity, clustering or other characteristics studied by those who are interested in networks per se.

In general, the diagrams showed the voluntarily childless to have relatively loose-knit networks. They do not include high proportions of kin among the inner segment of 'people who are important' (see table 13) and other studies[4] suggest that tight-knit networks are usually dominated by kin. Moreover, the diagrams tended not to connect up the points in a way typical of a dense network. Eric was the only person whose diagram linked everyone he knew to everybody else in the network, suggesting extreme density for at least a proportion of his social contacts.

Neither did the couples seem to rely on creating tightly supportive groups of other childless people (see table 13). Seven people had networks where more than half the members were childless, but none had totally childless networks. Their social circles were apparently not dominated by males, with whom children might be less of a preoccupation than with women. They do not appear to make efforts to develop a tight little set of like-minded persons around them for support.

Nonetheless, there is a sense of the networks consisting of 'birds of a feather' in terms of the values of the childless. I asked the couples to classify the people in their networks into the types they had diagrammed as sharing their world-views. On average, slightly more than half the people listed in the diagrams were shown as the same type as the person drawing it. And in two cases (Chris and Eric) the network was made up entirely of 'people like me'. This implies a degree of support for one's position, even if the 'people like me' are not also childless.

Evidence about the strategies they use within their networks to maximize their feelings of support and minimize feelings of pressure is much clearer. It has already been suggested that the childless would use conversations and network management as part of their interaction with other people and hence as a way of negotiating with ideology. The data on how they and their networks deal with childlessness reveal that the childless are skilled in the art of maximizing support.

CONVERSATIONAL TECHNIQUES
There is no doubt that the childless talk about their state with other people. Seventy-four per cent of questionnaire respondents had discussed the issue with their spouses, 87% of them had families who knew

of their intentions and 92.5% had friends who knew. Clearly, there had been at least some conversations between the childless people, their kin and their friends about not having children. The case-study group were similar. As table 14 shows, everyone had discussed the issue at some level with more than half their network. The women seem to have had more discussion than the men (on average they discussed childlessness with 29% of the people they listed, compared to 18.5% for the men), but there was no one who had not had some discussion. Only Eric and Evelyn indicated that they hadn't really discussed the matter much:

EVELYN: *I really don't think that it is something that we tend to talk about. Even friends with children, it is not something that we tend to talk about. I'm sure that there would be some comments occasionally, but I can't often remember having sat down and had a conversation on whether you should have children or you shouldn't have children.*

ERIC: *Nobody has been supportive to me—might have been to Evelyn. I've never discussed it with anybody or commented on it.*

The more common situation was the one depicted by Chris and Clare. There were specific people, such as Clare's father, with whom childlessness had not been discussed but, overall, as Clare said: 'Oh, everyone knows what we feel'. Not only did 'everyone know' but also almost everyone appeared relatively sympathetic. The general feeling of a supportive network (discussed in more detail later) was, I suggest, the result of the following conversational strategies.

Tactical decisions about confronting the issue

Depending on their particular situations, the childless might talk a lot about not having families or they might remain silent on the issue. Diane, especially when she was deciding to be sterilized, seems to have had lengthy conversations with most of her network. Gary, on the other hand, and more typically, would volunteer information rather cautiously:

I never go around talking about it. If somebody asks me, it depends on how close I feel to them as to what sort of an answer they get.

On the whole, women were less reticent than men about discussing childlessness, perhaps because the issue has more salience for them, or perhaps because it is more common for women to discuss children than for men to do so. And it could be that, for women, direct discussion is an effective technique for enlisting support or dampening opposition. This seems to be the view of the two women who worked as nurses. Judy, training as a midwife by the third interview, was in the interesting position of working with women whose major concerns as patients or nurses were babies. She said that enquiries about children were a slight embarrassment. With patients, she is cautious but with staff, she is more forthright:

> *... with most of the people now, and ... people I work with ... I told them straight out that I've had a tubal ligation and I'm not having children. Because I got sick and tired of the whole business of 'Oh, you'll be pregnant by the end of the course!'*

Clare, the other nurse (although not in a maternity ward), also responds directly to comments:

> *I say 'I don't want any', and they say 'Why? Doesn't Chris want them?' and I say 'No'. Then they say, 'Wouldn't you like them?' ... I always get on my soap-box ...*

Neither John, an executive, nor Chris, a teacher, feel a need to 'get on a soap-box' in response to comments from others. Chris simply says that, for him, any pressure is 'very mild' and does not need countering. John does get occasional polite queries about his domestic situation:

> *I would say on occasions, light-heartedly I guess, 'We've got a nine-year-old red setter and a two-year-old chinchilla cat' ... I haven't told people who are outside the circle of friends really that Judy has had a tubal ligation.*

Judy and Clare seem to be in situations where confrontation is useful—perhaps because of the sort of work they do. It is possible that they are by temperament blunter and more direct than their husbands but that is not my observation of the Cs, at least. What is clear, however, is that strategic decisions are made about how direct one should be on the issue of childlessness in order to defuse possibly embarrassing situations.

Avoiding opposition

The technique that was most commonly mentioned in discussions about interaction with networks was strategic avoidance of people, situations or topics which might produce opposition. So Evelyn would try to avoid the annoyance of comments by her friends' mothers:

> *Other people's mothers will say things like, 'You're leaving it too late', which annoys the hell out of me. It doesn't make me feel uncomfortable for not having children, it just makes me feel uncomfortable that other people are so bloody nosey.... It is an inevitable comment that they make ... it is not a case of I would try to avoid the people—I try to avoid the topic as much as possible.*

Judy and Kevin would both try to avoid talking about childlessness with particular members of their networks. But while Judy finds herself cutting short conversations on the issue, Kevin simply does not raise the topic because he feels it is likely that he will not be supported:

JUDY: *I love her dearly, but she aggravates me about this because every time we try to discuss it she just cries ... Well, every time we get on to this subject I just say, 'Look, R, it's just going to upset you, we won't talk about it'.*

KEVIN: *It probably hasn't come up because ... they have said something that had led me to believe that that is their view and there is no point in discussing it anyway ... [pointing to a name on his network] ... He is very anti-abortion, conservative ... traditional ... in terms of family and so forth.*

And Kate and Kevin agreed that conversations with new parents about children were a trial, which could lead to avoidance not just of the topic of children but also of encounters with the parents. Or situations where babies were likely to be present might be avoided because of possible embarrassment. Kevin argued that if he were asked to eat in a restaurant with small children present, he would rather not go. Fiona took a similar stand:

Where we were doing dinner parties and people were bringing brats along, I just dropped them from the dinner parties ... Certain social functions only. In other words, they are still welcome friends at an informal table but at formal entertaining they are not.

Her use of the past tense points up the fact that, as with decisions about confrontation, strategic avoidance is a technique produced in response to particular circumstances. At the last interview, she and Felix had moved interstate and knew few people with children who could be asked to dinner so that this avoidance technique was no longer necessary.

Interpreting conversation

Just as the childless interpret their past in terms of their current attitudes so they tend to interpret their interactions in ways that maximize their feelings of support. This can be done by taking any statement that can be seen as supportive at face value and by discounting the status of those who make unsupportive comments. An exchange between Felix and Fiona shows the first technique in operation:

FELIX: *The one who thought that it was most important to have children was my mother, or so I would have thought, and she has not said anything at all.*

FIONA: *Well, she had actually to me ... She says, 'I've got two grandchildren'.*

FELIX: *So I think there is no worry about keeping on the family name ...*

FIONA: *Your mother has actually discussed it with me ...*

FELIX: *She doesn't desperately want to become a grandmother.*

Initially, he has taken silence for support, or at least consent. As soon as he is told that his mother has spoken on the issue of childlessness, he amplifies her reported comment, making it more supportive. Henry and Heather, with opposite views about children by the last interview, listed some of the same names as supportive of their individual positions. For both of them, the simple fact that these people were friends made them also supporters. And for Kate and Kevin, the minutia of everyday conversation becomes a means of constructing and reinforcing the world-view that values childlessness so that casual remarks about daily arrangements or gossip about friends are felt as support for the status quo:

KEVIN: *... I mean, the topic comes up, and we obviously don't contradict each other about the issue. It comes up in the way we deal with topics about leisure and so forth ... 'Do you realize if we had kids we wouldn't be able to do that?'*

KATE: *Also, in talking about our friends who were having children or contemplating having children, I suppose we support each other because we start discussing what kids mean ... we get talking about friends who have children, or families who have children, and from there we give support to our decision. I think that is the way we do it.*

In addition to interpreting conversations in the most supportive light possible, the childless minimize the impact of negative comments through discounting their source. A remark that could be threatening if taken seriously can be discounted if its author can be categorized as a silly person. Trivializing or dismissing those who criticize is an effective way to neutralize their opposition. Judy, for example, has two friends who disapprove of her childlessness. One, who cries, she finds trying and, as we have seen, she avoids the topic when with this friend. Another friend becomes positively angry, but this response is airily dismissed:

JUDY: *This is the other person I was going to [indicate as opposing], and it's interesting that she is that far away from me [on the network diagram].*

INT: *Who is that?*

JUDY: *Susan. She can't comprehend, she gets angry about it.*

INT: *And how do you respond to that?*

JUDY: *I laugh, it's the best way around it. It's the only way to get Suze out of her anger.*

The use of a diminutive, and the suggestion that you might have to laugh at Susan because she's often angry, help to discount her opposition, in contrast to that of Judy's weepy friend R. John uses a similar discounting technique with the unsupportive member of his network:

JOHN: *In my fellow's case, you just can't talk to him about that sort of topic ... I think it has a lot to do with his upbringing and his religion ... he was going to be a priest at one stage, wasn't he?*

JUDY: *Thank heavens he wasn't.*

JOHN: *Yes. I think that has a lot to do with it. It's not resentment towards us, but just a lack of understanding, or wanting to understand ... Well, he is a very shallow person anyway. I mean, we love him dearly but he is very shallow.*

JUDY: *He can't talk about anything but sport.*

JOHN: *No ... and he has a problem about communicating with his own kids ... Unless they are talking about football or soccer or something. He is not a good communicator except in sport. He is a very successful coach.*

So the unsupportive friend is not so inept that John would not value him—he is, after all, a successful coach—but neither, because of his shallowness, is he a person whose implied opposition need be taken too seriously.

I found evidence of avoidance strategies in comments made by eleven people and evidence of strategies within conversations in all those cases. It is harder to be certain about 'interpretation' strategies. While I have quoted all the cases of discounting opposition which emerged, I suspect that there were people who were not 'important' enough to be listed in the network because of their opposition. And the tendency for couples to find their networks supportive suggests that interpreting comments as supportive may also be more common than my examples imply.

NETWORK MANAGEMENT

The conversational techniques of avoidance, confrontation or interpretation have, in the end, the effect of shaping a network so that support is maximized and opposition minimized. Relationships that might have developed between parents and childless couples never do develop since avoidance strategies preclude them, or existing relationships end as friends move into parenthood. Those whose opposition is painful or who cannot be discounted might cease to be part of the network, and those who are sympathetic might become more important within it. None of this happens by design, of course. Gary and Gabrielle described how potential friendships foundered if 'unacceptable' children were involved:

GABRIELLE: *We've had a few, I must admit, people who wouldn't have become friends because we didn't invite them ...*

GARY: *On the whole, whether you would find these people acceptable as friends would depend on how acceptable their kids were.*

INT: *So, in a sense, you don't let yourself become friends with anyone who is likely to be difficult because of their children?*

GABRIELLE: *It just happens.*

Similarly, once people become parents Eric and Evelyn find they have less contact with them, and the relationship tends to atrophy:

EVELYN: *We see less of our friends who have got children than we used to.*

ERIC: *Not deliberately.*

EVELYN: *Not deliberately, it's just that they don't have the time ... Also, it is more difficult to involve them in spur of the moment things. Often it is difficult to put up with their kids. So you see then only once or twice a year where you might have seen them previously every couple of months ... It is just that their lifestyles change so dramatically.*

Kate and Kevin, especially Kevin, are aware of the management technique by which networks are altered. He describes it uneasily as 'mercenary'—a word that hints at the bogey of selfishness (calculating rationality applied even to friendships), but goes on to point out that the 'chopping' of this branch of the network is not intended as an insult or unkindly meant. Rather, it is inevitable—the result of being unable to drop in on friends and feel comfortable about it:

[Pointing to friends on the network map who have had a baby in the last year] ... has affected our relationship a lot, because it chopped out a couple who we used to socialise quite a deal with ... We are being mercenary, but ... if it was any other couple we would have chopped them out ages ago ... the point is, if I hadn't heard from them normally, you know weekly, we would ring up and talk to them, or we would go around there. Now when they start having babies you stop ringing because it wakes the kid up; you don't go round there because of the door bell. I don't feel comfortable in a house where they have just had a new baby.

As with the conversational techniques, the degree of chopping or incorporating required to keep a useful network operating varies with individual circumstances. Kevin is extremely conscious of the part he plays in shaping his network; Eric and Evelyn are much less aware. This does not reflect different feelings about pressure on themselves. If table 13 is any guide, both the Es and Ks feel very little pressure, although the Es see more personal sources of pressure than the Ks. Perhaps Kate and Kevin are aware of the ways they dodge potential pressure simply because they have dodged it better than the Es, or perhaps because they live under different circumstances (being younger, they might have more friends who are becoming parents and are thus in a position to be 'chopped'), they have greater awareness of their network management.

The upshot of both the conversational techniques and the network management that flows from them is the creation of networks in which both parents and childless people are more supportive than opposition-al. While all the couples encountered some opposition to childlessness, only Henry had a network that was largely 'unsupportive'. And his cryptic comments suggested that in fact he did not feel unsupported, even if most of his network favoured parenthood as a general principle. The questionnaire group, too, seems to have friends who are support-ive, although families are seen as disapproving of childlessness more than they are seen as approving.

Among friends, 36.5% are mainly approving, 34.4% are neutral and 15.3% are mainly disapproving. Among family, only 17.6% are approv-ing, 25.8% are neutral and 35.1% tend to disapprove. (Also, more peo-ple did not know their families' views than were ignorant of how friends felt about their childlessness.) The network management tech-niques seem, on the whole, effective in helping the childless to maintain their stance towards the ideology of parenthood.

REFERENCE GROUPS AND IDEOLOGY

The previous section suggested that the networks of the childless pro-vide a high degree of support for their negotiation with the ideology of parenthood. I now turn to a related concept: that of *reference group*. Apart from the fact that several researchers on voluntary childlessness have invoked the term, it is obviously related to the concerns of this chapter. Making reference to other people is tied in with network manage-ment—decisions about asking people to dinner, such as the one men-tioned by Fiona, involve mental comparisons between them and 'our sort of people', and those decisions ultimately affect networks of impor-tant others. Moreover, the presence or absence of reference points in defence of childlessness might be a clue to the extent of pressure felt by couples—the more they are disapproved of and under pressure, the more likely they are to invoke supportive comparisons.

Like *network*, the term *reference group* has roots in the work of the early twentieth-century social scientists. The actual term came into vogue in mid century in the works of Hyman and Sherif.[5]

There have been three main strands of meaning in the way the term is used. It can refer to a group of real or imagined people who are a point of comparison or reference for an individual, or a group in which she or he aspires to gain or keep approval. Or, most broadly, it could mean 'a group whose perspective constitutes the frame of reference for the actor' (Shibutani 1955). The most common shade of meaning is of a group that constitutes a point of reference and is evoked to explain action. Bott (1971) defines *reference group* in these terms as:

> any group, real or fictitious, that is thought by an individual to have a real existence and is employed by him [sic] to compare and evaluate his position with that of others, and to justify or explain his actions.

In a complex society where individuals occupy a variety of disparate roles, there might be conflict for an individual between the values of different reference points (Merton 1968). Merton argues that some kinds of deviant behaviour (especially 'nonconformity') might be explained by adherence to the standards of one group rather than another. In spite of the differences between role theory (which underlies much of the work on reference groups) and the framework within which I approach childlessness, ideas derived from the study of reference groups can throw light on negotiation with ideology. Merton's work, for instance, suggests that an oppositional stance towards an ideology might be in part a response to the values of an important reference group. From this, it might be expected that people who disobey an ideological prescript might justify their behaviour by invoking reference points, either an admired one they wish to emulate or a despised one whose behaviour they spurn.

Previous research on the voluntarily childless has used the notion of reference groups in two ways. Houseknecht has developed a social–psychological model for understanding childlessness that includes the idea of support from reference groups who need not themselves be childless. She found that a small sample of single and intentionally childless female students did apparently make use of reference groups and had more support for childlessness from those groups than did a matched sample of women who intended to have children. This is consistent with the idea that reference group support is important in becoming childless.

Significantly, those who desired children tended to list more referents, and to say that they had considered a larger number of their opinions before deciding, than did the would-be childless women (Houseknecht 1977). Common sense suggests that they probably knew more supportive people than the childless did, since more people overall support parenthood than childlessness. That, in turn, suggests that the childless may not have much chance to refer to real people for support but will be forced to rely either on negative instances or on 'abstract categories', as might happen where loose-knit networks were involved (Bott 1971).

Veevers (1980) argues that spouses, above all, function as reference points for those who wish to avoid parenthood. She refers to the creation of a joint world by the couple as a process by which other people are gradually relegated to insignificant positions as arbiters of values and behaviour, and says: 'Among some childless couples, such processes are carried to their logical extreme, and the couple see in each other a reference group of one'.

While she is correct in suggesting that spouses are likely to be an important reference point since other researchers have found the same thing,[6] Veevers' comments grossly overemphasise the importance of the 'reference group of one'. This is partly because there is no indication of how many couples were in this position and partly because her view of the climate surrounding the couples is of a uniformly hostile pronatalist world, as the following quotation shows:

> The voluntarily childless couples we talked with were uniformly aware that their rejection of the parenthood mystique was very unusual, and that most persons would dismiss their views on parenthood as inaccurate and incomplete. Moreover, given a basically pronatalist society, they were also aware that most persons would consider their world-view to be morally offensive and would strongly disapprove of their rejection of parenthood. (Veevers 1980)

This picture of a monolithic ideology has already been shown to be false. Given that, the picture of childless couples as lonely dyads with only each other to refer to can also be rejected as an overstatement.

As well as overstating the isolation of the childless, Veevers' picture of the reference group of one tends to overemphasize the degree of consensus between couples.[7] An American survey of forty childless couples suggested that there was often disagreement on the issue of parenthood. If there was conflict, the pattern was that the husband's desires prevailed or the marriage disintegrated (Marciano 1978). This suggests that, at the very least, the idea of negotiation needs to be put alongside the idea of the spouse as a single reference point. More aptly, in the light of feminist-inspired studies of speech patterns and marital interaction,[8] the idea of negotiation from positions of unequal strength about an issue of unequal salience needs to be inserted.

REFERENCE GROUPS OF ONE?

Were the childless couples 'reference groups of one'? My case-study data show that the picture of a lonely dyad, supporting itself against a hostile world, is inaccurate. I have already shown that the couples felt more support than hostility from their networks and had developed a useful repertoire of techniques for dealing with interactions which had shaped networks which were, indeed, supportive. And while ten out of the fourteen people still married at the last interview agreed that their spouses were people with whom childlessness was often discussed only six of them listed a spouse as the 'most supportive' person in their network. This suggests that spouses are certainly not the sole supportive referent.

On the other hand, some data suggest that for some of the couples a shared frame of reference is so strong that there is almost no need to think about the spouse in thinking about support. It is as if the couple were so united that 'support' meant not 'support for me' but 'support for us'. So Chris and Clare agreed that Chris's mother was the most supportive person for both of them, with Clare saying that Chris was 'in total agreement' rather than offering support.

The two obvious ways of finding out whether an individual is making use of a particular reference group are (a) to ask questions about admired and emulated people, and (b) to look for a convergence of ideas between the individual and the group in question. In considering the question of spouses acting as a 'reference group of one' it is useful to look for convergence of ideas between husbands and wives.

Table 15 summarizes the reasons given by the case-study couples for not having children. These were collected in the first interviews, where husbands and wives were questioned separately, and show a degree of similarity, which one would expect where an issue has been discussed over time and become part of a joint biography. So Chris and Clare both see their busy lives as being disrupted by children, Gabrielle and Gary agree on the problems of travel if one had children, and so on.

The couple might interpret a theme in fairly different ways but still give it as a reason. So David and Diane were both fairly sure that parenthood would cause unpleasant changes to their lifestyle, but for David, the changes had to do with rows about children and limits on his freedom to go to the pub, and for Diane, they concerned economic dependence and the 'trapped' feeling which would follow from it.

Convergence was particularly noticeable in two cases, where from individual interviews I collected very similar accounts. The Js and Ks had each constructed a 'joint biography' that led them to tell a similar story, even when apart. While the Js' account, focusing on the incompatibility between their busy lifestyle and the demands parenthood would make, is probably 'her story', the Ks' joint biography is more recognisable as Kevin's account. There is agreement on how his temper would make him a bad father and on the instability of his family which might be passed on to his children. Kate then adds a parallel instance from her own background:

KEVIN: ... *I'm what can be modestly described as short-tempered, and I believe it would not take five seconds for me to pick up a baby and hurl it across the room if the circumstances were right. (Or wrong, depending on how you want to put that.) [After explaining that he had attempted suicide at one stage] ... despite the fact that you go around saying 'It's never going to happen to me (again) blah, blah', I think I'm intelligent enough to assume that it could happen. And once again, I don't think that's the right environment to start having kids in ... my mother was the same—I told you she was unstable. She's also tried to commit suicide on two or three occasions ... so we have an unstable background somewhere along the family line. I don't plan to propagate that.*

KATE: *I also know Kevin'd make a rotten parent. Because, you see, he's very possessive ... And also he's very short on temper, and I think although he'd never mean to hurt a child, he could. I think we'd be selfish, very selfish, to have children. On medical grounds. I feel on my side we've got a tendency towards petit-mal ... in fact one of my sister's kids has got it ... I had it when I was a kid. My eyesight's another one. Not that it's severe ... Kevin's folks. Oh, insanity—well, his mother's attempted suicide a couple of times, Kevin has himself. There's a very high tendency towards that sort of thing in their family. They're a really tense lot of people.*

The convergence of ideas between husbands and wives suggests that they do look to each other for validation and justification of their state and in that sense do constitute a 'reference group of one'. But there is no necessary connection between a *shared* frame of reference and Veevers' *single* referent. Kevin and Kate, for example, have clearly developed a joint frame of reference about why they do not want children and equally clearly find each other very supportive. They list each other as the 'most supportive' members of their networks and noted that their daily interaction helped them to shore up their decision. But they do not feel that they are an isolated couple, relying only on each other for support. Kevin felt that most of his network was supportive; Kate that it was mainly supportive or neutral. Despite their shared frame of reference, and their awareness of support for each other, this couple has referents in their network and possibly beyond it. They, and the other case-study couples, are clear proof that spouses are not the sole source of support for childless people.

POSITIVE REFERENTS OR AWFUL WARNINGS?

If the childless have reference groups besides their spouses, what are they? There is a little anecdotal evidence that some people move into childlessness by following a highly valued role model, who presumably offers a positive point of reference.[9] But in my study, there are no accounts of simple influence of that sort. Neither could I see evidence of highly valued abstract groups that the childless wished to emulate. The presentation of parents as somewhat sheepish in accounts of parenthood decisions (noted in chapter 5) certainly implies that the childless see themselves as sensible, but this is not the same as seeing a group of 'sensible and childless' people and emulating them. Like the practice of stereotyping parents, implying that childlessness is sensible is a tactic for maintaining a position vis-à-vis ideology rather than clear evidence for the existence of a positive reference group. In fact, the most typical form of reference was to what I call 'awful warnings'. They are summarized by Kevin, who noted that he and Kate had not met any role models:

We didn't look up to anyone else and say, 'Gee, we would like to be like him'. We were more likely to look around at all the people who had kids and say, 'My God, we don't want to end up like that'.

Thirteen of the twenty-two case-study people offered comments on how those they knew had been adversely affected by parenthood. These references, summarized in table 16, were spontaneous, not sought, and hence provide strong evidence for the use of 'awful warnings' as a technique. Sometimes, the references were simply descriptions; at other times, they included the idea that observations had been confirmed by the victims:

GABRIELLE: *A couple of my friends have actually admitted that their kids have been a tremendous disruption to their relationship and they've had to make tremendous adjustments. And that they just don't know each other as well as they did. And I have seen this in some relationships, I really have.*

Although the references to known examples of disaster were not always to people listed in the networks, friends and relatives featured often enough to suggest that the 'awful warnings' came from close to home, compared to the stereotypes of sheepish parents. And presumably, the closer they are, the greater their significance as warnings. The use of awful warnings is a tactic that enables the childless to justify themselves with cautionary tales (some more serious than others) which can be certified true; 'it really happened—I knew them personally'. This is not to say that the warnings alone caused the observers to stay childless. Accounts of the disasters of parenthood abound, and parents hear them as much as childless people. But the warnings are taken up by the childless and used as justification for their behaviour.

This chapter has shown the childless to be skilful in dealing with other people about childlessness. They have a more subtle awareness of the variations in pressure on them than do some researchers, and they are adept at managing conversations and networks and at using reference groups to support their position. They cannot be seen as beleaguered couples, desperately resisting social pressure towards parenthood. On the whole, they contrive very comfortably to get by with a little help from their (carefully chosen) friends.

This comparative ease is due in part at least to their social location in positions where they can appeal to countervailing ideas, and where they have access to potentially sympathetic others. I argue that it will be people whose location (in terms of class, geography, personal network and time) gives them most resources who will be best able to avoid a hegemonic acquiescence with ideology. But, as the last two chapters have shown, capacity to side-step an ideological demand is not the same as impetus to oppose ideology.

Because they do get by so successfully, these couples do not feel the moral outrage about the ideology of parenthood that would help to motivate opposition to it. In a sense, their very success in making use of the contradictory elements in the ideology prevents them from questioning it further. As they go through the process of managing their networks, gradually establishing for themselves a network and a joint biography in which they are not abnormal monsters but simply Chris and Clare who happen not to want children, the perception that 'that's just the way things are' helps to stop them from inquiring too deeply about why they are that way.

The implication of this is that choosing childlessness is by no means the 'ultimate liberation' suggested by some feminists. This, and other consequences of voluntary childlessness, will be explored in chapter 7.

7

. . . .

where

to

from

here?

I n order to pull together the threads of this study I shall briefly summarize my main findings and then return to the three sets of questions which sparked off the research in an attempt to show some of the implications of the study.

WHAT HAS BEEN SHOWN?

The findings of this study resemble those of other studies in some ways and differ from them in others. Like most of the other researchers, I found that the voluntarily childless couples in my sample were highly educated, relatively affluent, non-religious, professional 'dual-career' couples. While the difficulty of sampling from a population whose basic parameters are unknown means that we cannot be certain that all the voluntarily childless share these characteristics, it seems probable that they do.

Like some other studies, I found evidence that experiences in family of origin were related to voluntary childlessness but in a very complex fashion. My data do not support simple statements about position as an only or an eldest child or particular family climates leading to voluntary childlessness. Rather, they suggest that images of parenthood, based on a variety of earlier experiences, are evoked by childless people as partial explanations for their state. The experiences may well form 'motive antecedents' (Veevers 1980) for childlessness, but there are no straightforward causal links which are readily identifiable.

Like other researchers, I found that childless people came to their decision at different times. But I did not find clear evidence that they could be categorized as either 'early deciders' or 'postponers'. Rather, I found that childlessness was as much a state of becoming as a state of being and that commitment to the decision tended to ebb and flow, especially for women, for whom the issue is more salient than it is for men.

Moreover, this study has shown that the decision to avoid parenthood might not be irrevocable, even though all the participants in the research believed it to be so when they came into the research. The issue of the permanence of decisions about childlessness is one that only longitudinal studies (such as mine) can address. Several of the studies note the problem of our inability to predict whether couples self-defined as voluntarily childless will indeed stay that way. The fact that, of the eleven case-study couples, four now have children while a further three have split up, with at least one partner becoming a parent, is testimony to the reality of this problem. It suggests, incidentally, that most of the demographic studies that attempt to comment on 'voluntary' childlessness using random samples of people who expect no children are not only confusing chosen childlessness with known infertility but also taking as a permanent state what may well be highly temporary,[1] and that their findings should be interpreted as cautiously as those of the unrepresentative small studies the demographers criticize.

The most common solution to the problem of possible change over time is to set fairly stringent criteria (such as a lengthy marriage or sterilization) for inclusion in a sample. The fact that the Js, who now have two children, had been married for nine years at the start of the project, and that Judy had been sterilized, shows that such precautions will not always succeed and that only a retrospective study of couples who were no longer fertile would give a sample that we could describe with total conviction as voluntarily childless. Such a sample would be extremely difficult to collect and, even if it were possible to do so, it would not tell us anything about the proportions of couples who at some stage see themselves as voluntarily childless but later change their minds. The fact that commitment to childlessness may ebb to the point of reversal has implications for policy-makers which I will discuss later. It also relates to the study's most significant findings.

The most important findings of my study concern the relationship between the voluntarily childless and the ideology of parenthood. It is clear from my data that the childless couples are neither blind victims of a dominant ideology, living in 'cloud cuckoo land' (Comer 1975) nor radicalized and self-conscious opponents of it. Their refusal to obey the ideological 'parenthood prescription' (Veevers 1980) for some time or permanently is an act consistent with an oppositional stance towards the ideology of parenthood. But the evidence that the childless disobey this prescription because they accept broadly the notion that parenthood requires commitment, which in turn entails undesirable sacrifices, suggests that their stance is also hegemonic. They do not stand outside the ideology of parenthood, seeing it clearly as a social construction and refusing to accept it. They are located within it. Like parents, they see a rather dim set of 'social pressures' that impel most people into parenthood, and they accept it as inevitable that, should they become parents, their commitment would be manifested by sacrifices of time, energy, pleasure and (for women especially) precious elements of identity. Because they accept the sacrifices as what parenthood *is* rather than what parenthood *has been made*, they are inside the boundaries of ideology. But they have escaped those boundaries to the extent that they refuse to obey the prescription to have children, even if this refusal eventually changes into agreement.

They are able to negotiate this partial escape firstly because their social location provides them with opportunities either to use some of the ideas within the ideology of parenthood to counter other elements of the same ideology, or to appeal to other ideologies against it. Their relatively privileged position with regard to education and occupation gives them choices not available to others. At the same time it provides them with satisfactions and opportunities that may pull them away from parenthood. A second factor in their negotiation is the adroit use the couples make of dealings with other people. They have access to, and manage, relatively supportive networks.

They use a variety of techniques to deal with ideology. At times, they will appeal to one ideological statement against another—for example, invoking the prescription about commitment, and an added comment about their inability to live up to the required standards of commitment, against the prescription that they should have children. At other times, they will appeal to ideas outside the ideology of parenthood (for example, the ideal of professional dedication to work). Or they will manipulate language so that a word like *normal* applied to parents becomes faintly derogatory and their 'abnormal' position is given a positive value. Or a special meaning will be given to a word like *nature* so that the state of childlessness can be explained by the term usually applied as an explanation for parenthood. Techniques for negotiating with people include the 'conversational' techniques of confronting or avoiding people, situations or topics and the use of devices like humour to get around embarrassing situations; 'interpretation' of conversations as supportive wherever possible; and a range of 'network management' strategies. These include the 'chopping off' of some relationships and the discounting of opponents. Finally, techniques of reference, including the use of a spouse to help create an appropriate joint biography, and the habit of making reference to 'awful warnings' among the network, help to support and validate the childless identity.

Although previous studies have recorded some of the ways the childless maintain their world-views, they have taken for granted the idea that this is done in the teeth of strong opposition. My data strongly suggest that this is an oversimplification. The couples I observed are not fighting lonely battles against a pronatalist network and a hostile world, but are given sufficient support by networks which they have manipulated for that purpose to get by fairly comfortably.

All this suggests that it is not appropriate to see voluntary childlessness as the 'deviant' activity that various writers (those in sympathy with it as often as those against it) have made it out to be, nor as simply an outcome of individual psychology. People who decide not to have children should not be seen as deviant child-haters, nor as mentally unhealthy, nor as courageous social rebels. Voluntary childlessness is their response to the ideological and structural pushes and pulls they face and is thus socially created. To be sure, it is the outcome of some biographical factors but not of especially unusual ones (in every family some child has to be the eldest!). It is also a response to the demands placed on parents by the ideology of parenthood and to the broad social factors identified as 'structural antinatalism' (Huber 1980)—the material demands of parenthood as we understand it.

These demands have traditionally fallen more heavily on women than men. The women (and to some extent the men) in my study are aware of the sacrifices that mothers must make—especially where those sacrifices intersect with life in the paid workforce. Thus we should see voluntary childlessness as a response to the unfair way in which we have organized family life rather than as a manifestation of anybody's selfishness.

Having restated the main findings, I now want to return to my starting point. In chapter 1 I described the overlapping sets of ideas that lay behind the research. I started with my personal interest in the topic, then considered the public issue of childlessness and finally sketched out the theoretical question of structure and agency. I will reverse the order of these questions now and consider first the theoretical one, then the issue of future trends and finally the questions of most personal interest to me now, eight years after I began the study.

THEORETICAL ISSUES

I said in the first chapter that the issue behind the research was the one about individual agency and structural constraint. My research does no more than illustrate that both elements are involved in daily life. As I argued above, it shows that voluntary childlessness is socially created rather than being explicable in purely psychological terms, or even by the catch-all term 'family background'. It must be understood as an outcome of the interplay between complex matters of individual biography and equally complex social structures. Among those social structures, ideology is a crucial element. I shall now pick up from my study some pointers for those studying this element.

My research has shown that there are enormous difficulties in using ideology as a tool for research rather than a bumper-sticker signifying one's political or theoretical allegiance. I hope it has also shown that the enterprise is worthwhile. For years now, feminists (including me) have talked about 'the ideology of the family' as though it were monolithic, irresistible and driven by a single set of consistent interests. My data show that it is not monolithic or irresistible, and it could be argued that, as the outcome of negotiations, it does not represent one consistent set of interests. The attempt to clarify just what an ideology is, so that the concept can be used in empirical research, led me to a more sophisticated understanding of the term in general and of the structure/agency question.

Those who are interested in researching ideology, it seems to me, have several tasks to consider. First, they must spell out the ideology in question, its sources, content and dominance. Then they must look critically for evidence about the effect of ideology. At present, studies of particular ideologies seem to rely heavily on textual analysis—looking at a product such as a book or film for its ideological message, or offering an alternative 'reading' of the text. While there are areas of study where this technique is appropriate, when we are trying to explain social phenomena it seems to me that it is much less useful than asking about the reception of ideology: how people think and feel about particular issues and ideas, and how they act in response to them.

Research of this nature could be quantitative or qualitative. It is my belief that qualitative research is a necessary first step to understanding the workings of an ideology, since it is in words that messages are conveyed and therefore to respondents' own words that researchers must turn in order to comprehend the effect of messages. But if qualitative research has been done on an area, then quantitative surveys, carried out appropriately, could tell us much about the spread of ideas or the extent of dominance of an ideology.

As an aside, we might note the usefulness of 'deviant' groups in the study of ideology. Mills (1970) noted the importance of 'opposites' as a source of insight into social structure, and we could gain much understanding of ideology by looking at those who appear to have abandoned or escaped it, even if the escape is temporary.

Whatever kind of research is carried out, I think it important that ideology be seen as a complex phenomenon, dominating rather than dominant, and that explanations using this concept pay attention to both structure and agency. The idea of negotiation offers a kind of rapprochement between the two. Similarly, the notion of pressure deserves further exploration, along the lines of enquiry into what sort of people feel most pressure to conform to any given ideological prescription and who, if anyone, manages to evade it.

This kind of research takes us back to what I see as the central concern of sociology: the way in which we make our own histories, but within constraints outside our control. I also see it as essential for the concern to be investigated empirically as well as to be rigorously theorized. Rather than discussing the nature of ideology in general, we should be looking at the working of specific ideologies with a view to understanding the general concept through investigations of specific incidents.

Mild-mannered empiricism and belief in the usefulness of the concept of ideology sound dreadfully old-fashioned in the face of current theoretical enthusiasms for deconstructing meanings and the current political celebration of the end of communism. I persist in the belief that the end of *an* ideology (if indeed it is ended) is not the same as the end of ideology as such. Furthermore, I persist in the belief that to show that an ideology is a fractured complex rather than a monolithic whole, and that it is partially or highly contested, does not mean that we should abandon the concept. The move from talking about ideologies to talking about discourses seems to me frequently to involve a move towards metaphors in which power becomes invisible. Either discourses are in competition and there is not a sense that some of the competing voices have (social) amplifiers or, since all discourse is about power, even the critiques of discourse are located within the existing political/power parameters and there is no hope for change in them. Both stances have conservative implications; neither is particularly useful for the researcher who hopes that research might contribute towards the formation of social policy.

POLICY ISSUES

If the central intellectual concern of sociology is to understand the links between individual biography and historical social structure, the purpose of that concern for many sociologists is to enable social change. One way of creating change is for better social policy to be formed— policy that would make for happier biographies. In chapter 1 I sketched out the two policy issues that had caused concern about voluntary childlessness in the past. They were, first, concern about declining population and, second, the part played in family and public life by women.

The late 1980s have seen these concerns revived. In 1987 the Institute of Family Studies predicted that 20% of all Australian women born between 1951 and 1956 would remain childless. This estimate was based mainly on information about the increasing age at marriage of such women, their increasing age at first birth and the declining size of the average Australian family, and so did not mean that the proportion of voluntarily childless marriages would reach as high as 20%. It led, however, to a debate about voluntarily childless couples rather than a more general discussion about trends in family life.

The debate did not completely replicate the earlier concerns of the 1904 Royal Commission, but there were similar themes. One such theme was the idea that a declining birthrate would economically disadvantage the nation. Here, the defenders of tradition and the less conservative tended to agree. Michael Barnard, a columnist who identifies himself as writing from the political right rather than the left, argued that:

> Australia's declining birthrate is inextricably bound up with our present lamentable level of unemployment and other economic misfortunes. Smaller families reduce demand, whereas more children increase demand without immediately increasing the labour supply as does immigration. (Age 17/11/87)

Claude Forell, writing from a perspective more sympathetic to the voluntarily childless, and generally less overtly conservative than Barnard's, none the less agreed that smaller families created economic problems: 'Already, dire predictions are being made about the rising proportion of pensioners in the community and the declining proportions of taxpaying wage-earners to provide for them' (Age 11/11/87).

The assumption that a declining birthrate will be economically costly is worth questioning. Certainly, a decline in the proportion of children in a population means that there is a drop in demand for some social services (schools etc.) and a proportionate rise in the demand for others; as the population ages, the proportionate demand for services for the aged will also rise. But the extent to which falling birthrates cause economic decline is surely debatable, given all the many factors to be taken into account—automation, shifts in the economic base and so on. The view that the nation's economy needs more children is based on limited economic horizons and is one to be argued for rather than simply stated.

More importantly, it is worth questioning the notions behind this debatable assumption. Even if there is a clear link between the straightforward economic indicators of national prosperity and rates of reproduction, should policy be directed at preventing population decline in order to bolster GNP or even per capita income? The notion that economic growth is the sole or even the major indicator of social good is one that has been challenged by activists of various kinds. Two challenges have implications worth considering here.

First, environmental activists have been suggesting for two decades now that a fall in population is necessary in global terms for the survival of the planet, and that the Australian ecosystem might not sustain an increase in the local population even if there is enough geographic space for greater numbers. From this point of view, declining birthrates may well be something to welcome in the long term.

A second challenge to the idea that population growth is automatically and correctly needed for economic well-being comes from those who would see equitable distribution of resources as a better indicator of national financial health than the amount of growth in resources—from the proponents of EVE (economically viable everybody) rather than ERM (economically rational man).

Both challenges would make debate about voluntary childlessness as an economic problem somewhat irrelevant and therefore make the creation of any social policy to discourage childlessness irrelevant.

The 1980s debate about childlessness shares an economic assumption—that population increase is necessary—with the earlier debates. I have argued that this assumption is questionable in terms both of evidence and definition. Does the recent debate have anything else in common with earlier ones? Does it, for example, share the moral assumption that selfishness—and especially the selfishness of women— is the root cause of childlessness? The answer is both yes and no. There is a theme of voluntary childlessness indicating the selfishness of modern society, but the notion that heartless women are to blame for it is contested.

Newspaper reports on voluntary childlessness now make much of the notion that couples who chose not to have children do so because they are unwilling to make the sacrifices that parenthood demands. This easily extends to a lament for the abandonment of the virtues of altruism. Again, this lament may come from both sides of the political fence. Barnard, in the article quoted above, regards the moral and spiritual effect of decreasing fertility as even more serious than the economic effect. For him, childlessness is literally unnatural and places society at risk: 'Many of the ills of society ... are brought about by the same denial of caring instincts that operate in at least some cases of self-chosen childlessness'.

The basic solution to this evil for him is a moral regeneration of society. While Forell sees a solution in changes to social policy which would give more economic support to families with children, he, like Barnard, regrets that childlessness is symptomatic of an uncaring society 'in which possessions, individual satisfactions and stylish living are more highly prized than family life, and in which consumption is more desirable than reproduction'.

Comments like these hearken back to the idea of the family as 'haven in a heartless world' (Lasch 1977) and suggest that the theme of selfish childlessness is not dead. They also show the strength of the themes of parenthood as commitment and sacrifice (and Barnard's view shows that the biologically determinist view of parenthood as natural lingers on in the debate, too). But public response to the revived debate on voluntary childlessness suggests that there is not a clear consensus that childless couples are selfish. Letters to newspapers, as well as responses to talk-back shows, etc, show that many people regard the issue as less one of individual selfishness than of lack of support for parents. 'Support', of course, means different things to different people. Traditionalists tend to see the causes of voluntary childlessness in taxation policies which make it difficult for one-income families to afford the amenities we consider desirable in life. Feminists focus more on the lack of support for women who need or wish to combine motherhood with paid work. Both groups tend to argue that motherhood is not given a high enough status in practical terms—frequently giving the difficulty of using public transport systems with small children as an illustration. There are occasional grumbles from men who feel that fatherhood is downgraded. While much of this response defends the rights of the childless, it takes place within the same problematic as does the criticism—voluntary childlessness seems to be an issue of moral concern. This, of course, is what we would expect if there is an ideology of parenthood such as the one I describe.

I have already argued that the economic arguments for increasing the Australian birthrate that underlie concern about voluntary childlessness are not totally convincing. Is it appropriate for policy-makers to be concerned about any moral aspects of the choice not to parent?

The recent debate about couples with no children is based on information about families in general. Voluntarily childless couples are one of the factors contributing to declining birthrates in Australia and elsewhere, but they are not the only factor. Indeed, they would appear to be a relatively small factor, since the proportion of couples with zero completed fertility has rarely exceeded 10% of all Australian marriages over the first half of this century (Spencer 1979), and the number of such couples who would be voluntarily childless must be smaller still. In addition, my data show that childless people may change their minds—even after they have made a firm decision, taken dramatic action and lived happily for some time with the consequences. This suggests that to focus on the voluntarily childless as a cause, or even as a major symptom, of social ill is foolish simply in terms of numbers. In support of this view, I note a recent American study (Jacobson & Heaton 1991) which found that only 3.5% of the men and 2.8% of the women in a national survey reported that they were childless and expected not to have children.

Moreover, I, with other observers, have severe reservations about labelling those who choose not to parent as selfish. I found a variety of attitudes among the couples in my case-study group. Some couples, such as Gary and Gabrielle, the dedicated teachers, struck me as doing a great deal of good for society as a whole; others seemed to lead lives that could be called self-indulgent. The same is true of the parents I know. The argument that voluntary childlessness is significantly related to moral evil strikes me as overstated, at the very least.

I question the need to change the minds of voluntarily childless couples for either economic or moral gain, but, assuming that there were convincing reasons for policy-makers to seek an increase in the birthrate through trying to convince the voluntarily childless that they should become parents, can my study offer any guidelines on how this could be done?

I think it is imperative that we see decisions about parenthood as the result of negotiations with an ideology rather than as the choice of economically rational people who respond to carrots and sticks. Recently, several nations have tried to raise or limit population by decree or by incentive with relatively little success. The 'one-child' policy of China and the disastrous attempts to alter population figures in Rumania both show the futility of simply ordaining that people should have certain kinds of families and making all other choices illegal. Legislation will not, in this case as in many others, automatically condition action, even if severe sanctions are imposed. In the one case, there have been alarming reports of infanticide of girl babies, in the other a horrendous rise in the rates of death from illegal abortion. Basically, as the French have recognised in a series of pronatalist advertisements, babies are a socio-cultural phenomenon, and policies about parenthood need to recognize this fact.

My data suggest that if we wished to encourage the voluntarily childless into parenthood, we need to focus on the conflict between what the Institute of Family Studies has described as the 'ideal of autonomy' and the ideas that I have called the ideology of parenthood. This conflict creates disincentives for some people to become parents, namely those women whose class positions gives them the best chance of satisfying, autonomous careers outside family life.

The disincentives cluster around the ideal of sacrifice, which flows from the idea of commitment. Thus policies that made it possible for commitment to children to extend beyond the boundaries of the immediate family and eased the sacrifices required would remove some at least of the disincentives.

We must, for instance, make it easier for parents (male and female) to combine satisfying paid work with parenthood and to see the two as compatible rather than as opposed choices. This will require changes in attitude towards childcare (which will need to be much more widely available and in a wider range of options); permanent part-time work (as opposed to the use of casual labour); parental leave, as opposed simply to maternity leave (although maternity leave provisions will need to be much increased, too); negotiable working hours which would enable parents to meet their children's needs and so on. Some very recent developments, such as the 1990 decision to allow unpaid parenting leave to fathers as well as mothers, the 1991 signing of ILO Convention 156 about the rights of workers with family responsibilities, and the announcement in 1992 of federal legislation which will make discrimination on the grounds of family responsibility illegal, suggest that change is on the way. But there is still a long way to go. While paternity leave is now a legal principle, the majority of Australian women working for pay in the private sector do not have access to paid maternity leave. And at both federal and state levels, the Liberal Party's proposed dismantling of the existing structure by which working conditions are determined threatens gains that have been made.

While policies that help to reduce the division between the public world of work and the private world of the family by changing the structure of work will do some good, we will also require a change in many of our attitudes to parenting. We will, for example, need to change our views on fathering so that women are not left with the main responsibility for day-to-day care of children and men are not burdened with the total financial responsibility for supporting families. Again, there are some signs that this is happening. The attitude that household work should be shared when both parents are in paid work is well entrenched in public opinion, and the area where it seems that men are taking up some of the work done in the home is indeed that of looking after children. But overall, the bulk of domestic work is still done by women, just as, overall, most workplaces do not sufficiently recognize the fact that most workers have domestic responsibilities towards children, partners, aged parents or all three.

At present, parenting is an activity carried out by consenting adults behind the walls of the family home. The rest of the community is involved in the upbringing of any given child only when there is a major crisis in the home. If parenting were not such an isolated activity, and if it were better supported by the rest of the community, then some of the burdens of sacrifice would be lifted and parenting would become a more attractive option. This is not an unusual argument, but the most usual form of it is demand for financial support for the one-income family, for more helping services such as family counselling, or for some other measure which is seen as returning us to the imaginary good old days of the family-oriented 1950s. I recognize the need for income support for some of the community and have some sympathy for the call for increased services, but I have a rather different vision of how the community could support families. Since some of the steps needed to achieve my vision are not ones which can be taken by policy-makers, I will return to them in the final section of this chapter.

PERSONAL ISSUES: IMPLICATIONS FOR ACTIVISTS

As I noted in the first chapter, my interest in the topic of voluntary childlessness has a strong personal component. I was undecided about having children myself and therefore was interested in those who were childless by choice. I was also interested in them because, as a feminist, I am interested in strategies for liberation, and the issue of the impact of motherhood on women's lives has been much discussed in the women's movement.

Some feminists have suggested that if women avoid motherhood, they will find 'ultimate liberation'. Firestone (1972) suggested that technological changes that did away with the necessity for reproduction would be the forces which put an end to 'sex class' and, with it, female oppression. Movius (1976) argued that women who chose not to have children would be on an equal footing with men in terms of careers. And Wearing (1984), following Movius, suggested that the voluntarily childless could be seen as the utopian counter to ideological commitment to motherhood.

Others have argued that motherhood is a potential source of strength and power for women and that to forego it is dehumanizing rather than liberating.[2]

My study suggests that there is no necessary connection between deciding not to have children and a radical awareness of the ideology of parenthood; thus it is unlikely that the voluntarily childless will be a force for change. They decide not to have children because they in fact accept fully the prevailing ideas about what parenthood represents.

On a personal level, I liked and admired most of the people I interviewed, but the more I thought about their position, the clearer it became to me that I did not particularly wish to emulate their lives. Currently, I am facing the delights and terrors of early motherhood and both enjoying and bewailing the challenge they present. As a feminist, I have long been interested in promoting freedom of choice for women and in changes in ideas about how to behave towards children, either as as a parent or simply as a member of a community. As a novice mother, I am developing some more ideas about how I would like parenthood to be supported. This picks up the theme raised at the end of the last section and is, as I said, not so much a matter of policy as of revolutions in thought.

I have a vision—vague and inchoate because it is developing within the framework of the current ideology of parenthood—of a world that is not split into the two realms of public and private. In such a world, the kind of policy changes I discussed earlier would be automatic. So would many practices that cannot really be established by policy. I can best describe the kinds of thing I mean by talking about my own workplace.

I teach in a large-inner city tertiary institution. Since it is funded by the state, provisions about parental leave policies apply and there is a childcare centre available. In a formal sense, it is much easier for me to combine my paid work in the public sphere with the work of mothering than it is for many women. But every time I take my daughter in to my workplace (because, for example, I am working outside her crèche's hours) I am sharply aware of how much easier things could be if we assumed that private and public lives were not irrevocably divided and that children could be part of the public world.

In my imagined world, even entering the building in which I work would be easier than I currently find it. An architect who assumed that babies and children might sometimes need to be with their working parents would have designed a ramp suitable for prams, pushers and wheelchairs and would have thought about people other than adults using doors, lifts and toilets. Unfortunately, the building was designed before the Second World War and built in the 1950s, so the only access for such vehicles is a back entrance, down a dark and narrow alley well away from car-parking. People who need to bring babies to our workplace lump their carriages up the front stairs or haul toddlers up so that they can enjoy pushing the lift button set at adult chest height.

Once in the building, I am not too badly off. In addition to my own office, there is a large staffroom; so feeding and changing a baby was relatively easy for me, as is entertaining a child for a short time. Our students, however, have nowhere to do any of those things. When the interior of the building was renovated a few years ago it did not occur to anyone (least of all me) to suggest that a small table could be put into one or more of the toilets so that a student with a baby could change nappies there. I have in fact encountered students wrestling with this task on the tiled floor.

I am not the only person who sometimes finds it necessary to bring a child to work, and I am now struck by the number of offices in which there must be odd items of equipment—a packet of disposable nappies, a set of toddlers' blocks, a box of crayons and a colouring book—for such contingencies. Yet none of us have ever thought of collecting these supplies and leaving them available in the staffroom in the same way that we leave bottle-openers, salt shakers, an old saucepan and other useful bits and pieces for communal use. We accept that workers will bring some of their private needs (for the occasional drink after a long hard day, for example) into the public world, but our image of work does not include the presence of children. Even workplaces where there is formal provision for childcare have not managed to break down the barriers between paid work and the unpaid work of parenting, because all of us assume that commitment to a child is basically something that concerns only the family around that child. If we saw commitment as a social matter—if all of us took it for granted that whether we were parents or not we owed some responsibility to the next generation—workplaces would become very different. So would schools if they included not only teachers, children and parents but also had advice from visitors, volunteer workers and school council members who did not have children attending. And if the community as a whole took more responsibility for the safety and welfare of its children, some of the danger of assault which faces some children within or outside their homes might vanish. At the same time, the weight of anxiety about how to act as a parent might be eased for many if they felt that they could ask friends, fellow workers or acquaintances for advice or help in family matters as easily as asking them the way to the nearest post office.

And if attitudes towards responsibility for children changed, how debates about national budgets would alter! We might even find ourselves moving towards the great day, as a popular tea towel message notes, when family services and education funding would be a priority and the Air Force had to run cake stalls to buy bombers. Such policy changes could only arise if we indeed had a revolution in thought.

The question is, how would such a revolution be created? A necessary first step is for us to understand parenthood as a sociocultural phenomenon, one in which ideology plays a part, and for the recognition that we are all living within and negotiating with ideology. This is going to require rather different analyses from those traditionally produced by critics of ideology. Rather than telling the rest of the world that it lives in false consciousness, we need to start thinking about the ways in which all of us negotiate with reigning ideas.

My research began with one personal question, which has now been answered, but has left me with another set of questions. I have become convinced that the prevailing notion of what parenting means is the reason that some people choose not to be parents, and that their choice is thus not really a free one. Until we can re-imagine parenting so that the barriers (which are, above all, ideological) to genuinely social commitment disappear, choices about parenthood will be limited by our inability to imagine change. And if we cannot imagine change, how can we create it?

appendix 1 **METHODOLOGY**

. . . .

My initial strategy for locating couples was to ask friends whom I knew or suspected to be voluntarily childless. I obtained two couples in this way. A colleague at work volunteered herself and her husband, as did a friend of my husband. A friend in Canberra located two couples in her network, and two friends in Melbourne found one couple each. As the study became known, two couples contacted me and volunteered themselves.

I began interviewing in late 1979 and continued to study the couples until at least early 1984. In most cases I carried out four semi-structured interviews. The first was done individually, with husband and wife being asked the same questions on separate occasions. After about a year in most cases, a second, joint interview was held. After a further period of eighteen months to two years I did a final joint interview. In some cases, I kept in touch with couples or was given information about them by intermediaries right through the period of writing my thesis and up to the final draft of this book.

I used an interview schedule with structured questions and probes and tried to ask the major questions in the same words for each respondent. But I also pursued topics as they were raised and followed the themes suggested in conversation as much as possible. So I did not always ask the questions in the same order, and in each interview a different aspect of the questions might predominate.

The interviews were tape-recorded, with permission from the respondents. At the same time, I made notes of responses. In the third and final interview, in addition to questions, I asked the couples to make lists of people in their networks, to diagram their networks and to describe the characteristics of the people in their networks (using stick-on symbols). I also asked them to draw or diagram their views of the world and their perceptions of how people came to be parents or childless, as well as to respond to a series of cartoons on the subject.

These interviews provided a range of data in several forms. I had views from husbands and wives that permitted analysis on lines of gender—something that had been missing from some studies. I had data from different points in time that could allow me to see the changes brought about by the process of negotiating with ideology. Because I had used semi-structured interviews I could compare one couple with another, and I had data in several forms: diagrams, notes and transcripts. All interviews were transcribed in toto. I transcribed all of the individual interviews and most of the second interviews myself, putting them directly into a card file. The third interviews and a few of the second ones were professionally transcribed, and I then filed them. As the research went on, I began to develop headings based on themes as well as on questions and to cross-index material using coloured cards.

Most of the analysis was done in the time-honoured fashion (before the development of computerised text-coding) of shuffling cards or transcript sheets into piles on the floor, reshuffling them, losing some, discovering that I was sitting on them and shuffling them again. As themes began to emerge, it was possible to create new headings and further index material. At times, it was useful to summarise responses to a particular theme and work from the summary, going back to the cards as a check. As the research went on, the case-study group changed. While at the outset all eleven couples met my criteria for voluntary childlessness, by the third interview one couple had two children, one wife had decided she wanted children and three couples had separated. The third interviews were held with seven intact and childless couples, one of whom was now in dispute about parenthood, and two formerly married childless women.

Despite the frustrations of trying to deal with complex data and with data which kept changing rather than fitting my tidy definitions, the case-study method was the most suitable one for my purposes. It provided a sharp focus on how couples come to childlessness that a larger number of shallower interviews could not offer. Moreover, the range of information enabled detailed analysis of the world of the childless from a variety of perspectives. A theme could be examined in a variety of contexts as it emerged in response to different questions at different times.

Having a time-series of snap-shots (which in the end extended beyond the formal period of the research) rather than the single picture provided by one-off interviews is a useful and unique feature of my data, but the major use of the repeated interviews was that it enabled me to develop theory in interaction with data and to test my theories. The process of taking insights from 'the field', refining them intellectually, then returning to the field to try out the resultant theory is usually called 'grounded theory' (Glaser & Strauss 1968). While I did not begin in a spirit of total innocence and go on to develop theory from data alone, I did have the opportunity to collect some impressions and pieces of information, think about them and develop some kind of framework, then go back to try out the framework on some new data. By the time of the last interview, I was consciously seeking to test my ideas about ideology. In this way I was able to achieve something of the rigour that hypothesis-testing can bring to analysis. This last step would not have been possible without repeated interviews.

The case-study technique was also, I felt, ethically appropriate. Oakley (1981) and Finch (1984) have raised the question of exploitation of respondents, especially female ones, by interviewers who keep the traditional 'objective' distance between themselves and the researched. This distance is harder to maintain with repeated interviews. On the one hand, a series of interviews increases the researcher's feeling of indebtedness to the researched (especially if she has been given dinner and overnight accommodation by them, as happened to me several times). On the other, it enables the researched to insist that their own ideas be heard or to ask questions of the researcher as she becomes less of a stranger.

This lack of the traditional researcher's objectivity caused occasional dilemmas during the interviews, where I worried about biasing the responses, but in the end it strengthened the analysis in subtle ways. At one level, knowing the couples as people as well as subjects made it possible to pick up errors in transcription or filing ('Hang on, that doesn't sound like Kate'). At another level, it made me aware of deficiencies in data, especially where I was aware that personal reactions to my interviewees might affect my analytical judgement.

The core of the research was qualitative, but it contains some quantitative data as well. At times, I found it useful to count the number of statements made by my interviewees, and I report those figures because 'twelve out of the twenty-two' is a better basis for judging the plausibility of an account than 'most', 'some' or 'about half'. And the book also contains data from a questionnaire, filled in by ninety-seven voluntarily childless couples and analysed numerically. This subsidiary data is the result of more-or-less accidental circumstances but has been very useful for my purposes.

Some unexpected publicity for the study led to the collection of the questionnaire data. I had begun searching for couples to study and was considering strategies like advertising in family-planning clinics or writing to newspapers when I was interviewed by a local journalist, who published a story about the research, including my request that interested couples write to me care of the university. Rather to my surprise, within three or four weeks I had received nearly sixty letters. Moreover, other journalists were interested. I did several radio interviews where I repeated the appeal, and as a result received another ten or so letters. The original piece was reprinted in two other papers. All told I received about 120 letters from interested couples, plus a few from people who were not voluntarily childless in terms of my definition but wished to comment on the issue.

It was obviously impossible to handle so many case studies, and even single interviews would be difficult for an unfunded postgraduate with limited time, so I decided to send a questionnaire to the couples who contacted me. I drafted one and pretested it on colleagues for clarity. It reflected the questions I was asking in the first interview with the case-study group and the ideas I was playing with at that time and so said nothing about ideology.

All the couples who contacted me were sent a covering letter restating the criteria for inclusion as voluntarily childless, two copies of the questionnaire (one for each partner) and a stamped addressed envelope.

I received completed questionnaires from 106 couples, ninety-seven of whom met the criteria. Their responses were coded and analysed, using the SPSS package. Since the questionnaire group, like the respondents in all studies of voluntary childlessness, is a volunteer sample of a population whose parameters are unknown, complex statistical manipulation of the data was pointless. Cross-tabulations of frequencies were used to search for patterns. Chi-square was computed but must be interpreted in terms of the non-random nature of the sample.

The questionnaire adds breadth to the study, and the larger group provides a check for data coming from the case studies. It is used to complement and amplify some of the analysis of the case studies rather than to generate insights on its own account.

The methodology of the study seems to have worked reasonably well. I needed a method that could give me insights into hitherto unexplored questions about ideology. Since ideology works in and through language, a technique that would enable in-depth considerations of people's words would be especially useful. Since I was interested in a process that occurred over time, a longitudinal approach was needed. And the methodology had to be suitable for a single person with little funding.

The qualitative approach met the first two needs and the case studies the second two. The research has the strengths of qualitative research in general, of rich and complex data, and the added strength of longitudinal data, which may be analysed from a variety of perspectives. The major weakness of the methodology is that there is no comparison between the voluntarily childless and those who have children. I describe the interaction of the childless with the ideology of parenthood and draw inferences from other studies about the ways in which parents interact with the same ideology, but the research would be strengthened by data from a group of parents matched as closely as possible with the case-study couples. Without such data, I cannot tell whether the outcome of parents' interaction with the ideology of parenthood is different from that of the childless because there are two fundamentally different processes at work or because there is a similar process mediated in different ways.

The results of this study do not provide a good basis for certain sorts of generalization. They should not be regarded as definitely representing patterns among the entire population of the voluntarily childless in Australia unless further research can demonstrate that my sample is indeed representative of that population. But the understandings generated from this research can provide the basis for further exploration of the process by which some people choose to be childless and the broader processes by which people confront ideologies.

. . . .

Figure 1 *Occupation of sample*

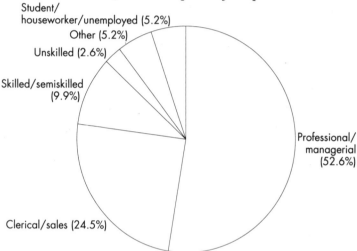

Student/
houseworker/unemployed (5.2%)

Other (5.2%)

Unskilled (2.6%)

Skilled/semiskilled
(9.9%)

Professional/
managerial
(52.6%)

Clerical/sales (24.5%)

Figure 2 *Education of sample*

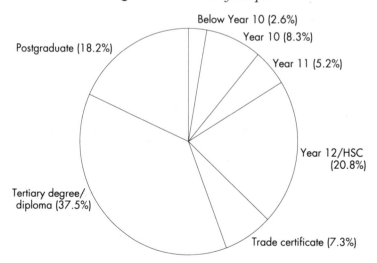

Below Year 10 (2.6%)

Year 10 (8.3%)

Year 11 (5.2%)

Postgraduate (18.2%)

Year 12/HSC
(20.8%)

Tertiary degree/
diploma (37.5%)

Trade certificate (7.3%)

Figure 3 *Father's occupation*

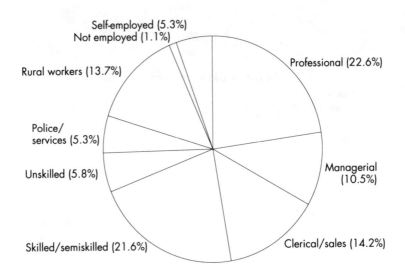

Figure 4 *Enjoyment of the job (questionnaire group)*

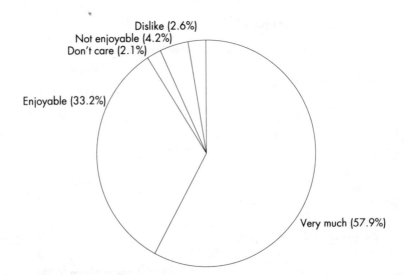

Figure 5 *Energy put into the job (questionnaire group)*

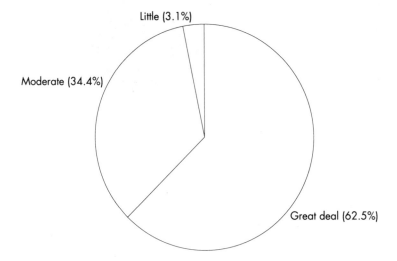

Figure 6 *Importance of the job (questionnaire group)*

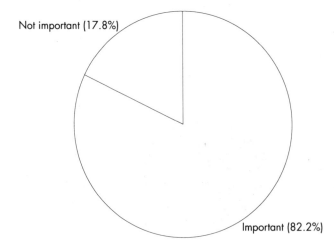

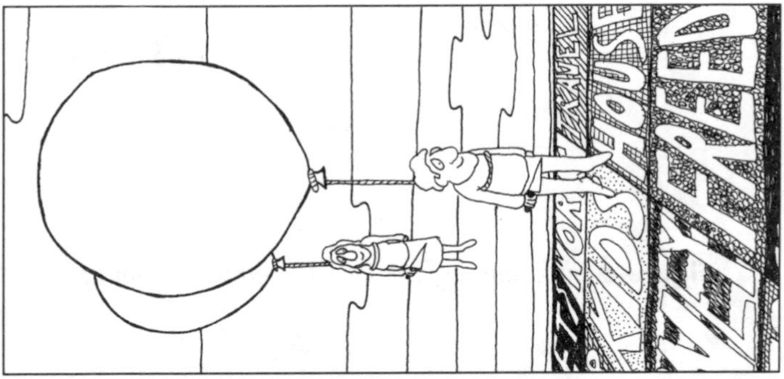

Figure 9 *The thinkers*

Figure 8 *The balloonists*

Figure 7 *The big black ball*

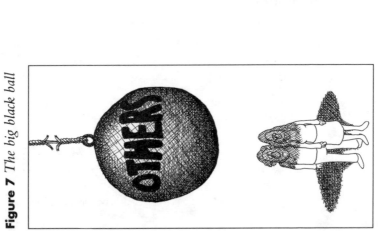

Table 1 *Case study identity statements summarized*

Husbands	Wives
Andrew 'I run a snooker parlour', well-educated, embittered with life, open and forthright.	**Alison** 'I'm me', 'the teaching identity is important' 'the home-maker image isn't as strong', 'Somebody who gets overextended', happy and optimistic, likes to read, cook, listen to music, sing, talk. Canadian, eastern suburbs, not western suburbs-type person (i.e. middle class rather than working class).
Bill Not descriptively outgoing. Librarian. Lives in an inner suburb. Aged 31, married, classical education, logical and orderly.	**Bridget** Married woman, academic, ambitious, likes to do things to the utmost of her ability.
Chris 'My own individual self', not affected by others, independence important, not worried about future, it's important to make sure that what you do benefits others.	**Clare** 'Don't think there's anything important to say', 24 years old, average, female, 'run of the mill, ordinary, nondescript individual'.
David 'A person', average intelligence, easy-going, nothing exciting, sports-minded.	**Diane** Values sincerity, cares about people, going through 'an incredible transition period' from preoccupation with domestic life, e.g. renovating to less 'superficial' concern with identity. 'I value people for trying ... if they've worked out who they think they are'.
Eric Eric, aged 33, male, nothing else.	**Evelyn** Public servant, has economics degree, 'work tends to be fairly all-consuming', interested in wine lifestyle—married with no children.
Felix 'Proud and lazy', takes things easy, physicist, an Englishman, scientist.	**Fiona** 'I am Fiona', 'wouldn't have a clue' what's important about her 'beyond the fact that I'm me'. If meeting new people, tells them she is a political scientist and a housewife. 'I've gained a lot of identity out of politics'.
Gary A perfectionist, easy-going, open-minded, but with certain likes and dislikes, not ambitious, enjoys leisure, believes we should help people.	**Gabrielle** 'If it was a person who didn't know anything, I would just say, I'm a teacher', married, very keen teacher, good unionist, slightly left-wing', keen on health, sport, loves animals, loves kids, gets on well with them, 'that's probably why I love teaching'. Happy, lucky.

cont. next page

Table 1 *cont.*

Husbands	Wives
Henry Individualist values.	**Heather** 'Sounds like the beginning of an application letter' Aged 38. Born in Melbourne, eldest of three, state school then scholarship to private school. Academically able, uncomfortable at university. Taught, married, then went into research positions; spent 6 months overseas with husband then back into research.
Ian 'I'm not a careerist'. Interested in chess and music. Likes 'comfortable' existence. Marriage is 'stable' component of his life. 'A gatherer of useless information', likes reading. Numerous hobbies: horticulture, boat-building, current affairs.	**Isabel** 'If it was a work-related matter. I suppose I'd introduce myself in terms my job'. Sociologist, interested in social change, 'a joiner', enjoys activities, interested in horticulture, likes writing letters, likes music, reading, current current affairs.
John Sales manager, loves job, successful in job. Interests—wife, sport, renovating. Came from very close family.	**Judy** 'I'm Judy and I work for a drug company, I do a nursing advisory service for them, which I love.' Enjoys working. 'Don't think of myself in terms of John' (i.e. as wife) 'I think the most important thing about me is that I work and enjoy working.' Close to parents.
Kevin 'Oh, I'm a 32-year-old economist who's got a 16-year-old brain'. Enjoys things that people his age don't normally do. Main passions, music, apart from his wife, then travel.	**Kate** 'Oh, I'm just me'. 'It's been years since I had to associate with anybody [who didn't already know me].' 'Usually I just tell 'em my job'. Musical interests.

Table 2 *Questionnaire group perceptions of marriage*

	Strongly Agree No.	%	Agree No.	%	Neutral No.	%	Disagree No.	%	Strongly Disagree No.	%
We argue a lot (a)	3	1.6	20	10.5	27	14	74	38.7	67	35.1
We agree on most things(b)	59	30.4	114	58.8	11	5.7	8	4.1	2	1
We tend to have separate groups of friends(c)	2	1.1	18	9.5	22	11.6	92	48.4	56	29.5
We have most of our friends in common(b)	63	32.5	92	47.4	24	12.4	13	6.7	2	1.0

(a) n=191 (b) n=194, (c) n = 190,

POWER IN OUR MARRIAGE

The wife has power in the marriage   9.7%

The husband has power   17.1%

We share power   73.2%

Table 3 *Attitudes of respondents from large families by position and sex (total %)*

| | Eldest | | | | Non-eldest | | | |
| | M | | F | | M | | F | |
	No.	%	No.	%	No.	%	No.	%
Certainty								
Absolute	3	18.8	4	23.5	8	50	2	11.8
Pretty determined	1	6.3	0	0	3	18.8	0	0
Not quite sure	1	6.3	2	11.8	0	0	1	5.9
Quality of decision								
Definitely decided	4	25.0	4	23.5	8	50.0	9	52.9
I drifted	0	0	0	0	2	12.5	2	11.8
Still deciding /drifting	1	6.3	2	11.8	1	6.3	0	0
Timing of decision								
When young	1	6.3	1	5.9	1	6.3	6	54.5
Adult—before marriage	1	6.3	3	17.6	6	37.5	1	9.1
Just before marriage	1	6.3	2	11.8	1	6.3	1	9.1
After marriage	2	12.5	0	0	3	18.8	3	17.6
I would make a bad parent								
Not a reason	3	18.8	1	6.3	7	43.8	3	18.8
Unimportant reason	0	0	1	6.3	1	6.3	1	6.3
Important reason	2	12.5	3	18.8	3	18.8	7	43.8

n = 33

Table 4 *Fears of parenthood by feelings about childhood*

'I would make a bad parent' as reason for childlessness

Feelings about childhood	Not a reason		Unimportant reason		Important reason	
	No.	%	No.	%	No.	(row %)
Childhood happy	84	50.3	31	18	52	31.1
Childhood not happy	2	8	5	20	18	72.0

Table 5 *Questionnaire group decisions and discussions (a)*

Decision made	No.	%
Before marriage—when young	43	22.5
Before marriage—when adult	50	26.2
When thinking of marrying	30	15.7
After marriage	66	34.6
Discussed often	44	23.0
Discussed sometimes	98	51.3
Discussed rarely	48	25.1

(a) Percentages total more than 100 because respondents could check more than one answer.

Table 6 *Reasons for not wanting children by sex (row %)*

Reason	Not a reason		An unimportant reason		An important reason		
	M	F	M	F	M	F	n
Overpopulation	65.6	51.5	29.2	37.1	5.2	11.3	193
Children don't fit with my career plans	48.4	35.1	27.4	38.1	24.2	26.8	192
My spouse doesn't want them	22.1	31.3	28.4	26.0	49.5	4.27	191
The sort of people I associate with don't consider children a priority	86.5	83.5	11.5	15.5	2.1	1.0	193
I don't think I'd make a good parent{a}	54.2	35.4	18.8	18.8	27.1	45.8	192
I like to be free of the constraints children impose	2.1	6.2	17.7	17.5	80.2	76.3	193
I want to travel	28.4	25.0	33.7	34.4	37.9	40.6	191
I don't want the responsibility of having children{b}	28.1	14.4	33.3	25.8	38.5	59.8	193
Financial	65.1	72.2	21.9	15.5	12.5	12.5	193

a Significant at .015
b Significant at .008

Table 7 *The varieties of commitment*

Husbands	Wives
Andrew Focus on moral responsibility. What will I teach a child about right and wrong? Clearly related to his occupation (academic philosopher who was unable to find a job in a tertiary institution and at the time of interview was running a billiard saloon). What if my child's personality is incompatible with mine? (Related to his experiences as an adopted child.) The unstated corollary is that you cannot give back a child once it is in your family.	**Alison** Long-term commitment needed. The child requires individual attention and so cannot be 'shunted' to day-care centres, and the commitment exists for years after infancy.
Bill You must be prepared to accept child regardless of how it turns out, even if it is handicapped.	**Bridget** Parents owe children more a than children owe parents, since children do not ask to be born. One should follow through the commitment to a job, conflicts arise and the commitment may be diluted, which is not a good thing for job or child, and which she would find unsatisfying.
Chris Parenting involves not just hard work but responsibility which takes over life and alters it completely. There is a need for an extended system, so that it's not just 'two parents who can't do anything else except look after the child'.	**Clare** In general, parenthood is an irrevocable commitment. Unlike buying a car or a house, it allows no change of mind. It is also a long-term prospect. 'The nine months while you are pregnant are not be too bad, it's the twenty years after.' Personally, 'I might be afraid of responsibility.'
David When he began thinking of having children 'I didn't have the responsibility'. Parents must be 'persistent' and 'patient'. Bad parents turn children into 'discarded toys' but they still have the duties of bringing them up and looking after intellectual and spiritual welfare, as well as physical care.	**Diane** Children are a 'tie'. So is having a dog, which she does. She sometimes wishes it would go away and leave her free of responsibility but 'I could never do anything about getting rid of it because it's there', and because she loves it. Having children would evoke the same feelings, only more strongly. Also, having children would be a greater tie. In particular, it would make working impossible. 'What I do I do completely' suggests that children would mean completely stopping outside work
Eric 'They [children] are a worry.'	**Evelyn** She cannot see herself able to 'do the right thing' by children—which probably means staying home to look after them.

cont. next page

Table 7 *cont.*

Husbands	Wives
Felix Children require long-term commitment from both spouses, though the wife is usually the more heavily tied-down member	**Fiona** 'Worries about how she would educate children. 'I'm a very disillusioned educationist' who would either have to teach her children at home or send the boys back to her husband's old school in England, where they would get a classical education. 'God knows where I would send girls.'
Gary & Gabrielle No discernible vision of commitment	
Henry Children carry with them a responsibility, just as his dog does. Because the dog is for 'my amusement not for its own' he should, as a moral responsibility, cater to its amusement by taking it for walks. This would be a more pressing demand if he had children. (This compares with Diane's attitude to her dog, and with Bridget's formulation that those who do not ask to be born owe less than those who in a sense demand their birth.)	**Heather** Recounts a 'responsibility' dream, in which she fears that she has forgotten to feed and care for a baby she has somehow acquired.
Ian Parents are obliged to look after a child's physical and spiritual needs. Parenthood is a 'lottery' because the personality of the child may or may not be compatible with those of the parents. (Cf. Andrew and Bill.) The implication here is that obligation includes being unable to give up a child once it arrives.	**Isabel** Parents must put children's demands first. 'I mean, if I had a child here now and it was screaming in the bedroom as I was talking to you, we couldn't as fellow human beings just sit here and ignore it!'
John Hard to discern the vision of commitment. John seems clear that he follows Judy's decision.	**Judy** Judy's account of why she would make, in here own eyes, a poor parent implies that parental responsibility extends beyond doing the best one can and that parents are in the end accountable for the actions of their children. (When her parents went to a psychiatrist for help after her sister's attempted suicide, they were 'devastated' to learn that their behaviour was at the root of the problem. Judy appears to accept that her parents did cause the suicide attempt, although she is quite clear that they had no intention of doing so. So parents who are loving and who do their best for their offspring are still held to be culpable if things go wrong.)

Table 7 *cont.*

Husbands	Wives
Kevin His comments on responsibility centre on the issue of whether he is a fit person to have children. He sees himself as having a quick temper, an unstable family background, and a desire for order and logic which makes him and children incompatible. The implication is that it is a more responsible action not to have any children.	**Kate** It is part of parental responsibility not to be unfair to children. It would be unfair of her to work and have children, but she is 'very career-oriented' and would not want to stop work. Since there are some health problems in her family, it would also be unfair to pass them on.

Table 8 *Perceptions of childlessness as selfish among the case-study couples*

TYPE 1 It's not selfish (and I'm not selfish for being childless)

Chris People say I'm selfish, but I don't think I am. It's not selfish because 'we are not affecting anybody else'. It's not selfish, it's 'sensible'.

Gary You can be selfish whether you have children or not. I'm not selfish because 'I spend more time with some kids than their own parents'.

Gabrielle In my job I give a lot of myself to the children I teach, so I am not selfish. I can be unselfish because I don't have children demanding things of me at home.

John I haven't ever been called selfish. I don't think I am.

Judy Great-grandmother accuses me of selfishness for depriving her of grand-children. I don't think I'm selfish.

Isabel The media paint the childless as selfish. Ian and I aren't selfish. We like children and we look after our friends' kids. I believe in community childcare.

Kate I'm not selfish. Parents make choices that affect others, but 'nobody misses out by the fact that I don't have children'.

TYPE 2 It depends on your definition

Diane It is a 'crummy' reason to give for having children that you will be selfish if you don't.

Evelyn 'I depends on your priorities.' Since ours are not having children, we are not selfish.

cont. next page

Table 8 *cont.*

TYPE 2 It depends on your definition

Isabel It can be a matter of selfishness or unselfishness, whatever you decide. We would be selfish if we just made money and didn't care about others. Parents may be 'parasites' just as much as the childless. A cousin who argued that it's selfish not to pass on wealth to descendants wasn't thinking of wider responsibilities.

Judy Others told me I was selfish, but eventually I decided that I had no need to defend my decision because it's not selfish to my mind!

Kevin Others may see us as selfish. That's their definition, not ours. We are 'mature' and have worked through the problem.

TYPE 3 It would be selfish to have them

Chris Is it unselfish to have children for no good reason?

Felix You can argue that it is selfish to have children if you mistreat them.

Fiona With my background as an only child 'I couldn't cope' with children [so by implication, it would be selfish to try].

Gary Lots of reasons given for having children are selfish—'to have somebody dependent on them', 'emulating themselves' or 'to look after them in old age'. Parents can be as much of a drain on society as dole-bludgers.

Henry It would be a poor reason to have children, just to avoid being selfish.

Heather Parents are just as likely as the childless to have selfish motives—'perhaps more likely'.

Ian It's both fallacious and selfish to say that a child will support you in old age, though it's only the childless who are accused of selfishness ... Having children to pass on property is selfish. Parents think only in terms of the family unit, and thus may be selfish.

Judy 'It would've been selfish to have turned round and had kids purely for my old age, as so many people were insinuating I should do.'

Kate If people are selfish they will be bad parents, so the notion that it's selfish to be childless is false. [By implication, if you had children to avoid the accusation of selfishness, then you'd be selfish.]

Table 8 *cont.*

TYPE 4 It is selfish and I'm selfish, but ...

Clare 'I think we are totally selfish' but that is just my personality, and I can't alter it.

Diane I'm selfish because I put personal growth first, but 'that's where I'm at' so it doesn't worry me.

Eric Has been called selfish 'and that's very true, I suppose' but 'we don't have to produce children to prove anything'. This accusation 'has been around for centuries' [and by implication is thus of no great account].

Evelyn Spoke of herself as selfish. When asked if she really was, said 'maybe that's just convention'.

Fiona We are selfish because we 'want each other to ourselves' but that is not 'nasty selfishness'.

TYPE 5 It's selfish, and I'm selfish

Clare It is selfish, because we don't want to give up our existing lifestyle.

David We are selfish, because money and lifestyle is a reason for us not having children.

Evelyn Since we like our lifestyle, and don't have children partly in order to maintain it, then we are selfish.

Gabrielle If it is selfish to want to maintain an interesting job which gives self-esteem, then I'm selfish.

John Having children would alter the social life I enjoy, and 'from a purely selfish point of view' that would be the biggest change.

Kevin 'I'm bloody selfish' because I don't want children 'imposing on me'.

Table 9 *World-views of the childless couples*

Type	Viewer	Divisions in the world	Where are parents located?	Where are the voluntarily childless located?	Where is viewer located?
SOCIAL LOCATION VIEW	**Chris**	*Fortunate* and *unfortunate* in terms of degree of choice	Either category. If they want and have children and the children live up to their expectations, they are fortunate	Always fortunate, having chosen	Fortunate
	Clare	*Haves* and *have nots* in terms of material conditions and experiences	Today, those who choose parenthood are haves. In the past, this was not true: some haves were parents against their intentions	All haves today	Haves
	Eric	*Haves* and *have nots* in material and emotional terms	More among the have nots. (But this is the larger group anyway)	More among the haves, because of 'educational and economic superiority ... they have alternatives available to them'	Haves
	John	*Haves*, *have mores* and *haven't gots*. The last group may never have had or may have voluntarily given away material resources	All groups	All groups	Haves

Table 9 *cont.*

Type	Viewer	Divisions in the world	Where are parents located?	Where are the voluntarily childless located?	Where is viewer located?
	Judy	There are three connected lines dividing the world into six types. On one line are *haves* or *steak-eaters* and *have nots* or *Chum-eaters*. On another those who try to change the world. *Flag wavers* vs the *apathetic*. Finally those who are *promoters* of women's independence and those who are *denigrators*	All groups	Mainly flag-wavers, steak-eaters and promoters of women's causes	Flag-waving, steak-eating, promoter of women
CHARACTER VIEW	*Diane*	Those who are *inner-directed* and question things and those who *accept* the status quo. A few move towards questioning, but get *wiped out*	Mostly accepting, though some make a conscious inner-directed choice	More likely to question, but may be locked into acceptance of materialism	Moving towards inner direction
	Evelyn	*Type A* achievers and *type B* non-achievers. While these are personalities, they are associated with background. Type A is largely middle-class and B is working-class	Mainly working-class (the larger group) and thus B	More likely to be As—middle-class educated 'achievement freak'	A middle-class 'overachiever'. (type A)
	Felix	You can only typify actions—as silly or sensible	Can be either sensible or silly	Tends to be sensible, because conscious of choice	No comment

cont. next page

Table 9 *cont.*

Type	Viewer	Divisions in the world	Where are parents located?	Where are the voluntarily childless located?	Where is viewer located?
	Fiona	*Intelligent* people and *idiots*. Also the (sexually) moral and immoral	Either	Tend to be intelligent	Intelligent
CHARACTER VIEW	**Gary**	Politically left *thinkers* and three kinds of conservatives: churchy moral ones, *Country Party* types and selfish greedy *Liberals*	All types	Mainly thinkers	Thinker
LIFESTYLE VIEW	**Gabrielle**	People who seek esteem and satisfaction through *work* (mainly male) or through *family* (mainly female) or *peer group* (the young) or creative pursuits—*fringe people*	Mainly family and fringe people, though some are peer people	Always work people	Work
	Henry	Those whose lives are dominated by *work* because they choose it. Those who do *not* choose it. Those whose lives are dominated by *hobbies* or *friends and family*	Mainly in the two work groups, since parenthood is a job	In all groups	Friends and family
	Heather	On one line of division, people *live alone* or are *companionate*. On another, they are oriented towards the *public* or the *private* sphere. A 2 x 2 table	All groups	Mainly public-oriented and living alone	Public-oriented and companionate

Table 9 *cont.*

Type	Viewer	Divisions in the world	Where are parents located?	Where are the voluntarily childless located?	Where is viewer located?
	Isabel	While there are many varieties of lifestyle, there are two main sets of values: *traditionalists* and *non-traditionalists*	Traditionalists	Non-traditionalists	Non-tradition-alist
	Kevin	The *work-oriented* who want money; the work-oriented who get *satisfaction* from the *job*; the *leisure-oriented*	Most are work- and money-oriented	Leisure-oriented	Leisure-oriented
	Kate	*Family-oriented*, who work to support their families; *security-oriented and independence valuing*	Security- or family-oriented	Security or independence valuing	Security-oriented

Table 10 *Use of the word* ideology

Chris	No, unless ideology is seen as 'culture'. And media are 'the culture of the day'.
Clare	No comment.
Diane	The problem is that most people lack a thought-out ideology to guide their decisions.
Eric	Ideology is just environmental conditioning. Wouldn't use the word.
Evelyn	Ideology is peer-group pressure.
Felix	Doesn't know what the word means. Anyway, it is a matter of choice rather than ideology.
Fiona	*Ideology* is a term used to describe political ideas only.
Gary	Ideology is not connected with childlessness.
Gabrielle	Ideology is not connected with childlessness.
Henry	Religion could provide ideological pressure to have children.
Heather	Once there was religious and social emphasizing that 'large families were your social duty'. That was ideology. No longer extant.
Isabel	A relevant word. But how you see ideology depends on the extent to which you have conformed to it—e.g. if married you will find the ideology of parenthood harder to see.
John	Not relevant.
Judy	Not relevant, because it's not ideology, it's 'society'.
Kevin	Ideology is present, but 'not in all cases'. Having children may be the result of 'inculcating' from family and peer group (ideology) or, by implication, the result of free choice (non-ideology).
Kate	Ideology 'can be' relevant. No further comment.

Table 11 *Questionnaire group response to question 'Do you think you are under pressure to have children?' by sex*

	Male No	%	Female No.	%
No	48	50	49	51.6
Yes	48	50	46	48.4
Total	96		96	

Table 12 *Sources of pressure to have children listed by the questionnaire group*

Source	Listed by (%)			
Mother	2.6)			
Father	0.5)			
Both parents	4.1)	Family in general 17.5%)		
Other close family	9.3)			
More distant family	1.0)	)		
Friends	5.7)		) Some source listed 67.5%	
Peers	4.1)	Peers in general 9.8%		
Social pressure	13.4)	Social pressure in general 13.4%		
Other (inc. more than 1 source)	26.8			
No pressure listed	32.5			

Table 13 *The network diagrams of the childless couples*

Individual (ego)	Size of network	Proportion of males	Proportion of kin	Proportion childless	Proportion with same values as ego
Clare	13	5 (38.4)	1 (7.6)	7 (53.8)	12 (92.3)
Chris	8	3 (37.5)	3 (37.5)	3 (37.5)	8 (100)
Diane	13	3 (23)	3 (23)	6 (46.1)	5 (38.4)
Evelyn	19	9 (47.3)	1 (5.2)	12 (63.1)	11 (57.8)
Eric	9	3 (33)	1 (11.1)	7 (77.7)	9 100)
Fiona	10	5 (50)	2 (20)	3 (30)	9 (90)
Felix	15	8 (46.6)	6 (40)	5 (33)	11 (73.3)
Gabrielle	22	9 (40.9)	1 (4.5)	3 (13.6)	8 (36.3)
Gary	13	6 (46.1)	1(7.6)	1 (7.6)	9 (69.2)
Heather	12	4 (33)	1 (8.3)	7 (58.3)	8 (66)
Henry	7	2 (28.5)	1 (14.2)	3 (42.8)	3 (42.8)
Isabel	9	3 (33)	3 (33)	3 (33)	3 (33)
Judy	13	3 (23)	3 (23)	7 (53.8)	3 (23)
John	11	9 (81.8)	5 (45.4)	4 (36.3)	8 (72.7)
Kate	19	9 (47.3)	6 (31.5)	13 (68.4)	9 (47.3)
Kevin	10	6 (60)	3 (30)	6 (60)	5 (50)

Note: Two couples, the As and the Bs, had dropped out of the project by this stage and therefore are not included in this table.

Table 14   *Discussion of childlessness with the network*

| | % With whom it was discussed | | |
	Ever	Sometimes	Often
Clare	84.6	23	61.5
Chris	87.5	37.5	50
Diane	53.7	15.3	38.4
Evelyn	94.7	73.6	21
Eric	33	33	0
Fiona	90	60	30
Felix	59.9	46.6	13.3
Gabrielle	100	36.3	63.6
Gary	100	84.6	15.3
Heather	74.9	66.6	8.3
Henry	100	85.7	14.2
Isabel	0	88.8	0
Judy	100	46.1	53.8
John	55.1	36.3	18.8
Kate	52.6	36.8	15.7
Kevin	60	40	20

Note: Two couples, the As and the Bs, had dropped out of the project by this stage and therefore are not included in this table.

Table 15 *Reasons for not wanting children—spouses compared*
(• = shared reason)

Andrew Worries about population	**Alison** Fear of pregnancy
• Dislikes children • Enjoys the freedom of childless life	• Dislikes some children • Lifestyle is satisfactory without them
Economics	Effect on her career
• Fears about 'messing kids up'	• Fears failure as a parent because of her temper, and fears 'to some extent' messing kids up
Bill • Commitment—you have to take whatever you get with kids	**Bridget** • Kids demand commitment which would dilute her commitment to work
Effect of children on the freedom of lifestyle	Fear of failure and not coping as a parent
No rational reason to have kids	Children would affect her marriage
• Found kids exhausting to be with	• Found kids exhausting to be with
Chris Kids demand commitment	**Clare** Effect on career
• Fears failure because of the examples he has seen	• Fear of failure based on examples seen
• Kids demand constant attention	• Kids demand attention
• Overpopulation	• World population problems (which are not, however, a problem for Australia)
• Busy lifestyle would be affected	• Children would cause 'lost opportunities' in a busy lifestyle
Economic reasons	No maternal instinct

Table 15 *cont.*

David	**Diane**
• He lacks the responsibility demanded of parents	• The demands of responsibility placed on parents are enormous, and the support small
• Fear of failure as a parent related to his own upbringing	• Fear of failure as a parent, because of lack of training.
• Changes to lifestyle (domestic ones)	• Changes to lifestyle—effect on her her career and the 'trapped' domestic life, dependent on David
	Already has a family which offers her emotional support
	Has no real reason to have children

Eric	**Evelyn**
Responsibility—kids are a worry	Demands placed on you—kids are a nuisance
• Economics	• Economics
• Disruption to lifestyle	• Disruption to lifestyle
	Fear of failure as a parent—couldn't cope
	Effect on career
	Dislikes kids

Felix	**Fiona**
Commitment too much	Fear of failure to cope and of pregnancy
• Economics	• Economics
Wife doesn't want them	
• Loss of freedom	• Lifestyle: loss of freedom, independence, antiques
	Effect on career
	Dislikes kids

cont. next page

Table 15   *cont.*

Gary	Gabrielle
Fear of failure—not coping	Degree of commitment demanded clash between work and motherhood
• Kids tie you down—loss of freedom	• Likes the freedom of life as it is
• Inability to travel	• Inability to travel
	Economics
	Lack of maternal instinct

Henry	Heather
• Kids demand too much responsibility and limit freedom	• Fear of responsibility
	Husband doesn't want them
	No biological need for children

Ian	Isabel
• Degree of responsibility	• Responsibility
• Effect on lifestyle—marriage and freedom	• Effect on domestic lifestyle
Ecological pressures	
No real reason to have children	

John	Judy
• Fear of what future holds for kids	• Fear of what future holds for kids
Effect on career	
Wife doesn't want kids	
• enjoys busy lifestyle and 'selfishness'	• enjoys 'irresponsible', free and busy lifestyle
Fear of failure as a parent, and of having a deformed child	

Kevin	Kate
This is a rotten world to bring kids into	Commitment demanded of parents
	Inability to cope with kids in any but 'small doses'
• Desire to travel	• Desire to travel
• Fear of failure as a parent, based partly on his temper and partly on his family's 'mental instability'	• Fear of own and Kevin's failure as parents. Health problems in her family and 'mental instability' in Kevin's

Table 16 *'Awful warnings'*

Repondent	Who was referred to?	How?
Bridget	'Friends'	The children become more important than the marital relationship
Clare	People in general, and males seen at hospital who are fathering their second family	When children arrive 'the woman stays at home and gets really boring, so finally the husband decides that he wants to nick off'
Chris	Woman next door	'There's that screaming brat again!' I keep saying, "how do they put up with it?" The poor mother, she is going berserk.'
	Kids taught at school	Unhappy or unpleasant kids are the result of bad or incompetent parents
Diane	Friends	Children create 'rocky roads' for marriages
	Sister	'I don't consider she's very happy'
	Friend	'I just watched her turn into a disaster area' with conflict over work and children
David	Sister-in-law	Has a 'hopeless' relationship with her children
	His parents	They 'fought about the children'
	Friends	One marriage broke down and one couple was 'disappointed' when they had children
Eric	'Other people who've been in that situation'	Marriage changes markedly—wife 'basically housebound for twelve months after they're born'
Felix	People he visited	Children lead to 'goo-goo-guk' talk
Gabrielle	Friends	Marriages are altered by children, but the tensions of an intense relationship with spouse may be dissipated by children
Heather	Mother	Having children caused marriage problems
Ian	Friends in general	Children have caused strain on relationships

cont. next page

Table 16 *cont.*

Repondent	Who was referred to?	How?
Isabel	Her parents	Children left them little time for communication between husband and wife
	Her mother	Didn't cope very well with four children and would have been happier with fewer
	Friend	Child had 'devastating impact'—now she is separated. (But the child is not the sole cause of separation)
	Friends with children	Have less time for communication than childless couples
Judy	Her parents	They worked hard and did all the right things but still 'failed' as parents. Mother kept anxious and busy by asthmatic son
	Cousin	Has become 'neurotic' since having children; marriage affected badly
Kate	Sister	Having five children 'to hold her marriage together' has not done the marriage good
	Marriages that I have seen	Damaged by disputes over child-rearing

e n d n o t e s

. . . .

CHAPTER 1   INTRODUCTION

[1]   'A vote against motherhood' (Greene 1963) and 'Why we don't want children' (Michels 1970) were both reprinted in Peck and Senderowitz (1974).

[2]   Examples are Peck (1971); Silverman and Silverman (1971); Peck and Senderowitz (1974); Radl (1974); Faux (1984) and Lewis (1987).

[3]   I wrestled with appropriate terms to describe the couples I was studying for some time and finally settled on 'voluntarily childless', which is cumbersome but manages to imply both freedom and lack. At times, I refer simply to the childless, for the sake of brevity.

[4]   See Ritchley and Stokes (1974) and Poston (1976).

[5]   See Freshnock and Cutright (1978) and Dietz (1984).

[6]   See Poston (1974); Ritchley and Stokes (1974); Cutright and Polonko (1977); Wolywa (1977); Freshnock and Cutright (1978) and Dietz (1984).

[7]   See Cutright and Polonko (1977) and Freshnock and Cutright (1978)

[8]   Moulton (1979) studies six women and Rowland (1982) studies 374 individuals.

[9]   Volunteers responding to media appeals were studied by Nason and Paloma (1976); Baum and Cope (1980); Veevers (1980); Rowland (1982); Baum (1983) and Callan (1985).

[10]   Barnett and MacDonald (1976) studied the (American) National Organization of Nonparents, which in 1978 became the National Alliance for Optional Parenthood. Houseknecht's (1978) study relied on college students.

[11]   See Nason and Paloma (1976); Moulton (1979); Veevers (1980) and Callan (1985).

[12]   See Barnett and MacDonald (1976); Nason and Paloma (1976); Goodbody (1977); Baum and Cope (1980); Den Bandt (1980); Veevers (1980) and Rowland (1982).

[13]   See Veevers (1980) and Rowland (1982).

[14]   See Bram (1978); Houseknecht (1979); Feldman (1981); Callan (1983b, 1985) and Callan (1984b; 1985).

[15]   See Den Bandt (1980); Veevers (1980); Margarick and Brown (1981); Carlisle (1982) and Callan and Hee (1984).

16 See Cooper (1978); Ory (1978); Veevers (1980); Baum (1983) and Campbell (1983, 1985).

17 See Nason and Paloma (1976); Den Bandt (1980); Rowland (1982) and Callan (1985).

18 See Barnett and MacDonald (1975); Bram (1978) and Ory (1978).

19 See Polit (1978); Richards (1978); Black (1979); Jamison (1979); Calhoun and Selby (1980) and Callan (1985).

CHAPTER 2 · IDEOLOGY: THE THEORETICAL CONTEXT

1 This discussion of ideology owes a great deal to the work of Larrain (1979, 1983). The comments on the 'dominant ideology thesis' are influenced by Abercrombie, Hill and Turner, although I do not share the interpretation of Marx offered by these authors. Readers interested in the theory of ideology are referred to these texts and to the discussion in Williams (1980).

2 There are two major problems usually ascribed to functionalist theory, and authors like Abercrombie et al. (1980) charge Marx with positing a functionalist view of ideology. The first problem is the teleological fallacy of attributing the cause of something to the function it fills (which leads in the end to the argument that it's there because it's there because it's there …). In my view, Larrain (1983) is right to argue that Marx does not say ideology comes into being because the ruling class needs to conceal truth—i.e his argument may entail a notion of functional fit, but it is not teleological.

A second criticism of functionalist theory is that it makes explanation of change difficult, if not impossible. (If something is in place because it contributes to the continuance of a system, what makes that something change?) I suggest here that a consideration of the complexity of both interests and the production of ideologies will help to overcome this problem.

3 See Abercrombie et al. (1980) and Chamberlain (1983).

4 This is the approach taken by Chamberlain (1983) in his study of class consciousness in Australia. In effect, he derives a set of attitudes from study of what he defines as ruling-class sources and argues that if these attitudes are held by the majority of the population (set at 80%) then there is a 'hegemony' or dominant ideology. His data show clear variations in attitudes along class lines which leads him to reject this hypothesis. The study is a pioneering attempt to catch an ideology in the field, so to speak, but seems to me to use the wrong kind of net.

5 This crude account ignores the many strengths of the psychoanalytic perspective and the differences between the two authors discussed. A full and sympathetically critical comment can be found in Eisenstein (1984). A shorter account is in Connell (1987).

6 See Aries (1962); Shorter (1975); Poster (1978); Badinter (1981) and Reiger (1984)

7 Busfield and Paddon (1977) give data from a qualitative (pilot) study of 50 wives and a full survey of 290 couples, of whom only 234 were interviewed jointly. In 43 cases only wives were interviewed. In addition, the researchers express doubts about the quality of some of their questions. Richards' study

involved couples, but women's voices feature much more heavily than men's in the published account. The criticism that family sociology has been carried out largely by women, on women, and has thus amassed only one of the two sets of data it needs, has been made many times.

8 See Shorter (1975); Mount (1982) and Badinter (1981).

CHAPTER 3 VOLUNTARILY CHILDLESS COUPLES

1 All population figures in this section are from ABS (1980).

2 For Australia, see Callan (1985); New Zealand, Rowland (1982); Canada, Veevers (1980); Britain, Baum and Cope (1980) and Campbell (1985); the US, Gustavus and Henley (1971); Barnett and MacDonald (1976); Nason and Paloma (1976); Poston (1976); Houseknecht (1978, 1979); Marciano (1978) and Feldman (1981). Note that Baum and Cope's findings about the class background of the voluntarily childless differ from the general trend — they did find some working class people who chose not to have children.

3 See Den Brandt (1980) and Feldman (1981).

4 See Callan (1982, 1985) and Houseknecht (1984).

5 See Gustavus and Henley (1971); Barnett and MacDonald (1974); Nason and Paloma (1976); Baum and Cope (1980) and Veevers (1980).

6 See Rossi (1968) and Glezer (1984).

7 See Harper and Richards (1979); Darroch and Mugford (1980); Gowland (1983) and Bittman (1991).

8 See Barnett and MacDonald (1976); Nason and Paloma (1976); Ory (1978); Veevers (1980) and Callan (1985).

9 The scale is very rough indeed. There is no way of knowing whether the words checked had the same values and connotations to all respondents, or if they meant to them what they mean to me. And the words are all given the same weight in the scale, which means that a fairly global term like *unhappy* could be (if it was the only response circled) read as evidence of a 'happy' childhood. In practice, this is unlikely to have occurred since the bulk of the group regarded their childhood as happy or neutral (only 12.4% circled *unhappy*). None the less, it represents a problem with an improvised scale.

CHAPTER 4 THE CHILDLESS AND IDEAS ABOUT PARENTHOOD

1 This version of the phrase 'it's natural' is common in our society as an explanation for a wide range of behaviour. It seems to mean something like: 'This behaviour has very deep roots. It feels or looks as though it comes from individual character rather than social pressure'. So my feelings about children, gendered aspects of my behaviour (like clumsiness with car engines and deftness with sewing machines), even my habits of leaving writing anything until the last moment, can all be explained as 'natural'. What this means is that I cannot be accused of wilfully being lazy, any more than I can be complimented for deliberately being nice to babies. My patterns are 'natural' to me so they cannot be helped. As feminists have noted, the appeal to nature is a

very comfortable way to defend an often unfair status quo. (See Richards 1982.)

2 Notably Houseknecht (1979); Veevers (1980) and Callan (1983).

3 See Barnett and MacDonald (1977); Richards (1978) and Veevers (1980).

4 The evidence from Barnett and MacDonald (1976) is that 52% of their sample had encountered the argument 'it is selfish not to have children' very often, with those reared as Catholics more likely to report this than any other group.

5 In the first interview I followed up the theme of good aspects of parenting only if it was raised. In interview 2 I asked, 'Would having children change your marriage? If so how? Would the changes be all good or all bad?' In interview 3 I asked the couples to tell me about their networks, and then 'When you're with friends with kids, what do you think you're missing out on by not having any?' followed by the probe 'What is it you'd like about having children? Don't you ever think about it in the middle of the night and wonder what you might be missing out on?'

CHAPTER 5   NEGOTIATING WITH IDEOLOGY

1 As Richards (1985) points out, this simply replicates the 'blind spot' in sociology about other aspects of family life. In particular, network studies have assumed that men and women are 'neighbours' in the same way. Other women have also pointed out the fallacy of describing marriage and family interaction as though it were the same for men as for the women, who are usually the source of data in family studies (Safilios-Rothschild 1969).

2 See Busfield and Paddon (1977) and Richards (1978).

3 Veevers' (1980) discussion of 'rejecting the rejectors' centres on redefinitions of *parenthood*. The technique described here, of redefining *childlessness* in terms of another valued characteristic is not one she considers (although she does describe the redefinition of childlessness as a neutral 'alternative lifestyle').

It is possible that her Canadian respondents did not use negotiation by appeal to the value of resistance, but I think it more likely that Veevers did not spot it because of her approach to ideology. She sees a fairly dominant ideology of parenthood, which is opposed by a 'counter ideology' of childlessness. So the sorts of statements that would show up during analysis are those which directly oppose pronatalism and say that 'parenthood is not good' rather than those which appeal to other ideas entirely. And her sympathy for the voluntarily childless leads her to accept too readily the picture of valiant couples facing an overwhelming ideology, which would reinforce the tendency to see only the most direct confrontations with it.

CHAPTER 6   NEGOTIATING WITH PEOPLE

1 See Barnett and MacDonald (1976); Nason and Paloma (1976); Veevers (1980) and Callan (1985).

2 See Stack (1975) and D'Abbs (1983a & b). Stack's account of the relationships between some black women and their 'kin' (genetic and notional), *All Our Kin*, stressed the way the networks that enabled survival also constrained the women to little but survival. For instance, an inheritance that could have enabled one family to purchase a house was quickly dissipated by the obli-

gation to meet the needs of the network. D'Abbs' account of networks in an Australian suburb stresses the way in which the type of network an individual inhabits is related to the resources available to him/her. The better off the individual in terms of resources like time, money and access to tradeable goods and services, the more 'diversified' her/his network and the less the reliance on the constraining aid of a small group of close friends and kin.

3   See Litwark and Szelinyi (1969); Stack (1975); D'Abbs (1983a & b); Richards (1983) and Wearing (1984).

4   See, for example, Fischer (1982).

5   See Shibutani (1955); Merton (1968) and Urry (1973).

6   See Nason and Paloma (1976) and Cooper et al. (1978).

7   I suspect that this is because of her sampling method as well as her view of coercive and omnipresent pronatalist pressure. While she notes that she has information on 127 childless marriages of at least five years' duration, she in fact interviewed only 29 pairs. Most of her data (on 91 marriages) come from women. Relying on one partner as a guide to issues involving negotiation may exaggerate the concord between husband and wife. (See Safilios-Rothschild 1969.)

8   See Gillespie (1970); Lakoff (1975); Bell and Newby (1976) and Spender (1980).

9   See Fabe and Wilker (1979) and Veevers (1980).

CHAPTER 7   WHERE TO FROM HERE?

1   See, for example, Heller et al. (1986) and Jacobsen and Heaton (1991).

2   See Rich (1977); Green (1985) and Mortimer (1985).

bibliography

· · · · · · · · · · · · · · · · · · · ·

Abercrombie, N., Hill, S. and Turner, B. (1980). *The Dominant Ideology Thesis* (George Allen & Unwin, London.)

Allan, G. (1979). *A Sociology of Friendship and Kinship.* (George Allen & Unwin, London.)

Althusser, L. (1969). *For Marx.* (Trans. B. Brewster). (Allen Lane, Penguin Press, London.)

——(1971). *Lenin and Philosophy and Other Essays.* (Trans. B. Brewster). (New Left Books, London.)

Aries, P. (1962). *Centuries of Childhood.* (Jonathan Cape, London.)

Austin, D. (1981). 'Ideology in class society: The contribution of Max Weber'. In Hiller, P. (ed.) (1981), *Class and Inequality in Australia.* (Harcourt Brace Jovanovich, Melbourne.)

Australian Bureau of Statistics (1980). *Social Indicators* No. 3.

Backett, K. (1980). 'Images of parenthood' in Anderson, M. (ed.), *Sociology of the Family: Selected Readings* (2nd ed., Penguin, Harmondsworth.)

——(1982). *Mothers and Fathers: A Study of the Development and Negotiation of Parental Behaviour.* (Macmillan, London.)

Badinter, E. (1981). *The Myth of Motherhood: An Historical View of the Maternal Instinct.* (Trans. R. Degaris.) (Souvenir Press, London.)

Barker, D. and Allen, S. (eds) (1976). *Dependence and Exploitation in Work and Marriage.* (Longman, London.)

Barnett, L. and MacDonald, R. (1976). 'A study of the membership of the National Organisation for Non-Parents'. *Social Biology* 23:4 pp. 297–310.

Baum, F. (1983). 'The future of voluntary childlessness in Australia'. *Aust. J. of Sex, Marriage & Family* 4:1, pp. 23–32.

Baum, F. and Cope, D. (1980). 'Some characteristics of intentionally childless wives in Britain'. *J. Biosocial Science,* 12: pp. 287–99.

Bell, C. and Newby, H. (1976). 'Husbands and wives and the dynamics of the deferential dialectic' in Barker, D. and Allen, S. (1976).

Bell, D. (1965). *The End of Ideology.* (Free Press, New York.)

Berger, P. and Kellner, H. (1970). 'Marriage and the construction of reality' in Dreitzel, H. (1970).

Berger, P. and Luckman, T. (1981). *The Social Construction of Reality* (Penguin, Harmondsworth.)

Bernard, J. (1973). *The Future of Marriage.* (Bantam, New York.)

——(1974). *The Future of Motherhood.* (Penguin, New York.)

Birrell, R. and Birrell, T. (1981). *An Issue of People* (Longman Cheshire, Melbourne.)

Bittman, M (1991). *Juggling Time: How Australian Families Use Time* (Office of the Status of Women, Canberra.)

Blake, J. (1979). 'Is zero preferred? American attitudes toward childlessness in the 1970s'. *J. Marriage & the Family* 41:2, pp. 245–56.

Boissevain, J. (1974). *Friends of Friends.* (Basil Blackwell, Oxford.)

Borrie Report *see* National Population Inquiry.

Bott, E. (1971). *Family and Social Network: Roles, Norms and External Relationships in Ordinary Urban Families.* (2nd ed., Free Press, New York.)

Boulton, G. (1983). *On Being a Mother.* (Tavistock, London.)

Bram, S. (1978). 'Through the looking glass: Voluntary childlessness as a mirror of contemporary changes in the meaning of parenthood' in Miller, W. and Newman, L. (eds) (1978), *The First Child and Family Formation* (Carolina Population Centre, University of North Carolina, Chapel Hill.)

Burns, A., Bottomley, G. and Jools, P. (eds) (1983). *The Family in the Modern World: Australian Perspectives.* (Allen & Unwin, Sydney.)

Burton, C. (1985). *Subordination: Feminism and Social Theory.* (Allen & Unwin, Sydney.)

Busfield, J. and Paddon, M. (1977). *Thinking About Children.* (Cambridge University Press, Cambridge.)

Caldwell, J. et al. (1976). *Towards an Understanding of Contemporary Demographic Change: A Report on Semi-structured Interviews.* (Australian Family Formation Project Monograph No. 4, ANU, Canberra.)

Calhoun, L. and Selby, J. (1980). 'Voluntary childlessness, involuntary childlessness and having children: A study of social perceptions'. *Family Relations,* 29:2, pp. 181–3.

Callan, V. (1983a). 'Factors affecting early and late deciders of voluntary childlessness'. *J. of Social Psychology.* 119: pp. 261–8.

——(1983b). 'Childlessness and partner selection'. *J. Marriage & the Family.* 45:1 Feb., pp. 181–6.

——(1985). *Choices about Children.* (Longman Cheshire, Melbourne.)

Callan, V. and Hee, Q. (1984). 'The choice of sterilization: Voluntarily childless couples, mothers of one child by choice, and males seeking reversal of vasectomy'. *J. Biosocial Science.* 16: pp. 241–8.

Campbell, E. (1983). 'Becoming voluntarily childless: An exploratory study in a Scottish city'. *Social Biology,* 30:3, pp. 307–17.

——(1985). *The Childless Marriage: An Exploratory Study of Couples who do not Want Children.* (Tavistock, London.)

Carlisle, E. (1982). 'Fertility control and the voluntarily childless: An exploratory study'. *J. Biosocial Science,* 14: pp. 203–12.

Carolina Population Centre, University of North Carolina. (1977). *Childlessness and One Child Families* (Popscan Bibliography No. 72. Chapel Hill, North Carolina.)

Carter, A. (1981). 'The quilt maker' in *Sex and Sensibility: Stories by Contemporary Women Writers from Nine Countries.* (Sidgwick & Jackson, London.)

Chamberlain, C. (1983). *Class Consciousness in Australia.* (Allen & Unwin, Sydney.)

Chester, R. (1974). 'Is there a relationship between childlessness and marriage Breakdown?' in Peck and Senderowitz (1974).

Chodorow, N. (1978). *The Reproduction of Mothering: Psychoanalysis and the Sociology of Gender.* (University of California Press, Berkeley.)

Clemenger, J. (1984). *Beyond the Stereotypes: An Illuminating Perspective on Australian Women.* (A Clemenger Report in Conjunction with Reark Research.) John Clemenger, (NSW) Pty Ltd, Milson's Point NSW.)

Comer, L. (1974). *Wedlocked Women.* (Feminist Books, Leeds.)

Connell, R. (1977). *Ruling Class Ruling Culture.* (Cambridge University Press, Cambridge.)

——(1979). 'The concept of role and what to do with it'. *Australian & New Zealand J. of Sociology,* 15:3, pp. 7–17.

——(1983). *Which Way Is Up? Essays on Class, Sex and Culture.* (Allen & Unwin, Sydney.)

——(1987). *Gender and Power.* (Allen & Unwin, Sydney.)

Cooper, P.E. (1978). 'Decision making patterns and postdecision adjustment of childfree husbands and wives'. *Alternative Lifestyles,* 1:1, pp. 71–94.

Cotton, S., Anhill, J. T. and Cunningham, J. (1983). 'Living together: Before, instead of or after marriage', in Burns et al. (1983).

Coulson, M. 'Role: A redundant concept in sociology? Some educational considerations', in Jackson, J. (ed.) (1972), *Role.* (Cambridge University Press, Cambridge.)

Cuff, E. and Payne, G. (eds) (1984). *Perspectives in Sociology.* (2nd ed., George Allen & Unwin, London.)

Cutright, P. and Polonko, K. (1977). 'Areal structure and rates of childlessness among American wives in 1970'. *Social Biology,* 24:1, pp. 52–61.

D'Abbs, P. (1983a). *Social Support Networks: A Critical Review of Models and Findings.* (Institute of Family Studies Monograph No. 3. IFS, Melbourne.)

——(1983b). *Give and Take: A Study of Support Networks and Social Strategies.* (PhD thesis, Department of Political Science, Melbourne University, Melbourne.)

Darroch, D. and Mugford, S. (1980). 'The division of domestic labour in Australia: A note on the distribution of housework'. *Social Science Quarterly* 60:4, pp. 685–90.

Den Bandt, M. (1980). 'Voluntary childlessness in the Netherlands'. *Alternative Lifestyles,* 3:3, pp. 329–49.

Dietz, N. (1984). 'Normative and microeconomic models of voluntary childlessness'. *Sociological Spectrum,* 4:23, pp. 209–27.

Dinnerstein, D. (1977). *The Mermaid and the Minotaur: Sexual Arrangements and the Human Malaise.* (Harper & Row, New York.)

Dixon, M. (1977). 'Women' in Davies, A., Encel, S., Berry, M. (eds) (1977), *Australian Society: A Sociological Introduction* (3rd ed., Longman Cheshire, Melbourne.)

Dowling, C. (1983). *The Cinderella Complex: Women's Hidden Fear of Independence.* (Fontana, London.)

Drietzel, H. (ed.) (1970). *Recent Sociology No. 2: Patterns of Communication Behaviour.* (Macmillan, London.)

——(ed.) (1972). *Family, Marriage and the Struggle of the Sexes.* (Macmillan, New York.)

Drucker, H. (1974). *The Political Uses of Ideology.* (Macmillan, London.)

Durkheim, E. (1964). *Rules of Sociological Method.* (Trans. S. Solovay and J. Mueller.) (Free Press, New York.)

Edwards, M. (1981). *Financial Arrangements within Families.* (National Women's

Advisory Council, Canberra.)

Eisenstein, H. (1984). *Contemporary Feminist Thought.* (Unwin Paperbacks, Sydney.)

Erenreich, B. (1983). *The Hearts of Men: American Dreams and the Flight from Commitment.* (Pluto Press, London.)

Fabe, M. and Wikler, N. (1979). *Up Against the Clock.* (Random House, New York.)

Faux, M. (1984). *Childless by Choice: Choosing Childlessness in the 80s.* (Anchor Press/Doubleday, New York.)

Feldman, H. (1981). 'A comparison of intentional parents and intentionally childless couples'. *J. Marriage & the Family,* 43:3, pp. 593–600.

Finch, J. ' "It's great to have someone to talk to": The ethics and politics of interviewing women' in Bell, C. and Roberts, H. (eds) (1984), *Social Researching: Politics, Problems, Practice.* (Routledge & Kegan Paul, London.)

Firestone, S. (1972). *The Dialectic of Sex: The Case for Feminist Revolution.* (Paladin, London.)

Fischer, C.S. (1982). *To Dwell Among Friends: Personal Networks in Town and City.* (University of Chicago Press, Chicago.)

Freshnock, L. and Cutright, P. (1978). 'Non-recursive analysis of 1970 U.S. rates'. *Social Biology* 25:3, pp. 169–78.

Friedan, B. (1968). *The Feminine Mystique.* (Penguin, Harmondsworth.)

Game, A. and Pringle, R. (1979). 'Sexuality and the suburban dream'. *Australian & New Zealand J. of Sociology* 15:2, pp. 4–15.

Gillespie, D. (1972). 'Who has the power? The marital struggle' in Dreitzel, H. (1972).

Glaser, B. and Strauss, A. (1968). *The Discovery of Grounded Research.* (Weidenfeld & Nicolson, London.)

Glasgow University Media Group (1976). *Bad News.* (Routledge & Kegan Paul, London.)

Glezer, H. (1984). *Antecedents and Correlates of Marriage and Family Attitudes in Young Australian Men and Women.* Paper presented to XXth International Committee on Family Research, International Sociological Association 'Social Change and Family Policies'. Melbourne, Australia, 19–24 August.

Goffman, E. (1968). *Stigma: Notes on the Management of Spoiled Identity.* (Penguin, Harmondsworth.)

Goodbody, S. (1977). 'The psychosocial implications of voluntary childlessness'. *Social Casework* 58: July, pp. 426–34.

Gowland, P. (1983). *Women in Families: The Sexual Division of Labour and Australian Family Policy.* (Knox Community Relations Group, Melbourne.)

Gramsci, A. (1976). *Selections from the Prison Notebooks.* (Trans. and ed. by Q. Hoare and G. Smith.) (Lawrence & Wishart, London.)

Greene, G. 'A vote against motherhood: A wife challenges the importance of childbearing' in Peck, E. and Senderowitz, J. (1974).

Greer, G. (1985). *Sex and Destiny: The Politics of Human Fertility.* (Picador, London.)

Gustavus, S. and Henley, J. (1971). 'Correlates of voluntary childlessness in a select population'. *Social Biology* 18:3, pp. 277–314.

Hall, S. (1980a). 'Cultural studies and the Centre: Some problematics and problems' in Hall et al. (1980).

——(1980b). 'Encoding/decoding' in Hall et al. (1980).

——(1983). *Ideology in the Modern World* (La Trobe Working Papers in

Sociology No. 65, La Trobe University, Bundoora, Vic.)

Hall, S. et al. (1980). *Culture, Media, Language*. (Hutchinson in association with CCCS Birmingham, London.)

Harper, J. and Richards, L. (1979, 1985). *Mothers and Working Mothers*. (Penguin, Ringwood.)

Headlam, F. (1985). 'Working wives'. *Australian Society* 4:2, pp. 5–7.

Heller, P., Tsai, Y.-M. and Chalfant, H.P. (1986) 'Voluntary and nonvoluntary childlessness: Personality vs. structural implications', *Int. J. of Sociology and the Family* 16: Spring, pp. 95–110.

Hicks, N. (1978). *This Sin and Scandal: Australia's Population Debate 1891–1911*. (ANU Press, Canberra.)

Hirst, P. (1976). 'Althusser and the theory of ideology'. *Economy and Society*, 5:4, pp. 385–412.

Hobson, D. (1980). 'Housewives and the mass media' in Hall, S. et al. (1980).

Hoit, J. (1970). 'Speaking of Spock'. *Up from Under*, 1:2, pp. 46–8.

Hollingsworth, L. 'Social devices for impelling women to bear and rear children' in Peck and Senderowitz (1974).

Houseknecht, S. (1977). 'Reference group support for voluntary childlessness: Evidence for conformity'. *J. Marriage & the Family*, 39:2, pp. 285–92.

——(1978). 'Voluntary childlessness: A social psychological model'. *Alternative Lifestyles*, 1:3, pp. 379–402.

——(1979). 'Childlessness and marital adjustment'. *J. Marriage & the Family*, 41:2, pp. 259–66.

——(1984). 'Understanding voluntary childlessness' in Sussman, M. and Steinmetz, S. (eds) (1974). *Handbook of Marriage and the Family*. (Plenum, New York.)

Huber, J. (1980). 'Will U.S. fertility decline toward zero?'. *Sociological Quarterly*, 21:3, pp. 481–92.

Institute of Family Studies (1982). *Selected Reading List No. 12 Voluntary Childlessness*. (IFS, Melbourne, December.)

Jacobson, C. and Heaton, T. (1991). 'Voluntary childlessness among American men and women in the late 1980s'. *Social Biology* 38:1–2. pp. 79–93.

Jamison, P. et al. (1979). 'Some assumed characteristics of voluntarily childfree women and men'. *Psychology of Women Quarterly*, 4:2, pp. 266–73.

Kaltreider, N. and Margolis, A. (1977). 'Childless by choice: A clinical study'. *American J. Psychiatry*, 134, pp. 179–82.

Kaplan, A. (1964). *The Conduct of Inquiry: Methodology for Behavioural Science*. (Chandler Publishing Co., San Francisco.)

Kelly, R. (1980). 'You don't have to be a parent'. *Guardian*, 3 September.

Lakoff, R. (1975). *Language and Woman's Place*. (Harper Colophon, New York.)

Larrain, J. (1979). *The Concept of Ideology*. (Hutchinson, London.)

——(1983). *Marxism and Ideology*. (Macmillan, London.)

Lasch, C. (1977). *Haven in a Heartless World*. (Basic Books, New York.)

Lewis, B. (1987). *No children by choice*. (Penguin, Ringwood.)

Lewis, R. (1984). 'Some changes in men's values, meanings, roles and attitudes towards marriage and the family in the USA'. Paper presented to XXth International Committee on Family Research, International Sociological Association: 'Social Change and Family Policies', Melbourne, August.

Litwark, E. and Szelenyi, J. (1969). 'Primary group structures and their functions: Kin, neighbours and friends'. *American Sociological Review*, 34:4, pp. 468–81.

Magarick, R. and Brown, R. (1981). 'Social and emotional aspects of voluntary childlessness in vasectomized childless men'. *J. Biosocial Science*, 13:2, pp. 157–67.

Mannheim, K. (1954). *Ideology and Utopia*. (Harcourt Brace, New York.)

Marciano, T. (1978). 'Male pressure in the decision to remain childfree'. *Alternative Lifestyles*, 1:1, pp. 95–112.

——(1979). 'Male influences on fertility: Needs for research'. *Family Coordinator*, 28:4, October, pp. 561–8.

Marsh, C. (1982). *The Survey Method*. (George Allen & Unwin, London.)

Marx, K. and Engels, F. (1852). *The German Ideology*. (Progress Publishers, Moscow, 1964).

McDonald, P. (1983). 'The baby boom generation as reproducers: fertility in Australia in the late 1970s and the 1980s'. Paper to the Australian Family Research Conference, 23–25 November, ANU, Canberra.

McKee, L. and O'Brien, M. (eds) (1982). *The Father Figure*. (Tavistock, London.)

McKirdy, G. (1978). *Bibliography on Voluntary Childlessness*. (National Organization for Non-Parents, Baltimore.)

Merquior, J. (1979). *The Veil and the Mask: Essays on Culture and Ideology*. (Routledge & Kegan Paul, London.)

Merton, R. (1968). *Social Theory and Social Structure*. (Free Press, New York.)

Michels, L. (1974). 'Why we don't want children' in Peck, E. and Senderowitz, J. (1974).

Michelson, J. and Gee, S. (1984). *Coming Late to Motherhood*. (Thorson, Wellingborough, UK).

Miles, M. and Huberman, A. (1984). *Qualitative Data Analysis: A Source Book of New Methods*. (Sage Publications, Beverly Hills, California.)

Mills, C. (1970). *The Sociological Imagination* (OUP, New York.)

Morgan, D. (1975). *Social Theory and the Family*. (Routledge & Kegan Paul, London.)

Mortimer, L. (1985). 'Feminism and motherhood'. *Arena*, 73, pp. 58–77.

Moulton, R. (1979). 'Ambivalence about motherhood in career women' *J. of the American Academy of Psychoanalysis*, 7:2, pp. 249–57.

Mount, P. (1983). *The Subversive Family*. (Unwin Paperbacks, London.)

Movius, M. (1976). 'Voluntary childlessness: The ultimate liberation'. *Family Co-ordinator*, 25:1, pp. 57–62.

Nason, E.M. and Paloma, M.M. (1976). *Voluntarily Childless Couples: The Emergence of a Variant Lifestyle*. (Sage Research Papers in the Social Sciences. Sage Publications, Beverly Hills.)

National Population Inquiry ('Borrie Report') (1975). *Population and Australia: A Demographic Analysis and Projection*. (AGPS, Canberra).

Oakley, A. (1981). 'Interviewing women: A contradiction in terms' in Roberts, H. (1981).

Ortner, S. (1974). 'Is female to male as nature is to culture?' in Rosaldo and Lamphere (1974).

Ory, M.G. (1978). 'The decision to parent or not: Normative and structural components'. *J. Marriage & the Family*, 40:3, pp. 531–9.

Owens, D. (1982). 'The desire to father: reproductive ideologies and involuntarily childless men' in McKee and O'Brien (1982).

Parsons, T. (1955). 'The American family: Its relations to personality and the social structure' in Parsons and Bales (1955).

Parsons, T. and Bales, R. (1955). *Family Socialization and Interaction Process.* (Free Press, New York.)

Patton, M. (1980). *Qualitative Evaluation Methods.* (Sage Publications, Beverly Hills.)

Peck, E. (1971). *The Baby Trap.* (Bernard Geis, New York.)

Peck, E. and Senderowitz, J. (eds) (1974). *Pronatalism: The Myth of Mom and Apple Pie.* (Thomas Y. Crowell, New York.)

Polit, D. (1978). 'Stereotypes relating to family size status'. *J. Marriage & the Family*, 40:1, pp. 105–14.

Poster, M. (1978). *Critical Theory of the Family.* (Pluto Press, London.)

Poston, D, (1976). 'Characteristics of voluntarily and involuntarily childless wives'. *Social Biology*, 23:3, pp. 198–209.

Pringle, R. (1973). 'Octavius Beale and the ideology of the birth rate'. *Refractory Girl*, Winter, pp. 19–27.

Radl, S. (1974). *The Motherhood Myth.* (Sun Books, Melbourne.)

Rainwater, L. (assisted by Weinstein, K.) (1969). *And the Poor Get Children.* (Quadrangle Books, Chicago.)

Rapoport, R., Rapoport, R. and Strelitz, Z., with Kew, S. (1977). *Fathers, Mothers and Others: Towards New Alliances.* (University of Queensland Press, St. Lucia.)

Refshauge, W.F. (1979). 'Population policy'. In United Nations Economic and Social Commission for Asia and the Pacific Monograph: *The Population of Australia*, Ch. 12.

Reiger, K. (1982). 'The disenchantment of the home: The rationalisation of domestic life in Victoria 1880–1940'. (PhD thesis, Departments of History and Sociology, La Trobe University, Bundoora, Vic.)

Rich, A. (1977). *Of Woman Born: Motherhood as Experience and Institution.* (Virago, London.)

Richards, J. (1982). *The Sceptical Feminist.* (Penguin, Harmondsworth.)

Richards, L. (1978, 1985). *Having Families: Marriage, Parenthood and Social Pressure in Australia.* (Penguin, Ringwood.)

——(1983). *Families in a Suburb: Network Management and its Varied Results.* (La Trobe Working Papers in Sociology No. 64, La Trobe University, Bundoora, Vic.)

——(1985). 'A man's not a neighbour: Gender and local relationships in a new estate'. Paper to SAANZ Conference, Brisbane, August.

——(1990). *Nobody's Home* (Oxford University Press, Melbourne.)

Ritchey, P. and Stokes, C. (1974). 'Correlates of childlessness and expectations to remain childless US 1967'. *Social Forces*, 52:3, pp. 349–56.

Roberts, H. (ed.) (1981). *Doing Feminist Research.* (Routledge & Kegan Paul, London.)

Rosaldo, M. and Lamphere, L. (eds) (1974). *Woman, Culture and Society.* (Stanford University Press, Stanford, California.)

Rossi, A. (1968). 'Transition to parenthood'. *J. Marriage & the Family*. 30:1, pp. 26–39.

Rowland, R. (1982). 'An exploratory study of the childfree lifestyle'. *Australian and New Zealand J. of Sociology*, 18:1, pp. 17–30.

Runciman, W.G. (1966). *Relative Deprivation and Social Justice.* (Routledge & Kegan Paul, London.)

Russell, G. (1979). 'Fathers! Incompetent or reluctant parents?' *Australian and New Zealand J. of Sociology*, 15:1, pp. 57–65.

Safilios-Rothschild, C. (1969). 'Family sociology or wives' family sociology? A cross-cultural examination of decision-making'. *J. of Marriage & the Family*. 31:2, pp. 290–301.

Salter, B. and Tapper, T. (1981). *Education, Politics and the State: The Theory and Practice of Educational Change*. (Grant McIntyre, London.)

Sarantakos, S. (1984). *Living Together in Australia*. (Longman Cheshire, Melbourne.)

Schapiro, B. (1980). 'Predicting the course of voluntary childlessness in the 21st century'. *J. of Clinical Psychology*, 9:2, pp. 155–7.

Shibutani, T. (1955). 'Reference groups as perspectives'. *American J. of Sociology*, 60:6, pp. 562–9.

Shorter, E. (1975). *The Making of the Modern Family*. (Fontana, London.)

Silverman, A. and Silverman, A. (1971). *The Case Against Having Children*. (David McKay, New York.)

Simmel, G. (1955). *Conflict and the Web of Group Affiliations*. (Trans. K. Wolff and R. Bendix.) (Free Press, Glencoe, Illinois.)

Spencer, G. (1979). *Fertility of Australian Marriages*. (Demographic Research Papers, R. Series) (ABS, Canberra.)

Spender, D. (1980). *Man Made Language*. (Routledge & Kegan Paul, London.)

Stack, C. (1975). *All Our Kin: Strategies for Survival in a Black Community*. (Harper Colophon, New York.)

Strawbridge, S. (1982). 'Althusser's theory of ideology and Durkheim's account of religion: An examination of some striking parallels'. *Sociological Review*, 30:1, pp. 125–40.

Summers, A. (1975). *Damned Whores and God's Police*. (Penguin, Ringwood.)

Thompson, J. (1984). *Studies in the Theory of Ideology*. (Polity Press, Cambridge.)

Urry, J. (1973). *Reference Groups and the Theory of Revolution*. (Routledge & Kegan Paul, London.)

Veevers, J. (1974). 'Voluntarily childless wives: An exploratory study' in Peck and Senderowitz (1974).

——(1980). *Childless by Choice*. (Butterworths, Toronto.)

Wadsworth, Y. (1984). *Do It Yourself Social Research*. (Victorian Council of Social Service/Melbourne Family Care Organization, Melbourne.)

Waller, J., Rao, B. and Li, C. (1973). 'Heterogeneity of childless families'. *Social Biology*, 20:2, pp. 133–8.

Wearing, B. (1984). *The Ideology of Motherhood: A Study of Sydney Suburban Mothers*. (Allen & Unwin, Sydney.)

Williams, R. (1980). *Keywords*. (Fontana, Glasgow.)

Willis, P. (1977). *Learning to Labour: How Working Class Kids Get Working Class Jobs*. (Gower, Aldershot, UK.)

Winship, J. (1978). 'A woman's world: "Woman" An ideology of femininity' in Women's Studies Group, *Women take Issue*. (CCCS/Hutchinson, London.)

Wishart, B. (1982). 'Motherhood within patriarchy: A radical feminist perspective' in 3rd Women and Labour Conference Papers (South Australian College of Advanced Education, Salisbury, South Australia), Vol. I.

Wrong, D. (1961). 'The oversocialized conception of man in modern sociology'. *American Sociological Review* 26:1, pp. 183–193.

Zweig, F. (1960). *The Quest for Fellowship*. (Heinemann, London.)

index

· ·

Abercrombie, N., Hill, S. and
    Turner, B.   15, 184 n1, 184 n2
Althusser, L.
    concept of ideology   22–4
    criticisms of   22, 23–4
    determinism   23–4
    ideology and individual identity
        23
    and structuralist theory   22
Australian Institute of Family Studies
    (IFS)   4, 6, 32–3, 35, 143, 146
autonomy, ideal of   146

Backett, K.   34
Barnard, M.   143, 144–5
Barnett, L. and MacDonald, R.
    115, 183 n10, 186 n4
Barret, M.   22
Baum, F.   183 n9
Baum, F. and Cope, D.   183 n9,
    185 n2
Bernard, J.   6, 29
Boissevain, J.   122
Borrie Report see National
    Population Inquiry
Bott, E.   131
Boulton, G.   34
Busfield, J. and Paddon, M.   31–2,
    34, 51, 91, 184 n7

Callan, V.   13, 51, 55, 57, 58, 62,
    115, 183 n9
Campbell, E.   51, 57, 63
Carter, A.   5
case study approach   12, 152–3
case study couples, changes in

marital and parental status   13,
    45, 138, 151–2
case study group explanations for
    childlessness   88–105
    'first nature'   99–103
    'natural' childlessness   98–103
    parenthood as the normal route
        89–92
    parenthood as silly   89–91
    parenthood as somewhat selfish
        82, 89–90
    resisters' character   95–8
    'second nature'   99–103
    social location of the childless   93–5
case study groups' perceptions of
    ideology of parenthood   69–84,
    105–12
    definitions of 'ideology'   107,
        111–12, 174
    existence of false ideas about the
        family   107–9
    transmission of ideology   109–11
    use of the word ideology   107,
        111–12
case study groups' reasons for not
    wanting children, convergence
    between spouses   72–84, 133–4,
    178–80
CCCS and ideology   24–5
Chamberlain, C.   184 n4
Chodorow, N.   29
Comer, L.   30, 139
Connell, R.   9
contraceptive behaviour and
    attitudes of the voluntarily
    childless   8

Cooper, P. 115

D'Abbs, P. 186 n2 ch6
decision to be childless as a process
40–5, 63–7, 138–9
declining birthrates, effect of
voluntarily childless on 145–6
decoding messages 25
demographic approach to studying
voluntary childlessness 6–7
Den Bandt, M. 6
Dinnerstein, D. 29
discourse theory 24
disreputable pleasures 77
dominant hegemonic position
towards ideology 25
dyadic intensity 7, 51–3, 78–9

early articulators 8, 63–7
Edwards, M. 53
encoding messages 25
Erenreich, B. 37

false consciousness 16
problems of definition 18
family experiences of the voluntarily
childless in other studies
eldest children 54–5
only children 54–5
family experiences of the voluntarily
childless in this study 54–63
'I had an unhappy childhood'
58–62
images of parenthood 58–62
position in family of origin
54–57
Family Formation Project
(Australian National University)
32–3, 34
Family Formation Survey (IFS)
32–3, 35
Feldman, H. 51, 57
feminist approach to voluntary
childlessness 10–11
feminist critiques of parenthood 4,
5, 10–11, 28–31, 148
Finch, J. 152
Firestone, S. 148
Forell, C. 143, 145
Foucault, M. 24, 25

Freudian theory in feminism 29

gaining support for childlessness,
conversational techniques 123–8
avoiding opposition 125–6
discounting opponents 127–8
interpreting conversation 126–7
tactical decisions about
confronting the issue 124–5
gaining support for childlessness,
network management 128–130
German Ideology, The 15, 16, 17
Glaser, B. and Strauss, A. 152
good sense, in Gramsci 20
Gramsci, A.
definition of ideology 19–20
influence on Althusser 22, 23
Greene, G. 183 n1
grounded theory 152

Hall, S. 24–5
hegemony, in Gramsci 20
Hobson, D. 24
Hoit, J. 30
Hollingsworth, L. 28–9
Houseknecht, S. 51, 57, 131
Huber, J. 140

idealist view of ideology. 17
Ideological State Apparatuses (ISAs)
22–3
ideology
concept in general 15–26
concept in Althusser 22–4
concept in CCCS 24–5
concept in Gramsci 19–20
concept in Mannheim 20–2
concept in Marx 15–19
implications of this study for
theory 141–3
in this study 26–7
operationalising the concept 27–8
ideology of parenthood
entails commitment and
responsibility 30–1, 33–5
is natural 30, 32–3
entails sacrifices, 35–6
Institute of Family Studies *see*
Australian Institute of Family
Studies

intellectuals
  Gramsci's view   20
  Marx's view   16, 18
interest, problems of definition   18
interpellation   24
interview techniques   12, 151–2

Jacobson, C. and Heaton, T.   146

Kaltreider, N. and Margolis, A.   57

language and ideology group   24
Larrain, J.   19, 184 n1
Lewis, R.   36
little mother syndrome,   54–7
longitudinal approach to research
  151, 152, 153

MacKellar, M. (Minister for
  Immigration)   4
Mannheim
  on ideology   20–2
  relationism   20, 22
  relativism   20, 21, 22
  on utopia   20–1
  weakness of concept of ideology
    21–2
Marciano, T.   10, 66, 132
Marx, K.   5
  concept of ideology   15–19
  on intellectuals   16, 18
  weaknesses of concept of ideology
    17–19
Marxist feminists   4
McDonald, P.   33
mental health of the voluntarily
  childless   8
methodology in this study
  described   11–13, 151–4
  weaknesses and strengths   153–4
Mills, C. W.   142
Mitchell, J.   22
motive antecedents for childlessness
  58
Moulton, R.   183 n8
Movius, M.   5, 10, 148

Nason, E. M. and Paloma, M. M.
  115, 183 n9
National Organisation of

Nonparents (NON) (USA)   10,
  183 n10
National Population Inquiry ('Borrie
  Report') (1975)   6
negotiating with ideology   24, 25,
  27
network(s)
  of the childless analysed   122–3,
    176
  defined   122
  management   122, 128–30
New South Wales Royal
  Commission on the Decline of
  the Birthrate and on Mortality of
  Infants (1904)   3, 4, 143
'new style' mothering   35, 73
'norm', concept of   9, 10

Oakley, A.   152
'old style' mothering   35
one child policy (China)   146
oppositional position towards
  ideology   25
Ortner, S.   102
oversocialized conception of
  humanity   9
Owens, D.   32

parenthood
  awful warnings of   134–6, 181–2
  fears of   57, 59, 62
parents' comments about the
  voluntarily childless   32
parents' perceptions of the ideology
  of parenthood   31–6
Parsons, T.   37
patriarchy   36–7
personal interests of author in
  studying voluntary childlessness
  2, 148–9
policy issues, voluntary childlessness
  and role of women   5, 143–8
policy makers   5, 146–8
population decline, economic debate
  on   143–4
Poster, M.   37
postmodernism   25–6
postponers   8, 63–7
pronatalist pressures on the childless
  in other studies

pronatalist pressures on the childless
in other studies (*cont.*)
differential impact   115
sources   115
pronatalist pressures on the childless
in this study
impact and reactions   116–19
perceived differentials: geographic
location   120–1; sex   119,
174; time   120
sources: family   117; friends
116, 117, 118; social pressure
117, 119; would-be
grandparents   117
pronatalist pressures, external   114,
121, 174, 175
pronatalist pressures, internal   114,
117, 121
psychoanalytic feminists, criticism of
29
public issue, voluntary childlessness
as a   3, 5, 143–5

qualitative approach to this study
11, 152–3
quantitative approach to this study
11, 152
questionnaire   153

radical feminists   4–5
Rapoport, R. Rapoport R., Strelitz,
Z. and Kew, S.   31
reasons for not wanting children
133–4, 178–80
reference group(s)
defined   131–2
of one   131, 132–4
in previous research on the
voluntarily childless   131–2
Reiger, K.   38
Repressive State Apparatuses (RSAs)
22
Rich, A.   30
Richards, J.   185 n1 ch4
Richards, L.   2, 32, 35, 91, 92,
122, 186 n1 ch5
role theory   9
Rowland, R.   183 n8, 183 n9
ruling class as creator of ideology
in Marx   16–17, 18

after Marx   20, 22–3
in this study   26
Rumania, attempts to alter
population   146
Runciman, W. G.   111
Russell, G.   29

Salter, B. and Tapper, T.   18
Scantlebury Brown, Dr V.   38
Sarantakos, C.   12
Schapiro, B.   115
selfish voluntary childlessness   32,
81–2, 91, 144–5, 146
Shibutani, T.   130
Simmel, G.   122
social attitudes towards the
voluntarily childless   8, 91–2
social-psychological approach
towards voluntary childlessness
7–10
social structure and human agency
5
Spencer, G.   145
Spock, Dr   30
Stack, C.   186 n2 ch6
stalking an invisible minority   8, 12
structural antinatalism   140

timing of decisions about
childlessness
early deciders and postponers
63–7
'his' and 'her' journey   64–7

utopia, in Mannheim   20–1

Veevers, J.   6, 7, 8, 12, 13, 48, 51,
55, 57, 58, 63, 77, 97, 115,
131–2, 134, 138, 139, 186 n3
ch5, 187 n7
voluntarily childless, definition of
12
voluntarily childless in other studies
attitudes to children   7
attitudes to marriage   7
attitudes to politics   47–8
attitudes to sterilization,   8
decision making process   8, 63
family backgrounds   7, 54–5,
57–8

voluntarily childless in other studies
(*cont.*)
  social location   6, 7, 47
voluntarily childless population,
  measuring it   6–7
voluntarily childless in this study
  attitudes to children   46, 82–3;
    decision making process
    63–7; family backgrounds
    46–7, 54–63
  commitments and allegiances:
    feminism   48–9; marriage
    51–4; politics   48; religion
    48; work   49–51
  explanations of the case-study
    couples   88–105: childlessness
    as choice   93–95; childlessness
    as natural   98–103;
    childlessness as resistance
    95–98
  perceptions about parenthood:
    commitment and responsibility
    72–6; dislike of children
    178–80; parenthood is natural
    69–72; parenthood is the
    proper path   89–92
  perceptions about parenthood,
    sacrifices: are the sacrifices
    rewarded?   82–3; sacrifice of
    emotional energy and dyadic

intensity   78–9; sacrifice of
  freedom and spontaneity
  77–8; sacrifices of money   77;
  sacrifice as moral demand or
  just part of the job?   81–2;
  sacrifice of personal autonomy
  78; sacrifice of self   78, 80–1;
  sacrifices of time and trouble
  76–7
social location: backgrounds
  46–7; education/occupation
  45–6; income   46;
  male/female differences   46;
  sample compared with others
  47
the world-views of the case-study
  couples   170–3: character as a
  world-view   87–8; and ideas
  about fertility   103–5; lifestyles
  as a world-view   87; social
  location as a world-view
  87–88
voluntary childlessness as liberation
  10, 136, 148

Wearing, B.   10, 33, 35–6, 91,
  148
Williams, R.   184 n1
women's liberation   47–9, 106–8
Wrong, D.   9